The Urban Racial State

Perspectives on a Multiracial America series
Joe R. Feagin, Texas A&M University, series editor

The racial composition of the United States is rapidly changing. Books in the series will explore various aspects of the coming multiracial society, one in which European-Americans are no longer the majority and where issues of white-on-black racism have been joined by many other challenges to white dominance.

Titles:

Leonard, David J. and C. Richard King, *Commodified and Criminalized: New Racism and African Americans in Contemporary Sports*

Melanie Bush, *Breaking the Code of Good Intentions*

Amir Mavasti and Karyn McKinney, *Middle Eastern Lives in America*

Richard Rees, *Shades of Difference: A History of Ethnicity in America*

Katheryn Russell-Brown, *Protecting Our Own: Race, Crime, and African Americans*

Elizabeth M. Aranda, *Emotional Bridges to Puerto Rico: Migration, Return Migration, and the Struggles of Incorporation*

Victoria Kaplan, *Structural Inequality: Black Architects in the United States*

Angela J. Hattery, David G. Embrick, and Earl Smith, *Globalization and America: Race, Human Rights, and Inequality*

Pamela Anne Quiroz, *Adoption in a Color-Blind Society*

Adia Harvey Wingfield, *Doing Business with Beauty: Black Women, Hair Salons, and the Racial Enclave Economy*

Erica Chito Childs, *Fade to Black and White: Interracial Images in Popular Culture*

Jessie Daniels, *Cyber Racism: White Supremacy Online and the New Attack on Civil Rights*

Teun A. van Dijk, *Racism and Discourse in Latin America*

Melanie E. L. Bush, *Everyday Forms of Whiteness: Understanding Race in a Post-Racial World*, 2nd edition

Noel A. Cazenave, *The Urban Racial State: Managing Race Relations in American Cities*

The Urban Racial State

Managing Race Relations in American Cities

Noel A. Cazenave

ROWMAN & LITTLEFIELD PUBLISHERS, INC.
Lanham • Boulder • New York • Toronto • Plymouth, UK

Published by Rowman & Littlefield Publishers, Inc.
A wholly owned subsidiary of The Rowman & Littlefield Publishing Group, Inc.
4501 Forbes Boulevard, Suite 200, Lanham, Maryland 20706
www.rowmanlittlefield.com

Estover Road, Plymouth PL6 7PY, United Kingdom

Copyright © 2011 by Rowman & Littlefield Publishers, Inc.

All rights reserved. No part of this book may be reproduced in any form or by any electronic or mechanical means, including information storage and retrieval systems, without written permission from the publisher, except by a reviewer who may quote passages in a review.

British Library Cataloguing in Publication Information Available

Library of Congress Cataloging-in-Publication Data

Cazenave, Noel A., 1948-
  The urban racial state : managing race relations in American cities / Noel A. Cazenave.
    p. cm. — (Perspectives on a multiracial America series)
  Includes bibliographical references and index.
  ISBN 978-1-4422-0775-2 (cloth : alk. paper) — ISBN 978-1-4422-0777-6 (electronic)
  1. United States—Race relations—Political aspects—Case studies. 2. United States—Race relations—Government policy—Case studies. 3. Urban policy—United States—Case studies. 4. Metropolitan government—United States—Case studies. 5. New Haven (Conn.)—Race relations—History—20th century. 6. New Haven (Conn.)—Politics and government—20th century. 7. Syracuse (N.Y.)—Race relations—History—20th century. 8. Syracuse (N.Y.)—Politics and government—20th century. I. Title.
  E184.A1C39 2010
  305.800973—dc22   2010048172

∞™ The paper used in this publication meets the minimum requirements of American National Standard for Information Sciences—Permanence of Paper for Printed Library Materials, ANSI/NISO Z39.48-1992. Printed in the United States of America

To my big sister, Andree, and the many fond memories we share of growing up in the Lower Ninth Ward of New Orleans.

Contents

List of Illustrations	ix
Preface and Acknowledgments	xi
Introduction: The Urban Racial State: An Overview	1
1 Understanding the Urban Racial State	15
2 Programming Race Relations through Community Action	33
3 The Civil Rights Movement, the War on Poverty, and Conflict over the Use of Community Action to Support African American Insurgency	57
4 Maximum Feasible Participation Meets "Black Power" and the White Backlash: The Struggle over Community Action in Syracuse	85
5 Black Rebellion, White Repression, and the Transformation of Community Progress, Inc., and Urban Politics in New Haven	103
6 Recent Examples of the Urban Racial State	135
Conclusion: Summaries of Findings, Lessons Learned for Understanding Today's Urban Racial State, and What We Still Need to Know	165
Notes	173

Index	209
About the Author	221

List of Illustrations

Table 1.1	Racial State Entities by Levels and Branches of Their Governmental Cores	27
Figure 1.1	The Urban Racial State's Use of Its Community Action Program to Mediate and Balance Race Relations within a City	28
Figure 1.2	The Urban Racial State, African American Protest, White Racial Backlash, and the Expansion and Contraction of the Social Protest and Resident Participation Activities of the URS Community Action Program	29
Figure 1.3	The Cycle of the Urban Racial State's Responses to Changing Race Relations	31

Preface and Acknowledgments
The Urban Racial State

In this book I introduce a new analytical concept, the urban racial state (URS). By the urban racial state I mean the political structure and processes of a city and its suburbs that manage race relations in ways that foster and sustain both its own immediate political interests and, ultimately, white racial supremacy. I hope the URS concept will prove useful in both contemporary and historical analyses of the workings of power and politics in cities and their suburbs by providing a conceptual bridge to three important bodies of social science literature—urban theory, racism theory, and state theory.

I realize, of course, that such an undertaking must overcome numerous conceptual challenges. Indeed, states are such complex phenomena that they can be analytically overwhelming. For example, they include governments and their various appendages and other links within both the public and private sectors. This complexity is also evident in the fact that their governmental cores exist at multiple levels (e.g., federal, individual state, and local governments) and through all three of their branches (the executive, judicial, and legislative). To simplify matters, my main focus in this book is the executive branch of city governments in its capacity as a manager of race relations, which I refer to as the URS administration.

I place racism at the center of my analysis of this book's New Haven and Syracuse case histories by examining the deployment of community action as a programmatic device to manage race relations. As you will see, one of the exciting things about any type of machinery, social or otherwise, is that once it is built and its switch is turned on it does not always function quite as designed. This will become evident when I examine what those two case histories and other more recent and noncommunity-action-focused examples of the urban racial state reveal about what its policies, programs, and practices actually do racially, how they do these things, for whom, and with what consequences.

The major funding for this project was provided by grants from the Ethics and Values Studies Program of the National Science Foundation. I also received supplemental funding through a grant-in-aid from Temple University to cover the expenses of data collection during the preliminary stage of my research. The Lyndon Baines Johnson Foundation provided funds for me to collect archival data from the Lyndon Baines Johnson Library in Austin, Texas. Special thanks are due to my research project consultants, Frances Fox Piven, Jill Quadagno, Martin Rein, and Ivan Szelenyi; to my oral history consultants, Ronald Grele and Sheldon Stern; and to Rachelle D. Hollinger of the National Science Foundation.

I would like to thank the following organizations and individuals of the University of Connecticut for their generosity: the Institute for African American Studies for providing research assistants, the Research Foundation for furnishing two supplemental grants for the transcriptions of oral histories, and the Center for Oral History for transcribing the oral histories cited in this book.

Dena Wallerson's work ethic and skills were extraordinary when she served as my research assistant during the project's data collection and the transcription of oral histories. I would also like to extend my appreciation to Karen Powell, David Nielsen, and Darlene Madden, who all worked as my research assistants during the project's various post–data collection stages. Thanks to Michelle Palmer and the transcribers of the University of Connecticut Center for Oral History for their important transcription work. I am also grateful to Mark Abrahamson of the sociology department and Louise Simmons of the Urban and Community Studies program for suggesting readings relevant to my conceptual approach. I appreciate the manuscript style advice I received from Tom Deans of the University of Connecticut Writing Center.

Thanks also to my Racism Theory graduate seminar students Angie Beeman and Mustafa Gurbuz for bringing to my attention articles that proved useful to me in my analysis, and to seminar member Bill Armaline's critical eye for forcing me to flesh out the reasons why I chose to use the term urban racial state. I am indebted to my University of Connecticut colleague Evelyn Simien for suggesting relevant readings as I formulated my conceptual approach. As usual, I am grateful to Katherine Covey, the department's program assistant, for coordinating the making of copies of drafts of the manuscript, and to Arlene Goodwin, the department's ad-

Preface and Acknowledgments   xiii

ministrative assistant, for assisting me with formatting problems, copying drafts of the manuscript, and ensuring that they were mailed out.

Thanks to Shannon Hassan for editing the manuscript down to a more manageable size. I am grateful to Zane Miller and David Stradling for their useful comments and suggestions on an early draft of the manuscript. I appreciate Joe Feagin's helpful feedback on a draft of the manuscript's preface, introduction, and chapter 1. Johnny E. Williams provided useful advice on a draft of the introduction. Both men also suggested readings relevant to my theoretical approach. I am very grateful for the comments I received from Carter A. Wilson, who read a draft of the introduction and chapter 1. Thanks also to Debra M. Lewis for the website link she sent me to a report on the progress of the post-Katrina recovery efforts in New Orleans.

Of course, I could not have written this book without the generous help of the following people who kindly consented to participate in oral history interviews: Betty Baer, Franklyn Barry, Richard Belford, Inez Blackshear, Mary Bonner, Ernest L. Boston, Richard Brooks, Edgar Cahn, Vi Chisolm, Richard Cloward, Thomas Costello, Robert Dahl, Irwin Deutscher, Don Dimenstein, Richard S. Dowdy, Edwin Edmonds, Joseph Einhorn, Jonathan Freedman, Joe Goldstein, Peter Gray, Howard Hallman, Fred Harris, Gwen Henderson, Norman Hill, William Johnston, Sanford Kravitz, Richard Lee, John Lascaris, Edward Logue, Frank Logue, Elmer Lutcherhand, Sherrill Moore, Russell Murphy, Robert S. Pickett, Nicolas Rezak, Walt Sheppard, Anita Sklarsky, Lawrence Spitz, Mitchell Sviridoff, Mary Norman Tillman, William Walsh, Anna Mae Williams, Earl Williams, Clifford Winters, Frank Woolever, and Ben Zimmerman. Copies of the transcribed oral histories are on deposit at the Columbia University Oral History Project in New York City and the John F. Kennedy Library in Boston, Massachusetts. I wish that I had the financial resources and time to have them all transcribed.

The research project from which this book was culled could not have been done without the help of these administrators and staff of the following archives: Amy S. Doherty, the George Arents Research Library, Syracuse University; Sharon B. Laist, Robert B. Colasacco, Allen Divack, Idelle Nissila-Stone, and Anthony Mahoney, the Ford Foundation Archives; Tina Houston, Linda Hanson, and Yolanda C. Boozer, the Lyndon Baines Johnson Library; Ronald E. Whealan, William Johnson, Michael Desmond, and June Payne, the John Fitzgerald Kennedy Library; and Mary Ann Bamberger, the University of Illinois at Chicago Library. There were, of course, many other helpful staff members of those institutions who are not mentioned here.

I also appreciate the help I received from administrators and staff of the following archives: New Haven Colony Historical Society, New Haven

Free Public Library, Onondaga County Public Library, Wisconsin Historical Society Library, and Manuscript and Archives, Yale University. They all made my work both productive and enjoyable. Thanks also to Jonathan Freedman for being kind enough to mail me two large boxes of Community Action Training Center memoranda, academic papers, and other documents he collected when he served as that project's research coordinator.

I would like to express my gratitude for the assistance I received from Joe Feagin as editor of the Perspectives on a Multiracial America Series, and from Sarah Stanton, acquisitions editor, Lynda Phung, production editor, Jin Yu, editorial assistant, and others associated with Rowman & Littlefield.

Introduction

The Urban Racial State: An Overview

From the mid- to early 2000s, racial tension over the police killings of Amadou Diallo and numerous other unarmed young men of color in New York City reached a breaking point. What pushed the United States's largest and most famous city to the brink of racial calamity was the racially divisive rule of Rudolph Giuliani, a mayor who many people came to believe operated both a police state and a racial state to punish and contain the city's African Americans, a solid voting block of opposition to his rule. As you will see, the existence of a racial state under the Giuliani administration was no aberration—that social entity began well before his time and continues today as cities draw battle lines over illegal immigration from the nation's southern borders.

In highly racialized[1] societies such as the United States one of the chief functions of cities and other urban governments[2] and their various institutional appendages is the regulation of race relations within their geopolitical boundaries. The aim of this book is to name and explain the workings of the political structure that does this. The name I have given this entity is the *urban racial state*[3] (URS). Although the specific objectives of a city government and other components of the urban racial state change in response to the vicissitudes of political objectives and race relations at any point in time, its ultimate function is the maintenance of the racial status quo within a metropolis to the benefit of the racially dominant group.[4]

The urban racial state component at the center of this analysis is the executive branch of city government. Because one of the major tasks of mayoral administrations is to ensure the political, economic, and social stability desired most by powerful individuals and organizations, racial harmony is essential. The task of maintaining racial peace can be quite a challenge, especially in the face of glaring racial inequality and changing racial demographics. Ironically, to maintain the racial status quo by forestalling the need for fundamental change, city-government administrations and their supporting organizations—what I refer to as the executive branch governmental core of the urban racial state, or more simply as the URS administration—must be nimble in their ability to structurally adapt to the demands generated by changing race relations. To this end, city governments, as well as other branches and levels of government that may cooperate with or oppose the racial actions of mayors, behave in three major ways at different times based on what their leaders deem to be politically prudent. First, there is the usual ignoring of the plight of the racially oppressed—the *racially oblivious URS*. What URS actors are oblivious to here is not the existence of racial categories and hierarchy but the need for any changes to the racial status quo, no matter how small. They may be blind to systemic racism, but they are definitely not color blind. Second, and less common, is the amelioration of the condition of those at the racial bottom of things through a change of racial policies and practices, or at least an expansion of services or opportunities—the *racially ameliorative URS*. Finally, when deemed necessary, there may be a strong crackdown on racial insurgency—the *racially repressive URS*.

Although this book devotes an entire chapter to more recent examples of the urban racial state, its main focus is on the nature, organization, and operation of the executive branch governmental component of the urban racial state in the two northeastern cities of New Haven, Connecticut, and Syracuse, New York, during the tumultuous 1960s when race relations changed quickly and significantly. A good way to set the stage for my study of the urban racial state and community action programs in New Haven and Syracuse is by examining the social and historical context in which those programs emerged and evolved.

SOCIAL AND HISTORICAL CONTEXT FOR THE NEW HAVEN AND SYRACUSE CASE HISTORIES

Who Is There? *What* Are They Doing? The Stage Is Set in New Haven and Syracuse

For some time now I have taught my sociology students about the nature and workings of social structures by asking them to observe two things as they approach a new social setting like an airport or bus station: *Who* is there? And *what* are they doing? Through this study's "who is there?"

lens I will first examine the continued migration of African Americans to racial ghettos in northern cities. And through its "what are they doing?" lens I will investigate the changing race relations during the rise and demise of the modern civil rights movement. As you will see, the answers to both questions profoundly affected the size, organization, and activities of the urban racial state.

The Migration of African Americans to Northern Cities and Their Ghettoization within Them

One of the key functions of the mayor's office as the most powerful command center of the urban racial state is *racially-targeted population control*;[5] that is the regulation of race relations through restrictions on the racial composition and/or location of a city's residents. This racial demographics management task of the URS is most pressing during times when population shifts threaten to upset what has become the accepted racial balance and relations of a city or other urban area.[6] This was the racially-targeted population control challenge the urban racial states of New Haven, Syracuse, and other northeastern cities faced with the increased in-migration of African Americans.[7] The URS response to such a threat can range from policies and practices that discourage the further in-migration of the racially oppressed and the reactive "white flight" out-migration of European Americans to social programs that more effectively govern the increased population of low-income residents of color within existing racial ghettos. By the time community action was tried as a remedy for this "Negro problem,"[8] the need for some type of local government response had been evident for some time.

Migration increased for African Americans during both world wars when the increased demand for labor in the defense industry, combined with restrictions on immigration into the United States, created attractive job opportunities in northern cities. The power of the "pull" from the North was intensified by the "push" out of the South by factors like racial terrorism and job losses due to the mechanization of southern agriculture.[9] World War I produced the beginning of what became known as the Great Migration, when between 1914 and 1920 a half million African Americans migrated from the rural South to highly industrialized northern cities.[10] Migration to the northern cities would continue dramatically as nearly 1.5 million African Americans left the South in each of the three decades from 1940 to 1970.[11] As a result of in-migration, African Americans as a percentage of the total population of the northeast increased from just 2 percent in 1910 to 4 percent in 1940 to 7 percent in 1960 and 9 percent in 1970. Moreover, whereas in 1910 73 percent of the African American population resided in rural areas, by 1970 only 19% of them did so.[12] And although the migration of African Americans was primarily to the nation's twelve largest cities, in the 1950s there was some diffusion of that migration away from large cities to smaller ones like New Haven and Syracuse.[13] The significance of those statistics rest, of course, in the profound social and political consequences of that geographic relocation of so many African American people.

Some scholars have made note of how African American migration impacted the forms and workings of American racism. For example, in his book, *Racism: From Slavery to Advanced Capitalism*, Carter A. Wilson observes that from 1865 to 1965 those African Americans who migrated away from the racially segregated Jim Crow South to the urban North in search of better job opportunities and greater freedom found that they now faced under industrial capitalism an *aversive* form of racism that included a rigid system of residential segregation. Through "violence, government actions, and institutional practices" like "restrictive covenants" and other means—many of which persist today—residential segregation was often more pronounced than in either the rural or the urban South.[14] And while not usually codified in law as was true for the de jure segregation of the South, the de facto segregation of schools, jobs, and other opportunities that followed racial ghettoization[15] up North could be quite devastating in its consequences.

This aversive-racism view fits well Richard Sennett's analogy to sixteenth century Venice, in which its Jewish ghetto provided anti-Semitic Venetians with an "urban condom" to protect themselves from what they perceived as the infectious touch of Jews.[16] Like slavery and Jim Crow, the "peculiar institution" of the ghetto "operated to define, confine, and control African Americans." Consequently, those who migrated to northern cities found no "'promised land' of equality and full citizenship but instead another system of racial enclosure, the ghetto, which Sennett deemed an "ethnoracial prison."[17]

As the African American migration continued, those racial reservations grew in both size and population density. This ghettoization was further intensified by white flight to the suburbs[18] and as a consequence of the belief held by most European Americans that it was their right to keep African Americans out of their neighborhoods,[19] be they in cities or suburbs. Moreover, it is likely that the intensification of racial segregation contributed to a further hardening of attitudes toward race relations.[20] The negative impact of that ghettoization was made worse by the fact that those northern cities were already in economic decline due to the loss of manufacturing jobs.[21] Unemployment and the wide range of social problems that came with it were especially prevalent in urban ghettos.

Public-policy-focused observers of these demographic trends in major U.S. cities found themselves searching for programmatic ways to address the social, political, and economic challenges posed by this highly visible racial population. The urgency to act came from the fact that ghetto residents seemed to be "controlled neither by existing neighborhood institutions nor the patronage apparatus of local politics which both had traditionally eased the assimilation of ethnic immigrants from Europe."[22] Community action programs were one of the urban reform initiatives private foundations and the federal and local governments—in their racial-state capacities—turned to in order to better manage potentially volatile race relations by socially and politically engaging ghetto residents in ways that would not provoke an immediate white backlash by threatening existing patterns of residential segregation. As you will see, this was often done by expanding the resident participation and social protest activities of community action when there were challenges by African Americans to the racial status quo and by contracting those community action armaments in response to white racial backlashes.[23]

The positive impact of that migration and ghettoization for African Americans manifested itself in two forms of political empowerment. First, the concentration of African Americans in northern ghettos significantly increased their clout as voters in electoral politics. Second, freed from the overt terrorism that enforced racial submission in the rural South and emboldened by their concentrated numbers in northern ghettos, African Americans could speak out about the bad conditions they endured in numerous ways, including soap box speeches, newspaper exposés and editorials, and even social protest.[24] And again, as was true for the migration itself, although the political consequences of population movement manifested themselves first and most dramatically in large cities, with help from community action programs social protest eventually would become commonplace in smaller cities like New Haven and Syracuse.[25]

Changing Race Relations during the Rise and Demise of the Civil Rights Movement

I have stressed two important reasons why changing race relations must be at the center of this book's New Haven and Syracuse case studies. First, the very reason for the existence of the urban racial state is the political management of race relations for the ultimate benefit of the white power structure, and especially its political leaders. Second, like a science fiction "shape shifter" or "transformer," URS is adept at fulfilling this function because of its ability to reconfigure both its organizational structure and its programmatic content to fit new challenges generated by changes in race relations.[26] These changing race relations and the difficulties they posed to different levels of the racial state[27] were evident during the rise and demise of the nation's modern civil rights movement.

During the short fourteen-year duration (1954–1968) of the modern civil rights movement, the era of the most concentrated and intense twentieth-century struggle for racial equality in the United States, African Americans challenged not only the racial status quo generally but also specific institutional structures within the various levels and branches of the racial state governmental core.[28] During this period the racial state was forced into overdrive as it strained to accommodate the conflicting demands of those groups that pushed for racial reform against those that circled their wagons to defend the racial status quo.

The Federal Racial State's Early Positive Responses to the Civil Rights Movement, 1954–1959.

The role of the courts as regulators of race relations was evident on May 17, 1954, when the U. S. Supreme Court finally issued its ruling in what became known as the Brown decision. The justices unanimously ruled that laws mandating legal segregation of public schools violated the Fourteenth Amendment of the Constitution and were therefore unconstitutional. The ruling had implications that went well beyond public schools since the "separate but equal" mandate was the linchpin for the entire system of Jim Crow segregation. As one historian put it, after the Brown decision it was widely believed among African Americans that "a new day in race relations had dawned."[29]

One of the ironic consequences of the 1954 Brown decision was that it helped shift the strategy and battleground of the civil rights movement from litigation in the courts to social protest in the streets. Although the Brown decision dramatically raised expectations of ordinary African Americans for social justice, its excruciatingly slow "with all deliberate speed" timeline for implementation caused great frustration and convinced those thirsty for freedom who were not already involved in the struggle that they could no longer wait for lawyers, judges, and other elites to act on their behalf. If they wanted change they would have to get it themselves through the only means available to most African Americans, social protest.[30] Although there were earlier protests involving ordinary African Americans, as a *mass* movement the modern civil rights movement is symbolically traced to the actions of Ms. Rosa Parks, who on December 1, 1955, refused to relinquish her bus seat to a European American male who had just boarded.[31] The magnificent ordinariness of the dignified and defiant Parks sent a clear message to African Americans. This movement is *our* movement. It is a movement for *all* of us, not just a few.

One of the most important civil rights events of the late 1950s was the integration of public schools in Little Rock, Arkansas, a crisis that pitted the federal racial state against its state and local racial state counterparts. After the Brown decision, states, cities, and local school boards throughout the South had to decide how they would respond, and what happened in Arkansas is a case in point of the volatility of the racial state during such trying times. When newly elected Governor Faubus went against the Brown decision and ordered Arkansas National Guard troops to Central High School in Little Rock to block the entrance of African American students, President Eisenhower enforced the federal court's order by sending in U.S. paratroopers and by later nationalizing that state's National Guard.[32]

Northern racial concerns manifested themselves in a different way among social policy and program elites. Their focus was on the sources of social volatility of urban neighborhoods that contained large concentrations of low-income people of color. For example, the same year as the showdown in Arkansas (1957), the planning for Mobilization for Youth (MFY), one of the nation's earliest and most influential community action programs, was initiated to fight juvenile delinquency in the increasingly Puerto Rican and African American neighborhoods on Manhattan's Lower East Side.[33] The planting of those early seeds of MFY was emblematic of the fact that juvenile delinquency was now emerging as an issue on the national scene.[34]

The Acceleration and Peaking of the Civil Rights Movement, 1960–1963.

In the early 1960s the civil rights movement accelerated as the highly publicized "sit in" movements and "freedom rides" were deployed to integrate various facilities.[35] Attracting much less public scrutiny was the growing concern among policy elites about the social conditions and behavior of African Americans and other people of color in the nation's urban ghettos. As I noted earlier, rather than deal with such worries directly, less controversial reasons such as juvenile delinquency and poverty were given for the need for urban reform. The Ford Foundation sponsored Gray Areas programs in New Haven and other cities in its attempt to apply community action to the problem of urban poverty while, through its President's Committee on Juvenile Delinquency and Youth Crimes projects, the federal government helped fund community action in New Haven, Syracuse, and elsewhere.[36]

The modern civil rights movement reached its peak in 1963 with the successful movement in Birmingham to integrate public facilities and increase jobs for African Americans. The Birmingham movement was followed by 758 demonstrations in 186 cities and the huge March on Washington for jobs and freedom.[37] That same year organizations like the Congress of Racial Equality organized protests in northern cities against targets like segregated schools, slum landlords, racist police departments, and job discrimination.[38] Increasingly, the goals of civil rights and economic justice were becoming indistinguishable in both the North and the South.

The Civil Rights Movement Provokes a White Backlash, 1964–1965.

By 1964 the impact of the civil rights movement in northern cities was evident. That year President Johnson signed not only a major civil rights bill but, consistent with the community action approach of providing some relief to African American constituents without directly attacking systemic racism and thus provoking a white backlash, also the Economic Opportunity Act, which authorized and funded his community action programs–centered War on Poverty. The symbiotic relationship between the War on Poverty community action programs (CAPs) and the civil rights movement soon became clear. Once established, the CAPs provided crucial organizational resources for protest in northern cities that had been slow in building their civil rights movement momentum. Equally important was their role in legitimizing and spreading the ideology of "maximum feasible participation" of the poor. This fueled the growth of the citizen participation movement, which challenged the very nature of urban government and its lack of responsiveness to its citizens, especially those who had been previously left out of decision-making processes that profoundly affected their neighborhoods, such as urban renewal and highway construction projects.[39] And, in turn, the citizen participation movement further enhanced the power of CAPs as battlegrounds for the redistribution of racial power in cities.[40]

The symbiotic relationship between CAPs and the civil rights movement was perhaps most evident in the association between urban rebellions and community action programs. The very summer the Economic Opportunity Act was signed civil disturbances erupted in numerous U.S. cities. In response to that urban unrest, both federal and local urban racial states would expand CAP resources and the maximum feasible participation scope of the CAPs as necessary to accommodate the rising expectations of African Americans. And they would later contract CAP material resources and participatory ideology as necessary to appease the white racial backlash to the use of CAPs to promote social protest involving African Americans.[41]

The emphasis on voting rights (i.e., the ability of African Americans to register to vote in the South without facing intimidation through bureaucratic trickery and physical treachery) continued into 1965 with the Selma movement, which was designed to force the federal racial state to remove the barriers that stopped many African Americans from voting.

In response to the racist violence against these and other civil rights activists, President Johnson asked Congress to pass a bill to protect voting rights, and in early August Johnson signed the Voting Rights Act of 1965.[42] Voting issues were not, however, confined to the Jim Crow South. One of the most controversial activities the CAPs would undertake was the initiation of voter registration drives that some mayors, such as Mayor Walsh in Syracuse, viewed as posing a federally sponsored threat to their local political regimes.

After Selma the civil rights movement began to focus more on issues involving economic justice. This trend was also fueled by urban rebellions in cities outside of the South, including the Watts section of Los Angeles.[43] The growing militancy of the civil rights movement and the broadening of its goals and geographic territory made the control of community action programs in cities like New Haven and Syracuse central to the northern struggles for African American political and economic empowerment.

The White Backlash Intensifies, 1966–1968.

By 1966 it was clear that the civil rights movement had largely transformed itself from Reverend King's nonviolent, southern civil rights–focused movement into a national black power movement that was now more in keeping with Malcolm X's call for racial liberation "by any means necessary." The militant and sometimes violent black power movement provoked a major white backlash in the white public's perception of who the poor where and what, if anything, should be done about their problems. This racialization of poverty as a social issue is evident in the findings of Martin Gilens's analysis of the photographs of poor people in stories about poverty in three major news magazines in the United States from 1952 through 1992, a period during which Africans Americans constituted, on average, 29 percent of the nation's poor. Gilens found that in the 1950s, when poverty was not considered to be an issue in the United States (and the modern civil rights movement was still in its early stages), only 18 percent of the people in photographs for stories about poverty were African American compared to 27 percent in 1964, the year the War on Poverty was begun with a big push from the now-intense civil rights movement. The percentage of African Americans in such photographs rose quickly and dramatically to 49 percent in 1965 and 53 percent in 1966 as both racial tensions and controversies over the community action programs of the War on Poverty increased. It is not surprising, therefore, that the number of African Americans depicted in those stories about poverty skyrocketed to 72 percent in 1967, the year of a major white backlash in the United States, which was fueled by a widespread perception that militant African Americans were using the

War on Poverty community action programs as command centers for the mobilization of urban unrest.[44]

Such views also manifested themselves in public opinion polls. For example, "a few months *prior* to the Watts insurgency in Los Angeles a large majority of European Americans (71 percent) agreed that the Johnson administration was 'pushing racial integration' either 'not fast enough' or 'about right,' with only 28 percent indicating that the push was 'too fast.'" However, "those responding 'too fast' increased to 36 percent the month of the Watts uprising, and to 52 percent in September of 1966, after the outbreak of civil disorders in forty-three communities" throughout the United States.[45]

In response to the white racial backlash, racial states operating at all levels and through all branches of government cracked down more intensely on organizations and leaders who enabled or actually encouraged African American social protest. The racial state's suppression of the civil rights movement was a major, although generally unacknowledged, factor in that movement's decline. Not only did foundations and governments begin to withdraw support from all but the most conservative civil rights organizations and social programs, but there was a well-orchestrated campaign by federal, state, and local police authorities to infiltrate, create dissension, and destroy the movement and its key leaders.[46] For example, in response to widespread civil unrest in the nation's African American ghettos, in 1967 the Federal Bureau of Investigation targeted its Counter Intelligence Program (COINTELPRO) against what its director deemed "black hate groups" "to expose, disrupt, misdirect, discredit, or otherwise neutralize the activities of black nationalist . . . leadership, spokesmen, membership, and supporters." COINTELPRO placed within its crosshairs the Black Panther Party, Martin Luther King Jr., and numerous other African American organizations and leaders.[47] And even in liberal urban racial states like New Haven, local mayors and police worked with the FBI to suppress local African American leadership and movements.[48]

Around that same time racial conflict over control of community action programs in places like New Haven and Syracuse became intense. White city governments were determined to retain control of those projects as a source of patronage and a mechanism of racial appeasement while African Americans envisioned them as command posts for racial insurgency. Although the mayors were able to regain nominal control over activist CAPs in 1967 through the passage of the Green Amendment to that year's reauthorization of the Economic Opportunity Act, which limited the representation of the poor and required that such programs be run by city or other local governments,[49] there remained very real battles for control at the local level of the racial state. The struggle intensified with the surge of African American anger and rebellion in the wake of the assassination of Martin Luther King Jr. in the spring of 1968 and the failure of his last initiative, the Poor People's Campaign. That same year the Kerner Commission report on civil disorders concluded that the United States was becoming divided into "two societies, one black, one white—separate and unequal."[50] Racial states at various levels of government reacted to that racial tension through their well-rehearsed pattern of appeasement and repression, which was especially evident in local struggles for control of community action in cities like New Haven and Syracuse.

The Study Period

For my two New Haven and Syracuse Case Histories, I stress the centrality of the modern civil rights movement from the Brown decision to the Kerner Report (1954–1968) to the federal, state-level, and local racial states' use of community action to mediate race relations. My analysis is especially concerned with the eleven years (1957–1968) of the modern civil rights movement, which witnessed the rise, growth, and demise of social-protest-focused community action. It is within this socio-historical context that you can better view the study's New Haven and Syracuse case histories.

THE NEW HAVEN AND SYRACUSE CASE HISTORIES

Although it provides both historical and contemporary examples of the urban racial state in various U.S. cities, this book is organized largely around case histories involving community action programs initiated in the two northeastern cities of New Haven, Connecticut, and Syracuse, New York.

Why New Haven and Syracuse? My primary reason for selecting these New Haven and Syracuse case histories as the analytical core of this book on the urban racial state is the intense and revealing racial conflicts over the control of community action programs in those two cities. The substantive focus of those case histories picks up where my previous book, *Impossible Democracy*, left off—with the explosion of racial conflict over control of the War on Poverty community action programs, which in the New Haven and Syracuse projects would not only continue but intensify. New Haven and Syracuse are also comparable in that they are both medium-sized northeastern cities, which in the 1960s experienced a rapid increase in their populations of low-income African Americans that the city government—in its urban racial state capacity—responded to programmatically. And although the New Haven and Syracuse projects are not as well known—or as well researched—as the New York City based Mobilization for Youth and Harlem Youth Opportunities Unlimited–Associated Community Teams projects I featured in *Impossible Democracy*, they were each influential alternatives to the conceptualization and implementation of community action as an instrument of local urban reform.

As you will see in the coming chapters, the New Haven and Syracuse case histories reveal important differences that offer valuable insights about the racial uses of community action. For example, the New Haven program was tightly controlled by a liberal Democratic mayor who used the agency to co-opt African American leadership, whereas it was in Syracuse, under a conservative Republican mayor, that city-government affiliated community action programs had enough independence and nerve to challenge city hall and other components of the local white power structure.

In this book I explicate the urban racial state concept through the methodology of qualitative historical sociology. The New Haven and Syracuse case history examples are constructed largely from archival and oral history data. The archival data was collected from the numerous archives listed in the book's preface and acknowledgments. Primary data includes memorandums, letters, grant proposal applications, project reviews, unpublished academic papers, newspaper clippings, and other foundation, government, and project data. Also included in this book's preface and acknowledgments is a list of the oral histories with various people involved with those projects, including government officials, community action program administrators and staff, social scientists, social workers, and community activists. For a more detailed discussion of the methodology used for those case histories please see the methodological appendix of my previous book, *Impossible Democracy*.[51] The New York City and New Orleans case examples and suggestions for additional urban racial state research discussed in chapter 6 are based primarily on newspaper clippings and secondary data sources such as published books and articles.[52]

CHAPTER OVERVIEWS

In chapter 1, I review three bodies of literature relevant to the conceptualization of the urban racial state, define the term, and introduce other concepts relevant to my analysis. I then introduce the study's major argument about the URS administration's use of community action programs to mediate race relations in New Haven and Syracuse.

In chapter 2, I examine how in their shift from a racially oblivious to a racially ameliorative urban racial state the URS administrations of New Haven and Syracuse were not inclined to acknowledge the significance of "race," much less systemic white racism. I also show how contrary to their stated goals, the real function of community action programs for the racially ameliorative URS was to provide a stealth form of racially targeted population control in which city governments appeared to address the problems associated with black ghettoization while maintaining existing patterns of racial segregation in housing.

In chapter 3, I explain how with the rise and increasing militancy of the civil rights movement came conflict over the use of the community action programs as instruments of African American insurgency and document how the immediate reaction of the racially ameliorative URS was to ratchet up the intensity and pace of its racial reform efforts.

In chapter 4, you will witness the transition from a racially ameliorative to a racially repressive URS administration. Here I show that when African Americans gained control of Syracuse's Crusade for Opportunity community action program the federal and urban racial states joined other national and local components of the white racial backlash to successfully suppress that challenge to the white power structure.

In chapter 5, the focus is New Haven during that same time period. Here I show how African American challenges for control of Community Progress, Inc., contributed to the transformation of urban politics in New Haven despite efforts by the Lee administration to deploy its community action program and its police force to co-opt and repress African American leadership and insurgency.

In chapter 6, I illustrate the usefulness of the urban racial state concept for analyzing more recent examples of the urban racial state in cases that don't involve community action programs, including racial conflict over police killings of African American and Latino men in the 1990s and early 2000s in New York City under the Rudy Giuliani administration and highly racialized battles over the rescue, relief, and rebuilding responses to the Hurricane Katrina flood disaster in New Orleans during the URS administration of Ray Nagin, an African American mayor. I also briefly outline a few additional studies that could be done on the urban racial state.

The conclusion chapter of this book has three main goals: it summarizes the findings of the book's previous chapters, discusses the lessons this research offers us about the usefulness of the urban racial state concept, and suggests work that remains to be done to provide a more complete understanding of the urban racial state.

1

Understanding the Urban Racial State

Among the numerous myths upon which American social science is built are that its activity is somehow value neutral and that the elimination of potential bias is largely a matter of doing good technical work, such as refining survey research questions and statistical techniques. Soothed by this intellectual balm, the eyes of social scientists typically remain narrowly focused downward on the minutiae of their work while the larger social context in which they operate goes mostly unexamined. Consequently, they overlook the simple fact that the greatest bias in the social sciences has nothing to do with matters of technical precision like the wording of survey research questions but instead with the questions that go unasked and therefore unanswered. In this chapter I examine both the questions typically unasked in existing research on urban politics and what a synthesis of some of the more critical bodies of relevant literature suggest in the way of a new, more racism-centered paradigm with its very different set of questions.

Of course, the ultimate goal of my review and critique is to introduce the core concept of that new paradigm, the urban racial state. To this end I will review the relevant existing theoretical literature and its limitations, define the concept of the urban racial state and its key components, and introduce my argument regarding this book's New Haven and Syracuse case histories.

LITERATURE RELEVANT TO CONCEPTUALIZING THE URBAN RACIAL STATE

The following three bodies of literature are most relevant to my conceptualization of the urban racial state: urban theory to understand its *urban* milieu; racism theory to flesh out its *racial* functions; and racial state theory to comprehend its *state* organization and dynamics.

Urban Theory

I begin my examination of the relevant urban theory literature with a brief look at the racism blindness within both U.S. society generally, and specifically its urban sociology. As you will see, that social structural sightlessness has been so extreme in its consequences as to help call into question the validity of the dominant urban sociology paradigm.

Racism Blindness in U.S. Society and Its Urban Sociology

Systemic racism—a highly organized system of "race"-based oppression in intensely racialized societies like the United States—remains largely invisible through "color-blind" and other ideologies that cloak the significance of "race," much less racism.[1] Not surprisingly, the same political denial is characteristic of the social sciences, which depend on individuals and organizations with a stake in maintaining the political and economic status quo for both their legitimacy and their funding.

In his book *The New Urban Paradigm*, Joe Feagin laments that the tendency in urban sociology since its Chicago School (University of Chicago) origins in the 1920s—which would remain true for the planners of the community action programs of the 1960s it influenced—has been to focus on the alleged culture of poverty of impoverished ghetto residents that was, in turn, assumed to have its roots in the social disorganization of their neighborhoods. In this human ecology model of urban structures and processes, such social disorganization was further assumed to be the result of natural and inevitable cycles of land use driven by free-market forces rather than the consequence of the social, political, and economic decisions that kept the residents of such areas both racially ghettoized and economically impoverished. In this way issues of racial and economic oppression were reduced to technical problems, such as how to best provide more adequate and affordable housing in adversely affected neighborhoods or how to ameliorate their high rates of juvenile delinquency.[2]

Critics of this power-evasive approach in the 1960s included Marxist scholars. Manuel Castells and others hoped to rescue the field from what they saw as the tunnel vision of its Chicago School human ecology approach and to return it to the tradition of the classical sociology of Marx and others, which assumed that urban structures and processes cannot be understood independently of the larger social forces that shape them.[3] To his credit, Castells realized that, as important as it is to bring social class analysis into urban sociology, in highly racialized societies such as the United States, focusing on class relations is not enough.

Feagin has touted the importance of the "next generation" of urban paradigm researchers who are moving racial domination to "the center" of their analysis. He argues that with its potential to focus on both class and racial oppression the new paradigm in urban research is better equipped than the old power-evasive urban sociology to analyze how the oppressed "struggle to make cities their own."[4]

The failure of the urban sociology paradigm is evident in its inability to provide an adequate explanation of residential segregation, one of the basic facts of life facing African Americans in U.S. cities. Contrary to the reason traditionally offered by mainstream urban sociology, this hyper-segregation cannot be accounted for as a natural outcome of urban ecological processes. Its existence is, instead, better explained by Feagin, who notes that "for more than a century multiple and reinforcing practices of discrimination against Americans of color have guaranteed that cities are territorially and institutionally segregated."[5] And as Susan Smith has aptly noted, racial segregation is "a political phenomenon created and enforced by political power." Particularly relevant to this book's New Haven and Syracuse case histories is Smith's observation that racial segregation is "a form of political exclusion which can isolate and marginalize the demands of a minority too small to make any serious political challenge."[6]

Of course, the politics of racial ghettoization is not limited to the local level. In tracing the roots of the racialization of federal government social policies, some scholars pay particular attention to President Roosevelt's New Deal "social welfare programs, labor policy, and housing policy," which "reinforced racial segregation."[7] Others have noted that through its various housing and transportation policies the federal racial state has promoted residential segregation between cities and suburbs and among city neighborhoods, whereas city government's primary urban racial state function has been to manage racial segregation solely within the political boundaries of cities.[8] Following the new urban paradigm then, not only is this racial ghettoization not natural, but power as manifested in elite decision making must be placed at the center of its analysis. Moreover, intense racial segregation in cities is a major form of what I refer to as the *racially-targeted population control* that "lies at the core of racial politics in the United States" and shapes not only the physical structure of cities but the racial relations both within them and elsewhere.[9] Indeed, if there were no "black ghettos," there would be no need for private foundations, the federal government, and local city administrations to devise various reform programs to better manage them. For example, as I will make clear in later chapters, it was the existence of such racial segregation and its consequences, plus the unwillingness of racial state leaders at various levels of its governmental core to tackle this problem directly that made the community action programs of the 1960s, and the later community development schemes they influenced, popular and safe urban reform alternatives.[10]

American Urban Politics, Bureaucracies, and "Urban Racial State Managers"

As useful as Marxist and neo-Marxist urban theory are to the conceptualization of the urban racial state, they have tended to ignore "the internal functioning of the local state."[11] To comprehend the workings of the urban racial state, it is therefore necessary to also examine the literature on local state bureaucracies. A useful approach to government bureaucracies for this study of the urban racial state is to view them as "adaptive systems responding to forces in their environments as they influence these forces."[12] The value of this perspective rests in its potential to explain the actions of *urban racial state bureaucracies* in response to changing race relations. And of course the activities of those local bureaucracies cannot be assumed to be separate and distinct from the policies and practices of federal government bureaucracies and private foundations at the national level.

In the 1960s both private foundations and federal and city governments sponsored activist bureaucrats in various community-action-related initiatives to reform local social service agencies that had proven themselves inept in serving low-income people of color. Clarence Stone, Robert Whelan, and William Murin noted that those actions, which were fueled by and in turn propelled the civil rights movement and a movement for greater citizen participation in decision making, helped usher in an era of more participatory urban politics in the United States. At the core of their analysis was the transformation of race relations. That is, dramatic changes in race relations helped trigger the shift from the "good government" reform era to the post-reform period of urban politics, which posed major challenges to mayors and their community action programs. No longer was it acceptable for decision making that affected the residents of low-income neighborhoods to be limited to the reform politicians and their elite social problems experts, who were assumed to operate on the basis of a citywide consensus as to what was good for a singular public interest. As the 1960s became more tumultuous because of the increasingly militant civil rights movement and other social protest, it was now expected that mayors, their URS administrations, and their community action programs would be responsive to the ethnically and neighborhood-specific demands of low-income ghetto residents.[13]

This proximity of urban racial state managers to racial conflict of various sorts is congruent with the fact I mentioned earlier that one of the strengths of the new urban paradigm is that it allows us to bring into focus how the racially oppressed can organize themselves to fight back. And more specific to this book's New Haven and Syracuse case histories, such analysis helps us to understand how, regardless of their intentions, the actions of racial state managers can spark and fuel racial insurgency. Moreover, the vulnerability of urban racial states to being commandeered to support movements for racial insurgency is in large part determined by the "solution-sets" their urban regimes employ to address the various social problems that accrue from the local ghettoization of African Americans.[14]

Racism Theory

In order to show that the chief function of the urban racial state is the maintenance of the racial status quo, we need to understand the system of racial oppression in whose service the URS is employed. Fortunately, there is a small but growing body of interdisciplinary literature that, unlike the still dominant and racism-evasive race and ethnic relations paradigm of American sociology, examines systemic racism directly and explicitly. I refer to that scholarship as racism studies and to its theoretical component as racism theory.

Joe Feagin's Systemic Racism Approach

Joe Feagin has complained that what is missing from the dominant race and ethnic relations paradigm within American sociology is a "full" view of "the big picture" of racial oppression as a highly organized and enduring phenomenon. Such a view, what Feagin has referred to as a "systemic racism perspective," is needed to address the basic fact that "white-on-black oppression is systemic and has persisted over several centuries." In this analysis I will treat the urban racial state as an integral component of that racist system and its efforts to adapt to various and often conflicting racial demands.[15]

More recently, Professor Feagin has added a powerful tool for the analysis of systemic racism: his conceptualization of racial framing and counter-framing.[16] In the next chapter you will see that the dominant white racial frame or explanation of the condition of African Americans in ghettos and elsewhere throughout U.S. history has been some variant of the "Negro problem" of deficient culture and pathological behavior. That prevailing racial frame was challenged in the 1960s as African American intellectuals and activists increasingly reframed the relatively high rates of poverty and related social problems involving African Americans as, instead, a white problem of systemic racism, a frame that would later find its way into the Kerner Commission report on the causes of the racial unrest that hit scores of American cities in the mid- and late 1960s. The many racial battles discussed in this book over issues like the use of community action, explanations of the police killings of typically unarmed young African American and Latino American men, and disputes over how a flood-ravaged city should be rebuilt and for whom all involved dominant racial frames of those issues and counter-frames by the racially oppressed.

Internal Colonialism Theory

One of the best-known racism theories, the internal colonialism perspective, is important to the main analytical component of this study not just because of the intense racial ghettoization in New Haven, Syracuse, and other northern cities in the 1960s, but equally because at that time it was an influential ideological view of racial oppression espoused by African American intellectuals and grassroots activists. Rather than being an actual theory, internal (or domestic) colonialism theory is a perspective on institutionalized racism that deploys a colonial analogy, articulated as follows in 1967 in Stokely Carmichael and Charles Hamilton's influential book, *Black Power*: "black people in this country form a colony.... [T]hey stand as colonial subjects in relation to the white society. Thus institutional racism has another name: colonialism."[17]

Chief among numerous criticisms of the internal colonialism perspective is its tendency to discount important differences between racial oppression within the same society and the classic model of colonialism. In the latter case colonialism is an externally imposed system of exploitation in which a powerful nation uses its military and economic might to dominate people living in a less developed region of the world.[18]

Despite its limitations, the internal colonialism perspective is an appealing analytical tool. One of the major advantages of the analogy is the accuracy of its treatment of racial oppression as a systemic and multidimensional phenomenon that is embedded in every institution and sphere of society, including the social, the political, and the cultural.[19] From this perspective the political core of the racial state can best be viewed as a colonial state, the political institution charged with the management of white racial hegemony over the entire colony. In this racial or colonial state, rather than rely on their ultimate resource of brute force, politicians normally mobilize various highly racialized cultural ideologies and images to protect their own power interests, the assorted racial benefits of the white public generally, and of course the economic welfare of the wealthy upon whom they are highly dependent for financial support in their election campaigns.[20]

As African American intellectuals and activists of the 1960s were well aware, the internal colonialism perspective is especially insightful for analyses of both the social situations and the political struggles of residents of "black ghettos" in the United States.[21] According to Robert Blauner, the key to racial control is the curtailment of the mobility of the racially oppressed, both physically and socio-economically. For example, Blauner roots racial discrimination in housing to the policies and practices of real estate interests that are buttressed by the actions of local government, which in turn are supported by the "majority sentiments of the white population"[22] and by racist cultural images of black ghetto residents.[23] With such highly institutional stakes in residential segregation, it seems much wiser politically for governments and private foundations to sponsor programs within racial ghettos than to tackle residential segregation as the root cause of their various and numerous problems. Blauner's work suggests that African Americans are confined to racial ghettos as a way of literally keeping them in their "place," both physically and socio-economically.[24] Community action programs and other place-based programs support this colonial agenda by providing the appearance of reform while respecting that normative mandate.

Racial State Theory

The third key conceptual component of the urban racial state idea is, of course, the state. Within political sociology there is a large body of literature on the organization and operation of the state, and recently there has emerged some scholarship specifically on what has been called the racial state.

The term *state* refers to the political structure of a society or one of its geopolitical components and all of its various institutional and organizational appendages and connections, including but not limited to government, which serves as its administrative core. States operate at all levels (e.g., federal, state, and local) and branches (i.e., executive, legislative, and judicial) of government and interface in ways that are either congruent or in conflict. At the level of a city or its metropolis—relatively uncharted territory for scholars of the state[25]—the state includes the various branches of city government and their many bureaucratic agencies, numerous boards and commissions, laws, policies, and links through grants and contracts and in other ways to federal and state government agencies, private foundations, policy institutes, university-based research centers, professional associations, and political parties.

The Managerial Perspective on the State

As I noted earlier, the analytical focus of this study is the executive branch governmental core of the urban racial state. Consistent with this

URS-administration focus, it is the managerial perspective on the state that works best in explaining the role of community action agency bureaucrats and other local government officials as managers of race relations within a city. This perspective assumes that, although their actions are limited by political restrictions, professional norms, and policy guidelines, URS managers are free to make choices that help shape certain policies and programs. "Thus how the state operates depends on how the relevant managers interpret their roles in particular circumstances."[26] This means that it matters who designs and operates community action programs, and that fact helps explain why racial conflict over their control can be so intense.[27]

Theories of the Racial State

The term racial state may have been used first in the 1940s to help explain the atrocities committed by Nazi Germany in its attempt to deploy that nation's military might to establish the world dominance of Hitler's vision of the Aryan race.[28] It would only be in the mid-1980s, however, that scholars who studied race and ethnic relations and state theory would try to develop the concept theoretically.[29] Unfortunately, that theoretical development has not only been slow; it has also been intellectually disappointing. Much of the work in the area is descriptive, with little attempt to flesh out what precisely is meant by the racial state, how it works, and why. Indeed, in some of the most insightful work on the state as a racial actor, the term *racial state* is not even used.[30] Although the very term *racial state* implies its value as an analytical bridge in articulating the relationship between the racial order of a society and its state, perhaps the major weakness of the racial state literature is that it largely ignores this crucial conceptual connection.

There are, however, a few scholars who have attempted to forge a link between sociological literatures in the United States on the state and on race and ethnic relations. One of the earliest of these was published in 1995 by Jack Niemonen, who lamented the tendency of "the American sociology of racial and ethnic relations" to fail "to make explicit the assumptions which define the nature of the state and its relationship to racial inequality." Niemonen rooted this failure in the assumptions that the nation's racial problems are best addressed through the assimilation of racial groups and that the state is "a neutral arbiter between competing interests." In this view racism is the aberrant attitudes and behaviors of individuals, not a key component of the social system, and the state, as simply a mediator of race relations, has no real stake in the maintenance of the racial status quo. Building upon this critique, Niemonen offered an alternative "structuralist" view of the relationship between race relations and the state, with the state playing a key and multidimensional role in race and ethnic group relations.[31]

In a more recent article, Jarvis A. Hall also offers a critique and an alternative perspective. Hall's model treats the racial state as both an intervening and an independent variable in which the state "is both the locus of conflict between dominant and subordinate groups in economic, social, and political spaces and a significant actor in those spaces." Moreover, the magnitude and influence of the state in its racial capacity changes over time in response to various racial conditions and issues. Finally, although the state serves to maintain the existing system of racial domination, how the state acts racially is dependent on not simply the wishes of the dominant racialized group, but more specifically on those of its political leaders. This could entail, for example, responding to the pressures of the civil rights movement by allowing some minor reforms that benefit low-income African Americans generally or certain segments of the African American leadership.[32]

One of the most fruitful attempts to synthesize a comprehensive theory of racism is Carter A. Wilson's *Racism: From Slavery to Advanced Capitalism*. Wilson's eclectic model of racism integrates Marxist-Gramscian, radical psychoanalytical, and Weberian theory as an explanation of both the persistence and the changing nature of racism—and the state's response to it—during different periods of U.S. history in a way that stresses its overlapping economic, political, and cultural dimensions.

Although Wilson did not develop an explicit theory of the racial state, his ideas are especially useful in explaining how the state responds to such challenges. In Wilson's model, state actions are indeterminate in that they are "alterable" by a number of factors, including social movements. In response to pressure from social movements, for example, the state has sometimes resembled a "divided and contested battleground" with not only changing, but sometimes conflicting, orientations to the racial order. You may recall that earlier in my discussion of the literature on systemic racism I mentioned that Feagin suggested that at the core of such battles are struggles over dominant and contesting racial frames. Wilson refers to this volatility as "the paradoxical role of the state" in that "on the one hand, there is a general tendency for the state to protect and legitimize oppressive relations. On the other hand, under special circumstances, it mobilizes resources to ameliorate oppression and to protect the interests of oppressed people."[33] It is because of the state's indeterminate and paradoxical nature that community action programs were useful to URSs in their efforts to manage the rapidly changing race relations of the 1960s. Those projects soon became themselves sites of bitter contention between groups who, with control of those programs, could use them to maintain the racial status quo, to initiate minor reforms, or to launch more serious challenges to the city government and other components of the local white power structure with which the URS was usually aligned.

Thus far my primary focus in reviewing the literature on the racial state has been *what* the racial state does. Equally important, is *how*; that is, the way the racial state is organized or structured to carry out its work. One of the most useful conceptualizations for explaining how states operate is Louis Althusser's explication of Marx's notion of state apparatus. More recently, the state apparatus concept has been further refined by Clark and Dear. Like Althusser, Clark and Dear stress that state apparatuses must be conceptually distinguished from state power generally. Borrowing from Antonio Gramsci's work on hegemony, Althusser argued that a state's power rests not only in repressive state apparatuses (RSAs) like the police, the courts, and prisons but in ideological state apparatuses (ISAs) like public schools and various social programs that can buttress its legitimacy without resorting to violence. For example, during the urban unrest of the 1960s, the federal, individual state level, and urban racial states relied on both repressive state apparatuses (e.g., the police and national guard) and ideological state apparatuses (e.g., opportunity- and participation-focused War on Poverty community action programs) to restore racial order.[34]

As Clark and Dear's notion of the "dual process" of state intervention suggests, however, such programs do not simply do what they are intended to do. Once established to respond to certain problems in their environment, the state apparatus is influenced by that environment and then in turn works to modify the state as a whole. For example, after a mayor's URS administration sets up community action programs to manage race relations, it is then itself subject to the influence of such programs, which based on a combination of program leadership and external pressure factors, may push for changes much greater than what was originally intended.[35]

In brief, borrowing from Clark and Dear's work, I can say that in highly racialized societies like the United States, at the city level of its governmental core, the state takes the form of an urban racial state whose chief function is the regulation of race relations in order to preserve the racial status quo. This is done not only through repressive state apparatuses like the police and courts, when they are used to curb the sometimes violent protest of impoverished members of racially oppressed groups or to discredit or otherwise remove grassroots leadership, but also through ideological state apparatuses like community action programs. An example of the latter is when low-income African American activists are co-opted through employment as paraprofessionals in community action programs or through the receipt of summer grants of various sorts that are intended to ensure that there are no urban rebellions in the area. Another illustration is when African American professionals are enticed to acquiesce in support of the agenda of the urban racial state through professional-level employment in such programs or through board memberships. Who controls such programs and for what purpose is important not simply because of what they can do in the way of reforming or reinforcing the racial status quo but also because of their ability to directly reform the URS itself.

This review of the relevant literature on urban theory, racism theory, and racial state theory helps us to understand both the context and limitations of existing scholarship. With that work done, I am now ready to define the urban racial state and to introduce my argument as to how it explains this book's New Haven and Syracuse case histories.

DEFINING AND CONCEPTUALIZING THE URBAN RACIAL STATE

As I noted earlier, the main goal of this study is to introduce a new theoretical concept for urban analysis: the urban racial state. With that goal in mind, it makes sense to spend some time defining the urban racial state and its key components before I present the main argument for its New Haven and Syracuse case histories. By the *urban racial state* I mean *the political structure and processes of a city and its suburbs that manage race relations in ways that foster and sustain both its own immediate political interests, and ultimately, white racial supremacy.*

Although city government is usually at the core of the political organization of the urban racial state, and my focus here is on its executive branch, my use of the term *political structure* also includes numerous links to other organizations and institutions that overlap with the state and are essential to its operation (e.g., courts, city and regional commissions, school districts, private foundations, university-based research centers, various agencies of the federal racial state and of state-government-level racial states, etc.). And whereas the term *urban* typically refers to a city and its suburbs, the focus of this study is primarily the political boundaries of the cities analyzed. By focusing specifically on the urban racial state as a set of political substructures and *processes* that *manage* race relations I am also able to highlight the more explicit and specific processes of the political regulation of *race relations* in urban areas that are achieved through various bureaucratic state apparatuses like the police, human relations commissions, and community action programs that function to maintain the racial status quo of white racial supremacy.

It is important to note, however, that the mayoral administration component of the urban racial state is not just an appendage of white racial supremacy. By *white racial supremacy* I mean the highly organized system of color- and "race" based group privilege that was established and is maintained through both force (e.g., the police and the court system) and hegemonic means (i.e., widely held beliefs that provide the ideological justification for the attainment and sustenance of the racial status quo). Because it has *its own immediate political interests to foster and sustain*, the urban racial state sometimes functions independently of white racial supremacy and local economic elites more specifically. This is true because the URS must respond to other important social, economic, and political forces than just local racial demographics and politics. For example, it must accommodate itself to local, regional, and national business interests, to the political order at every branch and level of government, and to the attitudes of the larger white public in surrounding suburbs and towns, at the state level, and nationally. Notable exceptions may occur, however, when in the service of racial insurgency reforms are pushed beyond the intended goals of city mayors.

An extreme definition of the urban racial state would assume that the urban state is a racial state and only a racial state. Although my main focus is its racial function as the regulator of race relationships in the furtherance of white racial supremacy, my definition of the URS is more nuanced in that it recognizes that this is not the only task of the urban state. In my review of the literatures on urban theory and on the racial state, for example, I made it clear that not only are class relationships an important factor in state actions but some of the class-centered state theories offer valuable insights into the organization and workings of the urban racial state.[36] Also significant is the impact of gendered relations on state actions. As you will see in later chapters, because the largely male-dominated community action programs had low-income women and their children as their chief clients, gender is an important factor in this book's New Haven and Syracuse case histories and the many conflicts it details. So although the primary focus of this study is the urban state as a racial actor, class and gender are also significant and overlapping factors. In brief, an important feature of my nuanced conceptualization of the URS is that, while it clearly privileges the urban state as an urban *racial* state, it also allows for the intersection of systemic racism, class exploitation, and gender oppression.[37]

In addition, I am not concerned with accounting for the origins of the state and all of its many functions. I propose, instead, a "partial theory" of one important component of state activity. For this reason it may be more appropriate to refer to URS theory as a theory of "state action."[38]

Finally, it is also important to note that various actors, operating at different levels of government, may promote either complementary or conflicting racial goals. For example, the federal government's racially ameliorative states under the Kennedy and Johnson administrations of the 1960s were often at odds with southern congressman and northern mayors who opposed the use of community action programs to challenge normally unresponsive state and local-level white power structures. The different branches of government within the racial state may also act in unison or at cross purposes—for example, a mayor's office and city council. Table 1.1 illustrates the various relational complexities of the urban racial state. Although the primary focus of this study is cell 7, the executive branch of the urban racial state (what I call the URS administration), I will also refer to its various relationships with other levels and branches of the racial state's governmental core.

HOW THE URBAN RACIAL STATE WORKS FOR THIS BOOK'S NEW HAVEN AND SYRACUSE CASE HISTORIES

I began this chapter by stating that in highly racialized societies such as the United States one of the primarily functions of urban government and its various organizational appendages is the regulation of race relations within its borders. I then stated that the goal of this book is to name and explain the workings of that structure and its processes, which I have dubbed the urban racial state. Finally, I pointed out that although the actions of the URS change in response to challenges posed by shifting race relations, its ultimate aim is the furtherance of white racial supremacy. This I argue is the URS storyline behind the rise and demise of social-protest-focused community action programs in the 1960s.

As I also noted earlier, continued migration to and ghettoization in northern cities like New Haven and Syracuse set into play by the South's Jim Crow system of racial domination and maintained by housing, employment, and other forms of racial discrimination in the North led to the extreme concentration of poverty and to a host of related social problems that private foundations and racial states decided must be addressed to ensure social and political stability. In response to this need, URS managers deployed community action as a form of racially-targeted population control.[39] By doing so those URS managers were able to placate poor people of color and keep them physically and socially contained without risk-

Table 1.1   Racial State Entities by Levels and Branches of Their Governmental Cores

Level of Government	Branch of Government		
	1. Executive Branch of the Federal Racial State	2. Legislative Branch of the Federal Racial State	3. Judicial Branch of the Federal Racial State
	4. Executive Branch of the State-Level Racial State	5. Legislative Branch of the State-Level Racial State	6. Judicial Branch of the State-Level Racial State
	7. Executive Branch of the Local (Urban) Racial State	8. Legislative Branch of the Local (Urban) Racial State	9. Judicial Branch of the Local (Urban) Racial State

28 Chapter 1

ing the immediate white racial backlash that would likely be provoked by serious attempts to end racial ghettoization and the impoverishment it causes.[40] With the intensification and northward spread of the civil rights movement, however, African Americans came to see community action programs as a resource for their insurgency.[41] Through its New Haven and Syracuse case histories this book reveals the structure, processes, and nature of the URS as it shifts community action program objectives to meet these often conflicting racial demands without threatening the status quo of racial segregation and inequality.

GRAPHICAL REPRESENTATIONS OF THE URBAN RACIAL STATE

The following three graphics provide an overview of the actions, influences, and modes of the urban racial state relevant to this book's New Haven and Syracuse case histories. Figure 1.1 illustrates the urban racial state's use of community action programs to mediate African American aspirations and white racial resentment. Note the two-way relationship indicated by its arrows that are not limited to the URS administration's reciprocal relationship with African American aspirations and with white racial resentment. That is, consistent with Clark and Dear's conceptualization of the dual process of state intervention; not only does the urban racial state influence its community action program but that project, in

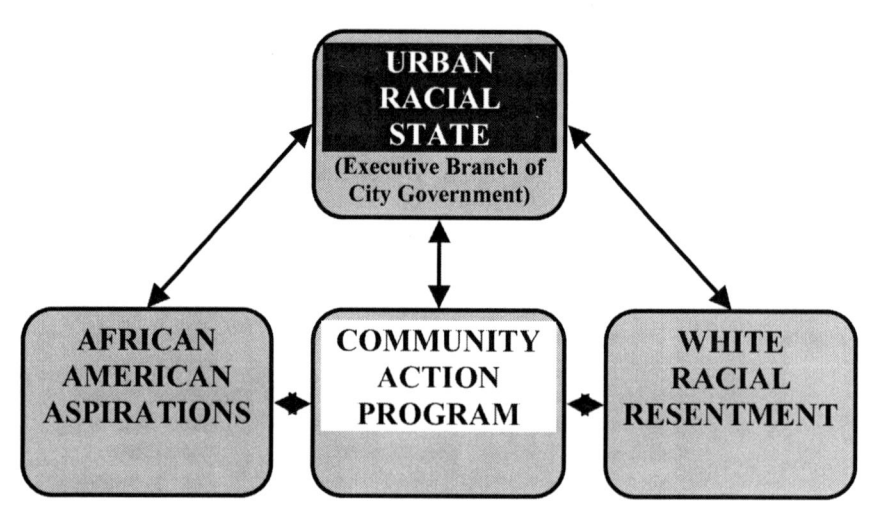

Figure 1.1 The Urban Racial State's Use of Its Community Action Program to Mediate and Balance Race Relations within a City.

turn, impacts the URS. And not only does the community action program mediate and balance African American aspirations and white racial resentment, but both, in turn, help shape—either directly or through the URS—the scope and focus of community action program activities.[42]

Figure 1.2 illustrates how a community action program operated by the executive branch of the urban racial state's governmental core expands or shrinks its social protest and resident participation activities in response to the shifting fortunes of African American protest and white racial backlash.[43] Again, be mindful of the complexity of this relationship as indicated by the two-way arrows; that is, the community action program not only responds to the wishes of the urban racial state but can influence the URS to change. And not only can African American protest and white racial backlash directly or indirectly help shape the urban racial state and its community action program, but the URS can in turn, directly or through its community action program, influence the racial behavior of the city's African American and European American residents.

To keep my graphics simple, I have limited their focus to the actions of only one branch and level of the racial state's governmental core, the executive branch of the urban racial state. Not represented here are the activities of the federal and state-level racial states and of actors representing different branches of government at a particular governmental core level. For example, if the sometimes competing entities composing the federal racial state (e.g., the White House, Congress, the Bureau of the Budget,

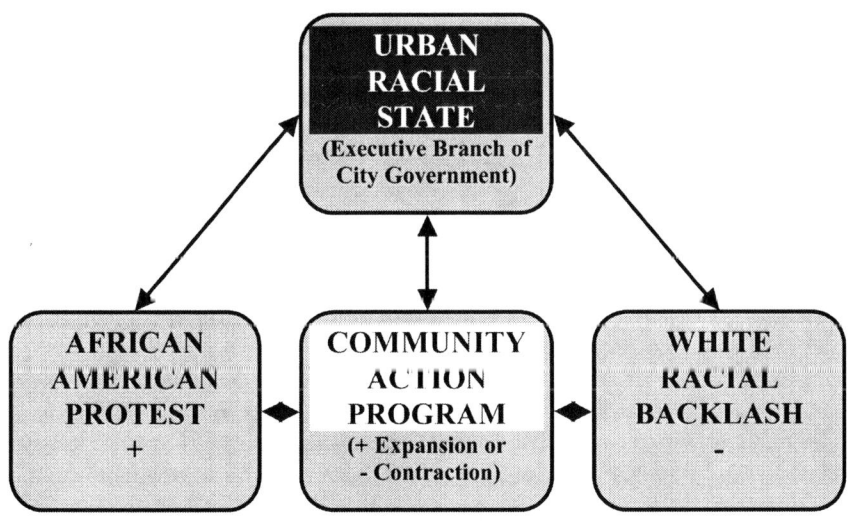

Figure 1.2 The Urban Racial State, African American Protest, White Racial Backlash, and the Expansion and Contraction of the Social Protest and Resident Participation Activities of the URS Community Action Program.

the President's Committee on Juvenile Delinquency and Youth Crime, and the Office of Economic Opportunity) were also included in both figures 1.1 and 1.2 they would be positioned above the urban racial state, with reciprocal lines and arrows linking the federal racial state directly and indirectly (e.g., through state government) to the urban racial state, to local community action programs, and to national and local African American and European American electoral constituencies. Additional complexity could be added by showing the relationships between actors from different branches of the same level of government (e.g., conflict between the mayor and city council over who should control local community action programs).

In discussing the nimbleness of the URS in making small, easily manageable adjustments in a way that forestalls the need to later allow farther-reaching changes in the race relations under its jurisdiction, I briefly explained Carter A. Wilson's concepts of the indeterminate and paradoxical nature of the state's handling of racial matters. These concepts suggest that the urban racial state can change its structure and functions depending on its needs at a particular point in time as it responds to the state of race relations within its geopolitical boundaries and the relative power of different groups of combatants in those racial battles. For example, depending on its changing needs and interests, the URS can configure or reconfigure itself to operate mainly (but not necessarily exclusively) as a racially oblivious state, a racially ameliorative state, or a racially repressive state.[44] By racially oblivious state I do not mean that in this mode of operation the urban racial state does not care about and is not engaged in the management of race relations. What it is oblivious to is the need to make changes in the racial status quo of white supremacy, whether that entails trying to accommodate some of the aspirations of residents of color, as is true for the racially ameliorative state, or aligning itself with a white racial backlash, as is the case for its racially repressive state mode. It is also important to note that not only can the form or modality of the urban racial state change over time under the right sociohistorical conditions, but so can its intensity. Figure 1.3 illustrates that in each of the aforementioned manifestations the urban racial state can elicit different racial control responses.

Again, it should be noted that there are also federal and state-level racial state governmental core cycles of responses to race relations. If I were to represent all three in one graphic they would somewhat resemble a set of three interlocking gears that could be in or out of synch at any given point in time. For example, the federal racial state may shift to its racially ameliorative mode with its initiation of social programs ahead of the urban racial state, which remains for a while in its racially oblivious mode, with the individual state level following even later.

```
      Racially                    Racially
      Oblivious                   Ameliorative
        URS                          URS


                    Racially
                    Repressive
                      URS
```

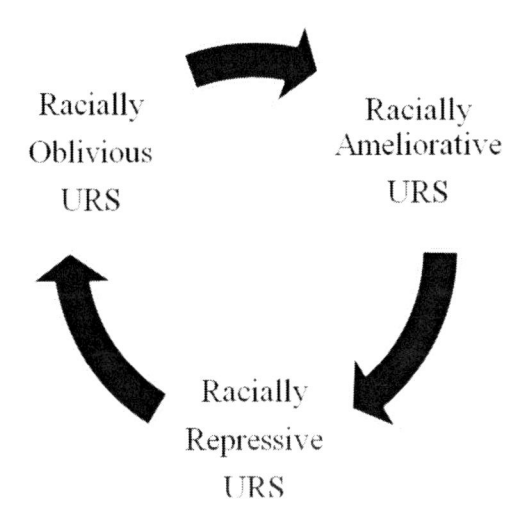

Figure 1.3 The Cycle of the Urban Racial State's Responses to Changing Race Relations.

And still later, in reaction to a white racial backlash, all three levels of the racial state may shift, either in unison or at different times, from a synchronized racially ameliorative mode to a racially repressive method of managing race relations.

CONCLUSION

Although the literature review, key concepts, argument, and graphics presented in this chapter do not capture the full complexity of the structure and operations of the urban racial state, they serve as a starting point to delve into the New Haven and Syracuse case histories. In the coming chapters, this book will reveal the structure, processes, and nature of the URS as it works to meet often-conflicting racial demands without threatening the status quo of racial segregation and inequality.

2

Programming Race Relations through Community Action

> There have been no cases in which CPI staff have helped to organize or have become active in militant protest movements. If such a case arose ... it is likely to be considered as exceeding the policy limitations placed upon CPI staff and the bounds of prudence necessary to hold the coalition together. Therefore, it would probably not be permitted.
>
> —Howard Hallman, deputy director, Community Progress, Inc.[1]

Mayors are like automobile enthusiasts who skillfully calibrate their cars' engines to ensure that they provide them the maximum performance possible. Of course, a finely tuned automobile can be driven fast or slowly in different directions and for many different reasons. Contrary to the stated goals of their funding proposals, the real function of community action programs (CAPs) for the racially ameliorative federal and urban racial states of the 1960s was to provide racially-targeted population control that appeared to address the problems associated with black ghettoization while, in fact, maintaining existing patterns of racial segregation in housing. In this way, such initiatives would program race relations. One goal of this chapter is to examine how mayoral administrations in their URS capacity came to see CAPs as public policy mechanisms through which they could manage the changing race relations within their political jurisdictions. In this chapter I also examine how, in their efforts to manage racial problems through racism-evasive place-based programs that focused on changing the attitudes and behaviors of ghetto residents, and to a lesser degree through some neighborhood reforms, mayors and their urban racial state managers found themselves entering into the terrain of treacherous social problems. The source of danger was the growing militancy of the civil rights movement in northern cities like New Haven and Syracuse and its efforts to commandeer every available resource for ghetto insurgency.

THE "NEGRO PROBLEM" AND THE DENIAL OF SYSTEMIC WHITE RACISM

Throughout the history of the United States, systemic white racism has been buttressed by the tendency of its European American beneficiaries to deny not only its pervasiveness and consequences, but indeed its very existence. Within white liberal policy discourse this racism blindness has often manifested itself in the presumption that the disproportionately numerous problems people of color face have their origins in social class and subcultural differences rather than in systemic racism.[2] Consequently, when the nation's racial problems have been acknowledged, the analytical and programmatic focus has usually been on the victims of racial oppression as the problem. This myopic and misplaced focus, an example of what Joe Feagin refers to as the white racial frame,[3] both obscures the existence of a highly organized system of racial oppression that benefits the racially privileged "white" group and justifies the continued subjugation of those deemed racially inferior.[4] In this way America's racism problem has been recast as its "Negro problem," with the spotlight of reform shone on the need to change the assumed pathological attitudes and behavior of miscreant Negroes, not the race-based system that oppresses them.[5]

PROGRAMMING RACE RELATIONS

By focusing on social problems such as juvenile delinquency and poverty that were prevalent in ghettos rather than on the racial dynamics that created such ghettos and kept them intact, antipoverty and antidelinquency programs of the early 1960s provided both a pretext and a mechanism for dealing with racial problems in a way that (1) kept the spotlight off systemic racism and (2) allowed the urban racial state flexibility in how it dealt with low-income African Americans it deemed to be problematic (e.g., more generously or more punitively as its racial challenges and political needs dictated).[6] In this way, community action came to be deployed by the executive branch governmental core of the urban racial state in its efforts to manage race relations without provoking the political backlash that would surely follow any perceptible threat to the racial status quo.

Such programming flexibility was especially needed by reform-oriented foundations and political elites as it became increasingly clear that northern ghettos would be sites of racial and class struggle as the civil rights movement expanded geographically and in scope, increasingly including economic justice as well as civil rights issues. Through such community-focused programming, social services and other stabilizing "carrots" could be delivered to those neighborhoods as part of what Louis Althusser referred to as an ideological state apparatus. This would be done under the politically safe policy ideology of addressing a city's racial problems by reforming the ghetto and its residents. However, the "stick" of police suppression by the URS's repressive state apparatus remained at the ready.[7]

And while I make no claim that such projects were initiated as instruments of racial control, by the mid-1960s it had become obvious how much they had been adapted to serve that function. The federal racial state's use of community action programs to regulate race relations was done—often in opposition to the wishes of the urban racial state—through the expansion of community action by the enforcement of the War on Poverty's maximum feasible participation mandate in response to black protest and later, with the encouragement of URS politicians, through its contraction as a reaction to the ensuing white racial backlash.[8]

Again, such racial regulation through community action would not have been needed had there been the political will to address racial oppression as the real cause of the social problems ghettoized African Americans faced. The need for such racially cautious urban reform was increasingly evident in New Haven. Whereas Mayor Richard Lee had previously been content to largely ignore the city's African American leaders as he dispensed some patronage goodies directly to African American constituents,[9] his assessment of the importance of better understanding and engaging that leadership changed with the profound trends evident in the city's racial demographics, mounting challenges from the civil rights movement, and the emerging pressures toward a more participatory urban politics. With those shifts, and the increasing conflict Mayor Lee was having with the leadership of African American organizations like the local chapter of the National Association for the Advancement of Colored People (NAACP),[10] African American leadership was now an issue for him, one which required study and reflection.

MITCHELL SVIRIDOFF'S MEMORANDUM
ON NEW HAVEN'S NEGRO LEADERSHIP

One of the earliest such efforts was a 1959 memorandum written by Mitchell Sviridoff, a state union leader, close advisor to the mayor, future school board president, and the future head of Community Progress, Inc. (CPI).[11] That document, "Memo on Problems of Leadership in the Negro Community,"[12] addressed the impact of the civil rights movement on New Haven and its mayor. In his memorandum to Mayor Lee, Sviridoff found each of three types of African American leaders in New Haven to be wanting and to require better management: Conservatives, Moderates, and Immoderates or Direct Actionists.

The Conservatives were portrayed as being comprised of personalities that ranged from "the apathetic, the obsequious, the compliant and the frightened" to the "highly rational but innately conformist or assimilationist." According to Sviridoff, while the Conservatives were once the city's dominant African American leadership, they were no longer influential enough to be useful agents of social and political control. "To rely on them today for practical assistance in coping with the potentially explosive social, economic and political problems of the Negro community would be an exercise in futility."[13]

Sviridoff's Moderates included "educators, ministers, professionals and intellectuals" who were objective in their thinking and active in their community. The moderates were a large, important, and apparently dominant African American leadership group. However, Sviridoff cautioned that while the Moderates appeared to be the type of leadership municipal officials would prefer to work with, they were unreliable in crisis situations, in which they seemed "to falter, hesitate, vacillate—and even run for cover."[14]

The city's small group of African American Immoderates/Direct Actionists included leadership types ranging from responsible, objective radicals to extreme fanatical nationalists. "Within the group, a large centrist element swings between the two extremes—depending on the nature of the crisis and *on how the crisis is being handled by the white community*." Sviridoff went on to express his concern that "all too frequently" it was the Immoderates/Direct Actionists who dominated leadership among New Haven's African American population. He attributed their leadership success to intense anger, bitterness, and "an insatiable appetite for progress" among African Americans; their ability to produce major victories for African Americans; and the ineptness of the city's white leadership.[15] As a case in point, Sviridoff contrasted the successes of the militant and aggressive NAACP to those of the quieter and more deliberate Urban League.[16]

Sviridoff concluded that city officials must consult with a wide range of African American leadership, including the responsible radical segment of the Immoderates/Direct Actionists, to identify "sore spots" at which to direct programs of action. "The alternative is simply to wait for the pressures to build up and eventually to explode—with the leadership inevitably passing into the waiting hands of the 'irresponsibles.'"[17]

Congruent with this view, social programs like CPI could have important social control and leadership-shaping functions in the city government's relationship with its African American population. This was the attitude toward African American leadership that informed Mayor Lee's URS administration in both its urban renewal efforts and its development of Community Progress, Inc., as its human renewal complement, with Mitchell Sviridoff as its head. That view would, of course, find itself in conflict with the growing Immoderate/Direct Actionist African American leadership of the city, which fought hard to keep CPI from having what it considered too much control of its community and leaders.

THE RISE OF THE RACIALLY AMELIORATIVE URS IN NEW HAVEN

The Lee administration initiated urban reforms like CPI in response to the city's changing social, economic, and political face—consistent with the leadership challenges it faced that were articulated in Sviridoff's memorandum. At the center of that change was the quantitative shift in the city's racial demographics, which by darkening the face of New Haven, triggered a profound qualitative transformation of race relations.[18] As was common in many northern cities at that time, African American migration was accompanied by "white flight" to the suburbs. Due to both a growth in births among the city's African American residents and an increase of about eight thousand African Americans who migrated to the city, largely from rural areas of the South, the number of African Americans in New Haven more than doubled in the 1950s to 15 percent of the city's population by 1960. Population projections put city officials on alert that if that trend continued, within the next two decades (by 1980) 40 percent of the city's population would be African American.[19] Moreover, African Americans tended to be concentrated in six densely populated New Haven neighborhoods. Those "inner city" neighborhoods were inundated with problems like poverty, single-parent families, substandard housing, and juvenile delinquency.[20] Clearly "there was no room for complacency." Unfortunately for the Lee URS administration, the city's private social agencies seemed not to have gotten the message. They were not inclined to shift their focus away from serving the needs of their traditional working- and middle-class European American clientele.[21] The attitudes of social service agencies were consistent with the discrimination African Americans faced in employment, in their ability to find credit, and in business ventures.[22]

The failure of the city's social services establishment to engage what politicians and policy elites saw as an increasingly volatile population was troubling. Indeed, due to the explosive mixture of an increasing African American population and rising expectations fueled by the civil rights movement, one scholar of New Haven politics referred to the profound change in the city's race relations during this period as "the social revolution."[23] This nascent revolution in New Haven race relations seemed always within the vision of Richard Lee, the city's most popular and enduring mayor. It was in this racial environment that Community Progress, Inc., was planned and implemented.

COMMUNITY PROGRESS, INC.

The CPI Planning Process and Initial Proposal

In January 1960 New Haven Redevelopment Agency staff member Howard Hallman and his associates wrote a seven-page proposal to the Ford Foundation called "A Program for Community Improvement in New Haven"[24] that provided the outline for what would become CPI and its innovative private, nonprofit corporation organizational structure. It would be another year however before the grant application process with the Ford Foundation would be advanced and the necessary communication with relevant New Haven institutions begun. Although Hallman broadened the planning process to bring in relevant schools and social agency officials,[25] his account does not mention any meetings scheduled with CPI focus-area residents.[26] In April of 1962 the Ford Foundation approved funding for the project, and a few weeks earlier the Kennedy administration, through its President's Committee on Juvenile Delinquency and Youth Crime, announced its award of a $155,825 planning grant to the City of New Haven.[27]

With these grants the urban racial state managers of the Lee administration had an ostensibly color-blind community action initiative. In shifting to its racially ameliorative mode, New Haven's URS administration accomplished this form of racially-targeted population control by ignoring the racially contentious issue of racial ghettoization and choosing instead a policy-frame ideology that limited action to the relatively safe social problem of the assumed cultural deficiency and bad behavior of the ghetto residents themselves. Community action also provided the Lee administration with a way of keeping the focus off the social dislocations caused by its urban renewal policies and practices. That strong link to urban renewal was evident in the Lee administration's choice of the CPI project focus area: the inner-city neighborhoods already impacted by or to be targeted by the city's urban renewal program. Most African Americans were concentrated in the inner-city neighborhoods to be served by CPI. In fact, one of those neighborhoods, Dixwell, was already 73 percent African

American, while an adjoining neighborhood was composed of 42 percent African American residents.[28]

The CPI Vision

The reform mantra CPI shared with other early federal-government sponsored community action programs could be summed up in one word: *opportunity*. As was true for the influential Manhattan-based Mobilization for Youth (MFY) project precursor to the War on Poverty community action programs, the primary program emphasis of CPI was to enhance the educational and employment training opportunities of its clients.[29] In stark contrast, however, to the MFY and Syracuse Action for Youth (SAY) visions, which were each spelled out in a "telephone book" of details,[30] the "Opening Opportunities" proposal section of New Haven's April 2, 1962, Ford Foundation application was only about fifty pages. The brevity of the "Opening Opportunities" proposal and the "Initial Programs" and "Program Development" titles of its second and third chapters suggest that the project's Ford Foundation application was intended to be a sketch of a work in progress, not a carefully fleshed-out plan. This difference reflected the divergent philosophies held by the Ford Foundation and the President's Committee—a major MFY funding source and relative newcomer in its influence on the New Haven project—as to the importance of strong executive leadership versus a significant role for social science planning.[31] It was also indicative of the strong presence and preferences of CPI's first executive director, Mitchell Sviridoff, who took a very practical, plan-as-you-go approach to the development of CPI's programs. Social science theory ("opportunity theory") was useful only to the extent that it legitimized the practical (i.e., Sviridoff's preferred programs in education and job training).[32]

Although the CPI proposal explicitly acknowledged the problem of "racial discrimination," its "opportunity" program focus, like that of the Mobilization for Youth project and most of the later community action programs of the War on Poverty, was on changing the attitudes, behaviors, and skill sets of low-income people of color, not on challenging systemic white racism. As we will see in the next section, when the project's bold rhetorical wrapping of expanding opportunities is removed, what is left is a set of very traditional programs.

CPI Program Components

Seven categories of "initial programs" are listed in the "Opening Opportunities" table of contents. Consistent with the project's emphasis on expanding opportunities and the interests of its first executive director, education and employment programs are mentioned first. They are followed by programs related to leisure-time activities, coordinated community services, the prevention and control of juvenile delinquency, housing opportunity, and opportunity for older people.[33]

Although Mobilization for Youth and Community Progress, Inc., were alike in that both stressed education and employment training programs as the way to realize the expanding-opportunities vision they shared, unlike the MFY project proposal, CPI's proposal contained no distinct community organization division. In the CPI proposal "community workers" and "neighborhood organizations" were components of a fairly conventional set of community services.[34] And the chief job of community workers was to "serve as a bridge" between area residents and local social service agencies. This would be accomplished through the community workers' (preferably area residents) ability "to 'speak' the language of the neighborhood."[35] The goal of the neighborhood organizations program was to work with indigenous area organizations that were already committed to solving community problems. It was further expected that this program would obtain for CPI needed support and cooperation from neighborhood organizations.[36]

The legal services program of the project's Coordinated Community Services component did, however, have built into it the potential for controversy. As we will see later, it was CPI's emergent legal services program that would embroil the project in its earliest racial conflicts. The New Haven proposal was different from the MFY plan in that two of CPI's employment programs and one of its housing programs were designed specifically to address the problem of racial inequality. But this would be done by working within, rather than challenging, the racial order of things. Project funds would be used to set up an Urban League chapter in New Haven to engage in activities in furtherance of a program of equal employment opportunity. Those program activities would also be advanced through the establishment of a Committee on Employment Opportunity composed of leaders representing both labor and management.[37] There would also be a housing for minorities component of the Housing Opportunity program, which with its rather narrow focus could nimbly skirt around the real reason—systemic white racism—such a program was needed in the first place.[38]

As you will see, CPI's brand of community action would prove too timid even for the cautious Ford Foundation.

CPI's Timid Community Action Plans

Despite its facade of independence, Community Progress, Inc., was a city hall program, an appendage of Mayor Lee's URS administration. Therefore, as the epigraph for this chapter makes clear, it would not be allowed to organize residents to challenge city hall and other components of New

Haven's white power structure the mayor counted on for support. And because CPI was to be coadministered by the board of education, the project would not rally parents to challenge the school system, one of the city's major institutions in need of reform. Consequently, community action for CPI was envisioned as a comprehensive plan of neighborhood-based community services rather than as the organization of local residents to challenge local institutions through social protest.[39] Those ideas were consistent with the traditional social work professionals' councils strategy of community organization, a model that elsewhere had been challenged by the more militant and grassroots approach of Saul Alinsky, the famous Chicago-based community organizer.[40]

The Community Progress, Inc., community reform strategy was to use the political clout of the mayor and the grant money and prestige of the Ford Foundation to co-opt local institutions so as to change them. Consequently, community organization or "action" was deemed not to be necessary for CPI to achieve its institutional reform goals. Instead, community action was largely the method of dispensing CPI social services to the neighborhoods served and of soliciting neighborhood support for the project and its programs. The Lee administration would soon realize, however, that timid community action could not guarantee CPI and city hall a snug harbor from the riptides caused by the crashing against the city's racial status quo of the rapidly rising aspirations of some of New Haven's most impatient African American citizens. That tension soon became evident as the controversies over the trial of Harold Cloud, an African American man accused of raping a European American woman, threatened to engulf the fledgling CPI before it could gain its footing as an effective programmer of race relations.

CPI's Collision Course with the Civil Rights Movement

Especially troubling to Mayor Lee and his supporters was their belief that CPI staff involvement with that racially charged case jeopardized the mayor's "governing coalition," which included much of the city's white power structure. As you saw in the chapter's epigraph, the CPI leadership was determined to quickly squash any such challenges from within the project's ranks.[11] And although they did just that, as you will see, their victory revealed the Lee administration's Achilles' heel.

A Challenge to the Ideology of a Common, Racially Transcendent Public Interest

As was true for other reform city governments at that time, the Lee administration was leery of being perceived as serving the interests of specific ethnic groups as had been the common practice under earlier machine politics regimes that had specific white ethnic groups as their core constituencies. The racially convenient ideology of these good government regimes had them serving, by consensus, only one interest—a common, racially transcendent, public interest.[42] Although such apparent color blindness may have seemed laudatory to economically and racially secure liberal reformers and intellectuals, for poor people of color it meant that their specific circumstances and needs, which had long been ignored by political machines and other regimes that served largely white ethnic constituencies, continued to be disregarded. In the name of good government, mayors and planning experts tended to be not only racially distant, but miles apart from low-income African American and Puerto Rican ghetto residents in their class background and worldviews. In this way, like today's color-blind ideology, the myth of a singular and racially transcendent public interest helped to sustain the racial status quo through its highfalutin touting of a democratic ideal that encouraged politicians and policy makers to ignore the social and political consequences of systemic white racism.

As the civil rights movement became a force to be reckoned with in northern ghettos in the early 1960s, that struggle and the philosophies, goals, strategies, and tactics of the Lee administration in its URS capacity were now on a collision course. In examining the Cloud rape trial controversies, I place the civil rights movement and community action programs at the center of the shift in post–World War II urban politics in the United States from the reform era of the 1950s characterized by both racial and class paternalism in racism-blind decision making to a more participatory, conflict-ridden, and more racism-cognizant[43] post-reform period that began in the 1960s and continues today.[44]

CPI AND THE CLOUD RAPE TRIAL CASE

Next I examine what the controversies involving CPI in the trial of Harold Cloud, an African American, for the rape of a European American nurse offer in helping us to understand how the Lee administration, in its urban racial state capacity, handled the conundrum of managing race relations without acknowledging the existence of systemic racial oppression and the centrality of racial ghettoization to its persistence. It was no coincidence that the Cloud rape trial controversies occurred in 1963, after the civil rights movement reached its peak with the successful Birmingham movement and the March on Washington for Jobs and Freedom. Indeed, the summer before those controversies *Connecticut Life* magazine featured an article titled "New Battle for Connecticut Negroes: Birmingham Stirs Demands for Civil Rights, and Comprehensive Attacks on Slum Living," which notes, "as Alabama exploded, Connecticut felt the tremor." The prime example of the "comprehensive attacks on slum living" given in that article was the work of Community Progress, Inc., which was expected—under the impressive leadership of its director, Mitchell Sviridoff—to do what the civil rights movement could not, by addressing the more intractable problems of ghetto life.[45] Once again, the programmatic focus of white liberals was on improving life *within* racial ghettos; not the more controversial, civil-rights-focused goal of the demolition of the highly racialized structures and processes that actually created and maintained them.

As you will see, the Cloud rape trial actually generated two conflicts involving two different African American professionals affiliated with the project whose actions were seen as threatening to the Lee administration and its governing coalition. The first of those disputes, involved Jean Cahn, an attorney on the CPI staff who would later coauthor with her husband a scathing critique in the *Yale Law Journal* that depicted Sviridoff's militaristic rule of CPI as a case in point of a design flaw in the community action programs of the newly initiated War on Poverty.[46] The other controversy involved Richard Dowdy, the city's human relations adviser, who had multiple connections to Community Progress, Inc. Not only was Dowdy involved in the early planning of CPI, but he received part of his salary from CPI and had an office in its headquarters.[47] When Dowdy took actions in support of Cloud's legal defense, Mayor Lee's URS administration quickly found itself the target of intense local news coverage, including newspaper articles and editorials.

Within public policy circles the most influential account of Jean Cahn's dispute with the Lee administration is probably the one published in Peter Marris and Martin Rein's book *Dilemmas of Social Reform*. In their strong racism and power-evasive defense of Mitchell Sviridoff, Marris and Rein appear to have signed on uncritically to the underlying assumptions of the reform urban politics paradigm. Although the authors portray Cahn as a principled person who was concerned about the inexperience of the public defender assigned to the Cloud rape case, his apparent lack of concern, and his unwillingness to pursue evidence pertinent to that case, they made it clear that it was Sviridoff's "prudence" they favored. Sviridoff was said to have insisted that Cahn remove herself from any involvement with the case and to have "strongly discouraged his staff from attending the meetings in the Negro community, where the question of injustice was being raised with growing concern." Because Cahn and other staff members persisted, Marris and Rein lamented that "principle would not yield to prudence."[48] As evidence in support of Sviridoff's decision not to become publicly associated with the defense, they note that "the Mayor was being harassed by anonymous letters and abusive telephone calls," and the reason that "if this public outrage found its target in CPI, his whole programme was in danger."[49]

In stressing the lesson learned from this dispute, the authors draw the same conclusion about the limits of reform government I attributed earlier to CPI deputy director Howard Hallman, a view that was legitimized by *Who Governs?*, Yale University political science professor Robert Dahl's influential study of New Haven.[50] Note their racism-evasive reference to "public outrage" instead of the more accurate term *white backlash* and their ultimate buildup of Sviridoff's wise "practical politics of effective reform" compared to what they depicted as Cahn's foolish "quixotic idealism." "Could CPI at once champion the disadvantaged, in the face of public outrage and the embarrassment of its political allies, and maintain the coalition of institutional support on which its programmes depended? Mitchell Sviridoff believed not. Forced to choose, he sacrificed quixotic idealism to the practical politics of effective reform. Jean Cahn resigned, and the legal programme was temporarily laid aside."[51]

Finally, decades later, Sviridoff talked to me more openly about the racial dynamics involved and how he and the rest of the Lee administration, in its urban racial state capacity, managed what I refer to as the URS conundrum of how to address racial issues without appearing to do so.

> The program served not only minority populations, but served white ethnic populations. So every attempt that was made from the right to attack the program met this powerful coalition of support, right across the community. The reform community, the black community, the white ethnic community. And so I was not prepared to allow that to be undermined by a thoughtless, adventurous, unwise involvement in this criminal case; which is why I stood fast on this one, despite the pressures, even from my major banker.[52]

Unlike Jean Cahn, Richard Dowdy was clearly no troublemaker. He was educated as an economist, was a star basketball player in college, and later played professionally for the Harlem Globetrotters.[53] Before coming to New Haven as the city's human relations adviser in 1959 Dowdy worked with the Urban League chapter in Pittsburgh, and one of his earliest assignments in New Haven was—in line with a goal of the CPI proposal discussed earlier—to develop a local chapter of the National Urban League, a middle-class dominated, social-work orientated, and politically moderate, organization concerned with African American advancement.[54] Unfortunately for the Lee administration, Dowdy's access to the African American community also attracted the interest of European Americans affiliated with Yale University Law School, another powerful New Haven institution that had an interest in the Cloud rape trial. At that time Yale's law school had an arrangement whereby some of its students worked largely as researchers and investigators for the local public defender's office. Those students and their professor, Abraham Goldstein, turned to Dowdy for help when they needed someone who could reach potential witnesses in New Haven's African American ghetto and convince them to testify to a possible relationship between Harold Cloud and the European American nurse he was accused of raping.[55]

Controversy regarding Dowdy's assistance to the Yale law students exploded like a bombshell when a witness—the owner of a barbershop on Dixwell Avenue, New Haven's main ghetto thoroughfare—stated under cross examination that it was "Mr. Dowdy of the mayor's office" who asked him to testify in the Cloud trial.[56] A March 13, 1963, editorial in the *New Haven Register*, "A Sound Sentence—And a Serious Question," congratulated the criminal justice system for imposing "swift and stiff sentences" in the Cloud trial for Cloud and for Harry Reed, another defendant who had previously pleaded guilty, and called for an examination of Dowdy's behavior in the case:

> With the sentence in, we feel that something must now be done to explain the peculiar activities of the Mayor's human relations adviser, Richard Dowdy. "Mr. Dowdy of the mayor's office" emerged, in the testimony of one witness, as a participant in defense moves which have since been described by the State's Attorney Gorman as "rape" of the victim's reputation. Is such activity a function of the municipal human relations adviser? We'd like to know. And we think that Mr. Dowdy has some explaining to do—in terms as open and obvious as those of his courtroom activity.[57]

In its second editorial on Dowdy's involvement in the Cloud rape trial, the newspaper questioned the wisdom of having one city entity, the human relations adviser's office—as "a new and unexpected authority" (a part of the URS administration's ideological state apparatus)—at odds with another city agency, the police department (the chief component of the URS administration's repressive state apparatus).[58] Finally, like Marris and Rein, without ever speaking directly to the issue of the racial conflict involved, the editorial expresses the ideology of city government serving only one common public interest: "Mr. Dowdy's performance was, in our opinion, deficient in an understanding of community-wide tensions."[59]

This was certainly not the view shared by *all* of *the* public. A letter from the local branch of the NAACP to Mayor Lee criticized what its leaders considered to be the lackadaisical defense by the local defender's office and supported Dowdy's involvement in the case. That organization also promised that because it saw "such assistance as being consonant with the functions of his position in city government" it would, in the future, seek the aid of the city's human relation's adviser as it played a more active role in cases that involved indigent defenders from the community.⁶⁰ The stage was now set for serious racial conflict over what community action programs and other apparatuses of the urban racial state should and should not do as the civil rights movement pushed the aspirations of African Americans forward in New Haven and many other American cities.

In the next section I explore the origins of the Syracuse Action for Youth (SAY) anti–juvenile delinquency project proposal in Syracuse, New York, and the various issues that proposal raised as it laid the foundation in that city for other community action program challenges to Mayor Walsh's URS administration.

THE ORIGINS OF COMMUNITY ACTION IN SYRACUSE

Changing Racial Demographics and Race Relations

Throughout much of Syracuse's history, the number of African Americans was very small and scattered. Whereas this near invisibility served to keep African Americans powerless politically, it also shielded them somewhat from racial competition and animus. Indeed, just as New Haven had once been a center for abolitionist activities, Syracuse was at one time a station for the Underground Railroad movement of escaped slaves to freedom in Canada. That attitude changed in the beginning of the twentieth century with the emergence of a white racist reaction after the African American population of the city increased to about five hundred and African Americans were hired as domestics and construction workers. As the African American population increased, it faced ghettoization due to housing discrimination and the city's failure to enforce housing codes.⁶¹ By 1960, Syracuse's population was on the decline, and despite rapid growth in the 1940s and 1950s, its 11,000 African Americans still made up only 5 percent of the city's total population.⁶² Consequently, African Americans in Syracuse found themselves in the precarious situation of being large enough to be perceived as a racial problem by the city's establishment but too small to have any real political clout.

The Syracuse Action for Youth anti-delinquency program proposal makes specific reference to the racist treatment of African Americans in the 1960s. For example, it notes that interviews revealed "that Negroes are belittled" because "they are thought to be invading neighborhoods occupied by white, native American or established immigrant groups."⁶³ Apparently, decades of the white power structure's acquiescence to the "usual prejudice" against African Americans contributed to a vicious racist cycle in which systemic white racism produced racial ghettoization, and the increased migration of African Americans to such areas that were in essence racial reservations resulted in an intensification of racist hostility and efforts to contain them. This likelihood is supported by a study conducted in the 1960s that found not only employment and housing discrimination against African Americans in Syracuse, but that those concrete manifestations of systemic white racism were greater than what African Americans experienced in other upstate New York cities.[64] The racism included employment discrimination against African Americans: "General Electric had never promoted a black to foreman. The Niagara-Mohawk Power Company employed less than a handful of blacks and offered a black college graduate a job as a janitor," and "in 1963, not one single black man belonged to any of the skilled craft unions."[65] These were just some of the statistics that suggested to national policy elites that Syracuse could benefit from racially noncontroversial social programs like those designed to tackle the problem of juvenile delinquency.

The Early Years of the Youth Development Center

Just as the Ford Foundation had a significant reform presence in New Haven, it was also involved in Syracuse by way of its provision in 1958 of a five-year grant to fund the Syracuse University–based Youth Development Center.[66] This center provided social science ideas and legitimacy that helped implant the more activist, Saul Alinsky–style community organizing seeds into later anti-delinquency (Syracuse Action for Youth) and antipoverty (Crusade for Opportunity CFO) projects initiated by the city administration, as well as another activist Syracuse University project—the Community Action Training Center (CATC).

As you saw earlier, in addressing urban problems foundation officials, politicians, and other reformers typically tried to manage racial inequality in a racially blind fashion. This racism-evasive approach would prevail until the civil rights movement flushed the problem out into the open as it shifted its framing from a Negro problem to a civil rights issue. Youth Development Center director Irwin Deutscher recalled how his ideas evolved from the time he arrived in Syracuse in 1959 to the peak of the civil rights movement in 1963:

> I scoffed at the suggestion that the Youth Development Center might be concerned to any large degree with the problems of race. I recall assuring our Community Citizens Board that race was only one of many variables that might enter into our search for understanding the process of growing up in the city. By 1963 we have come to realize that the urban problem of high rates of delinquency is inextricably tied to the urban problems of poverty, dependency, and race.[67]

The Goal of Community Action Programs in Syracuse: Challenge the White Power Structure

Unlike what was true for New Haven, Syracuse's various community action programs were designed, to one degree or another, to challenge the city's white power structure, including city hall. This was possible because, also unlike the situation in New Haven, in Syracuse the development of community action was never securely under the control of city government. As you will see in Syracuse, projects were designed by social scientists and other social-issues experts who sought to advance not only their own professional and organizational agendas but political goals that were meant to subvert the social and economic status quo. Indeed, much of the work on the Syracuse Action for Youth project proposal was done in 1963, at the peak of the civil rights movement. Of particular relevance for the African American residents of northern cities like New Haven and Syracuse were the racial and economic consequences of ghettoization and urban renewal.

Ghettoization and Urban Renewal

Racial ghettoization, the eight-hundred-pound gorilla most social-policy analysts and makers then and now choose not to see, was and is at the core of the problems faced by low-income African American residents of inner-city neighborhoods. Intense racial segregation can be explained neither by the living preferences of ghetto residents nor by the social isolation of the poor that results from the movement of more affluent residents to "better" neighborhoods. Instead, ghettoization is a dynamic process that is maintained by active segregationist attitudes, policies, and practices. In the early 1960s, 90 percent of Syracuse's African American residents were confined to the city's Fifteenth Ward ghetto. The appropriateness of the term "confined" is supported by a survey that found that not only did 80 percent of the city's African American population prefer to live elsewhere but most actually paid rents high enough to allow them to do so if their way had not been "blocked by a racial alliance of landlords, owners, realtors, and bankers."[68]

Campbell et al., who reported that 88 percent of Syracuse's African American residents lived in only 8 percent of the city's census tracts, also found major racial differences in owner occupation rates that ran contrary to the city's reputation of offering its citizens extraordinary opportunities for home ownership. Whereas most "whites" (51 percent) owned the homes they occupied, this was true for only 16 percent of the study's "non-whites," the greatest white/nonwhite difference of any upstate New York city. The overwhelming majority of Syracuse's African American population remained renters in racial ghettos. Moreover, the city's African American citizens paid much more for much less, with a much higher proportion of their incomes going for homes and for rent. They also lived in more crowded conditions in housing units that were much more likely to be deteriorated or dilapidated. By every definition, the vast majority of Syracuse's African American population was ghettoized.[69]

In Syracuse the problems that accrued from racial ghettoization were greatly exacerbated by the racially disparate consequences of the city's urban renewal practices. When the land of the adjacent black ghetto proved valuable to downtown white business interests, Syracuse's URS administration acted decisively in its capacity as an agent of racially-targeted population control by forcing ghetto residents farther out into new ghetto areas.[70] Ghettoization and urban renewal proved to be the proverbial "rock and a hard place" as most low-income African Americans in Syracuse found themselves stuck "between the bulldozers knocking over their homes in the one area whites allowed them to live and discrimination in housing outside that area." Early on, with "most of the first 250 families relocated to different parts of the same ghetto or areas near it," it was clear that urban renewal would fortify Syracuse's ghetto, not demolish it.[71] Indeed, by 1963, statistics from the city government office charged with relocating families made homeless by the city's redevelopment practices revealed that "97 percent of relocation of Negroes had been in the Ghetto or adjacent areas, mostly in substandard neighborhoods."[72] Not surprisingly, the social and economic predicament of impoverished African Americans who resided in the Syracuse Action for Youth project focus area was especially bad.

The SAY Project Focus Area Ghetto

The four neighborhoods chosen for SAY programmatic action were simply those that had the highest juvenile delinquency rates.[73] Let's take a closer look at the social and economic conditions in those areas.

The ghettoization of African Americans in the SAY "action area" is strikingly clear in the following quotation from the project's proposal: "Of the total number of Negroes in Syracuse in 1960, 80 percent reside in our Action Area and nearly 70 percent in one specific neighborhood in the Action Area."[74] The neighborhood with the extremely high ghettoization was called Action Area A. Not surprisingly, Area A also had the lowest socio-economic status (SES) of its residents and the most serious social problems.[75]

Residential segregation has devastating consequences in the educational, employment, income, and other opportunities it denies its victims. Both historically and today—nationally and in specific places like Syracuse—residential segregation has been, and remains, a major cause of poverty among African Americans.[76] Among the many negative consequences are de facto school segregation and a greater civic and school system tolerance of educational failure involving inner-city schools and their students. Not surprisingly, the SAY proposal cites numerous indicators of such educational failure for the project's Action Area, especially for Area A.[77]

Considering the educational problems, patterns of ghettoization, and discrimination experienced by African Americans in Syracuse, it should come as no surprise that unemployment was a major problem for the residents of the SAY Action Area. Indeed, the proposal notes that in Area A, one out of six adult males was unemployed.[78] Of course, high unemployment was not just an issue for area adults. Low-income male boys who were not in school not only faced high rates of unemployment but were more likely to drop out of the labor force as well. Moreover, it was found that while being a high school dropout was devastating for Action Area youth, with nearly half (47 percent) being unemployed, a high school diploma was no ticket to employment for these youth. Ten percent of the boys who did graduate high school still faced unemployment.[79]

The community organization of the area, which is closely related to its economic, social, and physical well-being, was also lacking. This is evident in the fact that although Action Area residents were both aware of and dissatisfied with neighborhood problems, there was a low level of activity to address those problems. For example, they were less likely than the residents of the middle-class neighborhoods to be members of social organizations or to participate in electoral politics. In regard to political participation, only half of the residents of Area A voted in the last mayoral election, and a third never voted. This lack of political involvement was attributed to cynicism and a sense of powerlessness.[80] Socio-economic pressure was also cited as another factor associated with the high level of delinquency in the SAY Action Area. Here the authors bring in a blocked-opportunities emphasis compatible with Richard Cloward and Lloyd Ohlin's opportunity theory, which provided the ideological rationale for the War on Poverty.[81] Thus, the SAY proposal focuses on community disorganization and the paucity of opportunities available to area residents. This provided the rationale for subsequent community action programs that contained both the ideology and the resources for challenges to the city's URS administration and other elements of its white power structure.

The Social Protest Response

Clearly, African Americans in Syracuse had lots to complain about in the early 1960s. And as the civil rights movement advanced and spread those grievances, they found a voice in social protest. In August of 1963, the Congress of Racial Equality's (CORE) Syracuse chapter skipped the March on Washington and instead launched its own protest against urban renewal in Syracuse. This is how a history of CORE recorded the protest that was begun on that day: "Charging that Negroes were simply being shifted to other slums, nearly one hundred Syracuse CORE members and supporters protested during the summer of 1963 by blocking bulldozers, sitting on cranes, and halting demolition work at urban renewal sites."[82] The goal of these protests was much larger than urban renewal; the list of demands CORE leader George Wiley presented to Mayor Walsh included "construction of low-cost public housing outside the ghetto, relocation of blacks in safe, integrated housing, enforcement of housing codes, and passage of an ordinance prohibiting housing discrimination." In brief, CORE hoped to use that dramatic confrontation over a downtown redevelopment project that was highly valued by Syracuse's business and political elite to force the city to address all of its racial problems, including of course the one the local white power structure was least inclined to tackle, racial segregation in housing.[83]

In response to the protests, Mayor Walsh, acting in his capacity as head of Syracuse's URS administration, met with CORE leaders and offered some concessions, including the enforcement of housing codes, the establishment of a human rights commission, and a promise that "families of color would not have to move into a block already more than one-third people of color." But CORE could not forestall the devastating impact urban renewal (or "Negro removal," as it came to be known nationwide by many of its African American critics) would have on the African American community in Syracuse. Decades later a report by the Human Rights Commission of Syracuse and Onondaga County lamented that "the bulldozers were never stopped. Twenty-seven blocks of the 15th Ward were razed including the houses of about 75 percent of the city's black population. Four of the five major black churches, and most of the stores, businesses, and social centers owned by blacks were demolished."[84] In brief, with the encouragement of local business leaders and support from the federal government, city government, operating in its then racially oblivious URS administrative form, destroyed most of the African American community in Syracuse and the indigenous resources it might muster for racial protest.[85]

But that was not the only legacy of that urban renewal struggle. The protests radicalized CORE members and supporters, who came to agree with Wiley when at a large church rally following his release from jail he stressed that their struggle was much larger than urban renewal.[86] Among those CORE supporters who were politically transformed by the urban renewal protests were some of the designers of the city's insurgent community action programs. For example, those arrested in civil rights demonstrations in that city in September 1963 included "two members of the Mayor's Commission on Youth" and "the director and some staff members of the Youth Development Center."[87] "Professor Warren C. Haggstrom of the School of Social Work, Syracuse University, and Dr. Irwin Deutscher, Director of the Youth Development Center at Syracuse University and also Assistant Director of the Mayor's Commission on Youth" were arrested while holding protest signs next to buildings that were being demolished.[88]

The Youth Development Center Plants Seeds of Community Action Insurgency

A good place to begin my examination of the Syracuse University–based Youth Development Center's subversive role in the planning of community action in Syracuse is with the community reform philosophies and civil rights involvement of its social science activists, who were influential in the planning of the city's community action programs. They were Syracuse University professor Irvin Deutscher, the center's director, and psychologically oriented social work professor Warren Haggstrom, both of whom I have already mentioned, and sociologist S. M. Miller. The center's influence was stressed in an oral history interview with Betty Baer, a social worker who was assigned by the United Way to serve as the planning director of the SAY project and to work with the Youth Development Center in the crafting of that project, which later—with Office of Economic Opportunity funding—became Crusade for Opportunity. In stressing how she was "very much influenced by the sociologists at the Youth Development Center," Baer, who was also inspired directly by the civil rights movement, recalled, "My education really began with people like Irwin Deutscher."[89]

In his report on the Youth Development Center's first five years, Deutscher describes the differences in Professor Haggstrom's and Professor Miller's "action" schools. In doing so he raised some of the key issues and limitations of community action as an urban reform strategy that would later manifest themselves in controversies in cities like New Haven and Syracuse. Miller, who served as an adviser to the local CORE chapter, is described as "an economist and sociologist" interested in "lower and working class families," "in the labor movement, in political action, in social mobility, and in the consequences for a democratic society of a 'have' and 'have not' economy."[90] Deutscher describes Haggstrom as "a social worker and social psychologist" who had rejected the traditional social work goal to "help the poor" for a social action strategy. And he surmises that the basic rationale of Haggstrom's approach to social action was that the problem was "not so much poverty per se as enforced dependency." The solution was therefore to deploy social action in such a way as to help the poor "grow from dependency to interdependency with the larger community." In brief, social protest was valued largely for its socio-therapeutic effect. Because of his belief that many of the problems facing the poor could not be addressed at the local level, Miller took a more cautious approach to the potential of social action as a force for social change than did Haggstrom. In Miller's view social action is most effective when it links "local actions to broader national concerns though increased political activity and leverage."[91]

Like Haggstrom, Ben Zimmerman, the executive director of both SAY and its Crusade for Opportunity offspring, and Lloyd Ohlin, a sociologist and Ford Foundation consultant who was influential in helping craft the "opportunity" conceptual frame of such initiatives, Miller saw a key role for nonindigenous organizations in the development of indigenous leadership and organizations. Miller notes that "there is increasing talk about developing indigenous leadership in the areas of poverty in the large city. . . . Perhaps, as Ben Zimmerman has pointed out, the thing that can be done most effectively by outsiders—noncolored, nonpoor—coming into the impoverished areas is to try to develop the kinds of issues, crises and situations which permit, encourage, and engender the emergence of indigenous leadership."[92]

Miller's ultimate goal here was not to address racial oppression directly or to support African Americans who were already doing so, but to redirect the movement into what he saw as a more progressive, safer, and more manageable channel. Miller cautioned that unless African Americans were moved into class-based alliances with other working-class people "to fight for some common economic and political interests," they would "become a group narrowly attuned to race interests and mainly concerned with what happened to them." Moreover, in such a scenario groups like the "the Negro-Muslim movement" would grow in influence. Clearly, although Professor Miller was concerned about "improving the housing and communities of the poor," he and most of his professional colleagues were not inclined to take action that would increase the "the prominence of race" as an issue, such as a major assault on housing segregation and other forms of racial oppression.[93] Instead, the energy of the civil rights movement was to be diverted into the less racially explosive arena of community action, where "indigenous" movements were to be planned by outside elites who had other social issues and political agendas to pursue.

As you have seen, the relative radicalization[94] of these social problems professionals, who after their involvement with the urban renewal protests designed community action programs that likely incorporated the lessons they learned from that experience, came at a time when much of the indigenous organizational capacity of the African American community in Syracuse to challenge the white power structure had been destroyed by urban renewal. The combination of those two facts may have tempted these progressive European American professionals to believe that externally imposed schemes like community action were now needed.

The SAY Project Proposal as a Seedbed for African American Insurgency

As Aesop noted millennia ago in his fable about the wolf in sheep's clothing, "appearances often are deceiving."[95] Another apt metaphor for understanding the subversive intent of the SAY proposal is that of a Trojan horse. Hidden within the Syracuse Action for Youth project proposal was an activist philosophy of community action that developed into something quite different from what the city's political and social services establishment anticipated. Indeed, as I will show in the next chapter, the President's Committee on Juvenile Delinquency and Youth Crime project in Syracuse sowed the seeds of what would become the most explicit attempt in the nation to apply confrontational Alinsky-style community organization strategies and tactics to a War on Poverty community action program.[96]

CONCLUSION

The coming of the post-reform era of urban politics helped shape community action programs in New Haven and Syracuse as vehicles for programming race relations. This chapter's case history evidence shows that in both cities the more controversial and intractable problem of racial ghettoization was largely ignored for a safer focus on juvenile delinquency and poverty-centered programs of community action. Also, in both cities, the color-blind strategy for appearing to address what was, in fact, essentially a problem of systemic white racism would prove futile as the civil rights movement grew, became more militant, and boldly yanked the cloak off of racism-evasive politics, policies, and programs. There is, however, one important difference in the program administration in the two cities. Under the Lee administration, the New Haven URS administration forbade Community Progress, Inc., from being subverted into a tool for African American insurgency, while the more conservative URS administration in Syracuse, which unlike the racially ameliorative URS administration in New Haven was still operating mostly in its racially oblivious mode, seemed remarkably unaware of the racial implications of community action as the Syracuse Action for Youth project planners quietly plotted to deploy that organization in support of the civil rights movement and its challenges to the local white power structure, including of course city hall. In brief, whereas the designers and operators of the New Haven city government who ran Community Progress, Inc., were careful not to upset the racial status quo in their programming of race relations, this was precisely the goal of the Syracuse Action for Youth project and subsequent community action programs it influenced, which were relatively independent of the control of the local urban racial state.[97]

In chapter 3 I take a closer look at how over the next two years—fueled by the rising expectations of both civil rights movement activists and those community residents served by the War on Poverty community action programs—New Haven's Community Progress, Inc., and Syracuse Action for Youth, and the other community action programs SAY planners influenced, became centers of sometimes intense racial struggles for control of community action programs. You will see how—as I illustrated in figure 1.2—the federal and urban racial states, in response to African American demands, first expanded the War on Poverty community action programs' social protest and participatory democracy capabilities and later contracted those more activist components of community action as they capitulated to the demands of the white racial backlash.

3

The Civil Rights Movement, the War on Poverty, and Conflict over the Use of Community Action to Support African American Insurgency

> Here was the establishment on one side, and here were the ugly whites on the other side. And King and his movement . . . could sweep down the middle and could negotiate. It was that kind of a concept. So we imagined. . . .
>
> —Betty Baer, planning director, Syracuse Action for Youth[1]

The best laid plans of mice and men sometimes go astray.[2] As we have seen, community action programs were intended by foundation officials and politicians to offer both color- and racism-blind ways of managing the political, economic, and social volatility that was expected to accrue from profound demographic shifts in the racial and class composition of many cities. With a forceful push from the civil rights movement, however, they often had exactly the opposite effect. In this chapter I examine conflict over the use of the community action programs (CAPs) of the racially ameliorative urban racial state (URS) as instruments of African American insurgency. Here you will also get a glimpse of the consequences of that conflict for CAPs, the URS, city government, and urban politics.

COMMUNITY ACTION PROGRAMS AS ONE OF THREE TYPES OF RACIAL FORCES

In chapter 1, I introduced the challenges the urban racial state may face as it responds to conflicting racial demands. This chapter explores the complex and quickly shifting relationships among community action programs, the urban racial state, African American aspirations, and white resistance by building on and ultimately going beyond the simple graphics presented there in figures 1.1 and 1.2. Here I examine the confluence between the civil rights movement, the War on Poverty, and the use of community action programs in New Haven and Syracuse to understand how the rise and increasing militancy of the civil rights movement sparked conflict over the racial purposes to which those projects would be deployed. More specifically, in this chapter you will see how community action programs were used as racial forces in three different ways: (1) as a tool for racial control by the URS administration, (2) as a co-opted resource for African American insurgency, and (3) as a subversive facade of mediation between black struggle and white resistance, as illustrated in this chapter's epigraph.

Let's begin by examining criticism from both policy elites and the grassroots of the Lee URS administration's attempt to deploy community action in New Haven as a means of racial control.

COMMUNITY ACTION AND RACIAL CONFLICT IN NEW HAVEN

Elite Criticism of CPI

The year 1964 is important for the critical evaluation of community action programs for a number of reasons, not the least of which is that on August 20, President Johnson signed the Economic Opportunity Act, the bill that authorized and funded the War on Poverty community action programs.[3] It was also the year that Mobilization for Youth and Harlem Youth Opportunities Unlimited–Associated Community Teams, the two influential Manhattan-based precursors to the War on Poverty community action programs, endured major crises that gave politicians great concern about the ability of such projects to cause them political trouble through social protest challenges to their local white power structures.[4]

Crisis in Black and White

The first of the two critiques I will discuss here was influential because it was written as part of a book the Ford Foundation commissioned as an early assessment of its Gray Areas programs, which included CPI.[5] In *Crisis in Black and White* Charles Silberman criticized what he characterized as the top-down paternalism of Ford Foundation projects while he praised the indigenous community organization efforts advised by the renowned community organizer Saul Alinsky. Silberman specifically cited the planning of CPI as an example of that "grand fusion of paternalism and bureaucracy."

After quoting its executive director, Mitchell Sviridoff, on the type of programmatic vision that was needed and the various types of groups to be represented on the CPI board of directors, Silberman observed that "the crucial question raised by Sviridoff's oratory is, who is to do the planning for whom . . . everybody, in short except the people being planned for."[6]

Silberman rooted that paternalism in two basic assumptions about urban reform that were held by Paul Ylvisaker, the Ford Foundation official responsible for those projects: acculturation theory and a consensus-centered view of how urban government should operate. Silberman believed that in limiting its focus to the need for the acculturation of low-income African Americans migrants to northern cities, acculturation theory, which was popular among social scientists at that time, served "as a license to look away from the uncomfortable fact of race and so to avoid the hard and painful decisions."[7] As I noted earlier, the hardest and most painful decision that the very existence of CAPs helped avoid was what to do about residential segregation and the ghettoization it caused and sustained.

The second reason Silberman gave for the paternalism and fear of controversy embedded in Ford Foundation–sponsored programs like CPI was Paul Ylvisaker's consensus-centered view of how urban government should operate. This is an important issue because it is yet another articulation of the democratic theory of urban reform government I discussed in the previous chapter that allowed CPI to justify its alignment with the local white power structure as opposed to the growing aspirations of the city's African American citizens, under the ideological cover of serving some mythical common public interest. Silberman rooted Ylvisaker's "naïve" need for "community-wide consensus" in what he argued was that foundation official's misunderstanding of how American democracy was intended to work and does work both nationally and in cities. As his case in point, Silberman quoted Ylvisaker lamenting how American cities do not have the unifying democratic safeguards like those in the preamble to the U.S. constitution:

> "Without these soaring objects," he argues, "we become in the metropolis but a collection of warring self-interests concerned with the means rather than the ends of human existence" . . . "we the people" becomes "some of the people" and "some of you people."

Citing Martin Luther King Jr.'s famous letter from a Birmingham jail in which Reverend King chided white moderates and liberals for claiming to support the civil rights movement's means while rejecting its methods, Silberman argued that such a simplistic and unrealistic dichotomy would make it extremely difficult to address racial issues.[8] By definition, such issues, because they are rooted in social division, do not fit a consensus model. A similar assessment of such restrictions placed on community action programs was inherent in Jean and Edgar Cahn's influential essay on the community action programs of the War on Poverty, which was also published that year.

The Cahns' Essay on the War on Poverty

To say that the Cahns provided an early critique of the War on Poverty community action programs is a bit of an understatement. The July publication date of their influential[9] paper, "The War on Poverty: A Civilian Perspective," in the *Yale Law Journal* was actually a month prior to President Johnson's signing of the Economic Opportunity Act of 1964.[10] What they were really critiquing then were the plans for the War on Poverty that had been heavily influenced by the Ford Foundation and President's Committee on Juvenile Delinquency and Youth Crime (PCJD) project precursors to its community action programs. Although the Cahns' article rarely mentioned race, much less racism, their critique was a part of a then-emerging counter-ideology that, along with the civil rights movement, helped usher in our current—more racism-cognizant and participatory—post-reform era of urban politics. It was in this way that their essay had profound racial implications.

In *Urban Policy and Politics in a Bureaucratic Age*, Clarence Stone, Robert Whelan, and William Murin view the War on Poverty community action programs and their project precursors as part of that movement to what they referred to as the post-reform era of post–World War II urban politics. That shift was away from the consensus/one common public interest–oriented, top-down/experts decide, and white-dominated reform era of urban politics characteristic of many U.S. city governments in the 1950s to the more confrontational/competing interests, participatory, and racially and ethnically diverse mode of governance typical of the post-reform era of urban politics that emerged in the 1960s.[11] As I will show in this book, as a propellant in that movement, African American insurgency would place growing pressure on the urban racial state—especially its executive branch governmental core—for a racism and public-policy shift from the racism-driven or racism-blind policies and practices characteristic of the racially oblivious URS to a racially ameliorative URS that could, with sufficient pressure, engage in racism-cognizant, racism-sensitive, and even racism-targeted actions.[12] This post-reform ideological challenge to the underlying assumptions of the reform era of urban politics is obvious in the Cahns' description of the "essence" of their civilian perspective as "one of dissent, of critical scrutiny, of advocacy, and of impatience."[13] As you will see, however, the Cahns' argument was fundamentally flawed in one of its basic premises. They were wrong in their presumption that the militaristic and civilian approaches to urban governance and community reform were, indeed, compatible. They were not.

In their essay, the Cahns skillfully exploit what became the "maximum feasible participation of the poor" mandate of the Economic Opportunity Act of 1964 to make their public-policy case for the urgency of adding a more participatory "civilian" perspective to what they saw as the dominant militaristic ideology, policies, and practices of CPI and other project precursors to the War on Poverty community action programs. The significance of the Cahns' article is enhanced by their choice of the Office of Economic Opportunity's (OEO) "maximum feasible participation of the poor" mandate as their analytical focal point. Not only did that policy ensure representation of the poor on community action program boards, but it helped to shape the history of post–World War II U.S. urban politics and to expand the democratic processes of the entire nation.[14]

In a section titled, "The Strictly Military Approach to Urban Poverty—Community Progress, Inc.," the Cahns identified what they considered to be the "core" characteristics of CPI's "purely military approach." The first of those characteristics of the CPI strategy is that its war was "to be fought by professionals on behalf of the citizenry through service programs." That is, congruent with other reform-era urban government initiatives, the CPI war on poverty was top-down in its planning and administration and traditional in its programmatic content. The second military characteristic of CPI the Cahns identified was that the agency's "attempts to retain and utilize the support, energies, and resources of the incumbent political administration and major local commercial, charitable, and educational institutions." The third and final military characteristic of CPI the Cahns identified stressed the necessity of having a well-formulated project plan and sticking to it.[15] This meant that, again in accord with the top-down reform government approach, once the experts set into place their plan, with little or no participation of neighborhood residents, the CPI administrators would stay with that design regardless of demands by CPI project-area residents that were sparked by a combination of the increasing urgency of the civil rights movement and the maximum feasible participation mandate of the War on Poverty legislation. In brief, here the Cahns' main complaint about CPI was that by neglecting "the poverty of the spirit in ministering to the needs of the flesh" it had a disempowering impact on democratic participation.[16]

Further, the Cahns made an observation that had important implications for urban politics: CPI was *not* a neighborhood project. In its focus on the *majority* of the city's neighborhoods, the project reflected the tendency of reform government to design initiatives to benefit the entire city rather than its often-competing ethnic groups or neighborhoods. This meant that under this "overall perspective" the unique needs of specific neighborhoods were less likely to be met, especially when to do so might result in competition over resources or political opposition from other neighborhoods. More important politically, unlike other neighborhood-based community action programs like those in Syracuse, the neighborhood residents served by CPI were less likely to see themselves as pressure groups organized around neighborhood and ethnic issues and leadership. Consequently, because of their commitment to supporting the existing coalitional bias, projects like CPI could actually work against the national movement of low-income residents of color who pushed for a more participatory, post-reform era of urban government.[17]

This need to maintain a "citywide perspective" and an overall plan takes us back to what I quoted CPI deputy director Howard Hallman in the previous chapter as saying about the necessity of the project avoiding controversy in order to protect Mayor Lee's governing coalition. As the Cahns put it, "such a perspective of delicate balances has, in more than one comprehensive program, led to particular, and even general prohibitions, being placed on neighborhood attorneys' participating in litigation which might stir up antagonism and jeopardize other portions of the program." Specifically cited as examples of racial controversies were cases involving "the defense of a Negro accused of assaulting a white policeman or raping a white woman." Another example the Cahns gave of racism evasiveness as a form of "risk avoidance" had to do with any efforts that might threaten the existence of racial ghettos. Project actions to address the problem of residential segregation would tend to be limited to "finding homes in mixed and all-white neighborhoods for prospective Negro homeowners with steady incomes and middle-class backgrounds." With that narrow and relatively safe focus, the more important problem of "equal opportunity in rental housing for lower class Negroes with small incomes, large families, and poor housekeeping habits" would be ignored.[18] This is of course not surprising because, as I noted earlier, if the Ford Foundation, the federal racial state, and local URSs had been willing to tackle the intense residential segregation and other forms of racial oppression ghetto residents faced, there would have been no need for community action programs.

On December 7, 1964, Richard Oliver Brooks, a lawyer and special assistant to CPI director Mitchell Sviridoff, prepared a lengthy response to the Cahns' article for a University of Pennsylvania law professor, with a copy sent to the Ford Foundation. Not only was Brooks' letter an eloquent ideological defense of CPI's approach to community action and conceptualization of democratic theory by "a partisan defender of the 'faith' of Community Progress," but, equally important, like the arguments of Howard Hallman, it was a justification of the reform-government approach to reform and a response to the Cahns' challenges to its underlying assumptions. And as I noted earlier, the battle between the advocates of the post–World War II reform and post-reform eras of urban politics was anything but color-blind. In the first paragraph of his letter, Brooks stresses the racial context of his debate with the Cahns by indicating that his response would encompass his understanding of "the nature of the civil rights movement."[19]

Brooks did not waste much time in getting to the core of this disagreement with the Cahns for taking more of an ethnic-neighborhood than a citywide perspective that was sensitive to the needs of what, as I noted earlier, Hallman referred to as Mayor Lee's governing coalition. On page two of his reply he characterizes the Cahns' criticisms as being "irresponsible" because they were not "formulated in such a way to be *responsive to all* the factors and forces within a community."[20]

Later, in his reply to the Cahns' criticism of CPI taking a professional-service orientation in its military approach that resulted in "undercutting incipient protest," Brooks seems to speak directly to arguments I made in chapter 1 about community action programs serving as the URS's mediator of African American aspirations and white racial resentment and, more specifically, to the limitations faced by consensus-focused and racism-evasive reform city governments in addressing those growing African American aspirations:

> We are in the midst of a Negro revolution which is demanding an equal status for the Negro. At the same time, however, we are in the midst of a society in which the immediate recognition of these claims of the Negro are rejected in part or totally by some of the white community. The hard truth is that public officials, responsible for leadership of the entire community and elected by that whole community, must strike a balance between the groups in society, while moving toward the realization of equality.[21]

Brooks also discusses the nature of government and the civil rights movement and the appropriate relationship between the two:

> In essence, Community Progress, Inc. is a *public* program with, for the most part, *public* funds to spend on a program to relieve poverty. The program depends upon the cooperation of *public* officials for implementation of the program. It is not the Civil Rights movement, and to confuse the two, or to judge one another by a common standard, would be a disservice to both. Since Community Progress, Inc. must be responsive to the whole community, it must balance community claims.[22]

And for Brooks, balancing those claims meant the rejection of the Cahns' call for inclusion of a civilian community action program perspective that encouraged the direct participation of the poor and possibly the use of social protest as a means toward local reform as opposed to relying on representative democracy.[23]

As I noted earlier, the Cahns' article and Richard Brooks' response to it are emblematic of elites in conflict over whether city government should follow the post–World War II urban reform politics model characteristic of the Lee URS administration, CPI, and its racism-evasive coalitional bias[24] or the emerging, more participatory and conflict-responsive postreform approach. To further explore the issue of who should control community action programs, and for what racial purpose, I will now examine the emergence of a grassroots challenge to the model of governance deployed by the Lee administration and his CPI project as the civil rights movement gained the momentum that would help reshape urban politics in the United States.

THE RISE OF CPI's NEMESIS: THE HILL PARENTS ASSOCIATION

The negative attitude Mayor Lee held toward African American leaders I discussed in the previous chapter also manifested itself in his often-hostile relationship with them. This included his infiltration of the New Haven chapter of the National Association for the Advancement of Colored People (NAACP) with his own supporters and his marginalization of the local chapter of the Congress of Racial Equality (CORE). These and other actions by the mayor left a leadership vacuum in that city for African Americans who felt the need to challenge his administration and other elements of the local white power structure. That would be filled in the Hill neighborhood with the establishment of the Hill Parents Association (HPA), a grassroots organization that often found itself at odds with Community Progress, Inc.[25]

One of the places where reform was badly needed was New Haven's public schools. Indeed even CPI was committed to some level of school reform, although its reluctance to upset the local power structure and its strong ties to the school system made it unlikely that the project would either initiate or support significant challenges to the way the city's school system operated. Ironically, this Community Progress, Inc., failure became a source of neighborhood empowerment by making clear both the need and the opportunity for the formation of an indigenous neighborhood organization that could address such problems.

According to Fred Harris, one of its founders and its first president, the Hill Parents Association had its origins in the fact that the basic needs of some of the city's low-income African American school children were not being met by the public schools. One day Harris, an African American machinist, noticed his wife giving their two children toilet paper to take to school. When he asked her why she was doing that, she informed him that the children did not have toilet tissue at the school and that they had developed sores from using brown paper towels to wipe themselves. After Harris unsuccessfully confronted the Prince Street School principal and janitor about the issue, he was visited by a group of teachers from the school who informed him of the conditions there and of his rights as a parent. Harris was again disappointed when he took his concerns to the board of education. He then started organizing area parents with the help of the teachers and a group of Yale University students.[26]

Harris noted that from its first organizational meeting what became known as the Hill Parents Association received "opposition from people that were supposed to work for CPI . . . or were friends of CPI." He also recalled his suspicion when, while he was in front of a school, he was approached with advice by someone who worked for CPI. "I don't remember exactly what he said, but I had no trust for him, because he worked for CPI." In providing the context for that suspicion, Harris remarked, "Then I began to see CPI as a tool for the Mayor, and that they should have been instrumental in helping us, but it seemed like they were trying to mess up what we were doing. They'd make suggestions, and this and that, and we'd just ignore their suggestions."[27]

Among the parents' demands were the replacement of the school principal with an African American principal, the hiring of more African American teachers, and the establishment of a Parent-Teacher Association with parental involvement. Their criticisms were not, however, limited to what was happening at the Prince Street School. "At the same time, we began to talk about CPI, and how there was no real community involvement on their part." Although the parents experienced some successes from their efforts, like getting the principal replaced, they left with the unpleasant memory that "all through this thing, we were getting opposition from CPI." Harris recalled that people from CPI were sent to talk to him and to give assurances that the problems were being taken care of and to warn that there were communists and other radicals in the Hill Neighborhood Union, an organization of largely Yale University students with which HPA was closely associated.[28] It didn't take long for HPA's leadership to see CPI as emblematic of everything that was wrong with the Lee administration.

The Hill Parents Association Challenge to Community Progress, Inc., and the Lee Administration

Perhaps Mayor Lee set the context of the dispute between CPI and HPA best when he recalled, "That was a period when black leadership was not anointed by the white community, it was beginning to emerge on its own."[29] Indeed, what made HPA both unique and dangerous to the city's racial status quo was its success in pursuing neighborhood issues independent of Mayor Lee and his CPI project. As an indigenous, low-income, grassroots, and neighborhood-based organization, the Hill Parents Association would have influence and legitimacy unlike any other of the city's predominantly African American organizations. HPA's birth and early success signaled the beginning of what would become a period of black power–style militancy during which African American leadership was not so easily co-opted or ignored, as had been true for the local branches of the NAACP and CORE.[30]

The fact that the racially paternalistic Lee administration was not prepared for this type of African American organizational independence from its URS administration will be evident later in chapter 5 when I examine what happened when Richard Lee was unsuccessful in co-opting the HPA leadership at a time he thought he needed it to deal with the most racially explosive crisis he would face as mayor. As you will see, Mayor Lee's response would prove not only inept but ruthless as he turned matters over to the New Haven Police Department, the overtly repressive state apparatus of his executive branch URS governmental core.

In the next section I examine events in Syracuse during that same time period that reflected a very different use of community action. In Syracuse, community action was designed to promote African American insurgency against Mayor Walsh's URS administration.

COMMUNITY ACTION AND RACIAL CONFLICT IN SYRACUSE

The Origins of Community Action in Syracuse: The SAY Proposal

From the very beginning, Syracuse's Mayor Walsh had a very different relationship to community action than did Mayor Lee of New Haven. Whereas the liberal Democrat Richard Lee initiated a plan for "human renewal" as the city's Community Progress, Inc., project,[31] William Walsh responded to a request by Attorney General Robert Kennedy to apply for a PCJD planning grant by putting the issue to a "citizens' committee." That committee, whose members he selected, advised the Walsh administration to apply and recommended that the initiative be based on "a new model of community organization—independent of all existing structures, both public and private."[32] In brief, whereas it was Mayor Lee who was clearly in control of the conceptualization, formulation, and implementation of New Haven's community action program, Mayor Walsh's role was more as an elected official who was inclined to allow the project to go forward after having delegated its planning and operation to the appropriate social science and social services experts. Mayor Walsh's tendency to distance himself from the federally funded project is not surprising for a conservative Republican who was not dependent on the support of African Americans or the poor as part of his electoral coalition.

In the spring of 1962, the project planning committee established a forty-five-member policy-making body known as the Mayor's Commission for Youth. City government officials were but one of many groups represented on the Mayor's Commission. Among the other groups included were "the State Department of Social Welfare, the Onondaga County School Board, Syracuse University, Syracuse Herald-Journal, YMCA, AFL-CIO Labor Council, Syracuse Post-Standard, General Electric, Bristol Laboratories, Onondaga County Mental Health Department, the Police, the Family Court, Parochial Schools, and lawyers, doctors, and local businessmen."[33] Unlike what was true for the planning of the New Haven project, Mayor Walsh notes more than "150 lay and professional leaders" were involved in the planning of the SAY project action proposal.[34] The Mayor's Commission was similar to the board of New Haven's Community Progress, Inc., in that it also functioned as a board of directors for the project during both its planning and early implementation phrases and was initially composed of various city elites and not actual CPI project focus-area residents. The Mayor's Commission differed, however, from the CPI board in two important ways. First, the commission was to determine the project's policies "free from political influence." Second, as you will see later, the SAY planners made provisions to include commission members on various demonstration project proposal-planning task forces.[35] The Mayor's Commission's project-planning operations were officially delegated to the United Community Chest and Council of Onondaga County, whereas its research operations were placed in the hands of the Syracuse University–based Youth Development Center. It was executive director Ben Zimmerman's job to coordinate the work of those three groups.[36]

In early October 1962, PCJD awarded the Mayor's Commission a $152,552 grant to fund a fifteen-month planning period.[37] That planning period ended with the completion in April 1964 of *Syracuse Action for Youth: An Action Program for Disadvantaged Youth*.[38] Let's take a closer look at the SAY action proposal and its seeds for local African American insurgency.

The SAY Action Proposal.

In most ways, SAY's project demonstration or action proposal was similar to other PCJD- and Ford Foundation–sponsored community action project proposals. In a break with then popular conceptualizations of juvenile delinquency that focused on the bad attitudes and behaviors of wayward individuals, those community-centered project proposals rooted juvenile delinquency in social causes. SAY planners built on the work of the University of Chicago sociologists who found higher rates of juvenile delinquency in areas of the city where there was a rapid transition in land use, regardless of which racial or ethnic group happened to occupy that locale at a particular point in time. In this view, social disorganization was seen as a major cause of the high rates of juvenile delinquency and other social problems in the project's action areas. This perspective provided the rationale to target the entire community for programmatic action, including of course community organizing to strengthen the traditional neighborhood social controls that discouraged delinquency. Complementing this view was the opportunity theory of delinquency, which assumed that a major social cause of the relatively high rates of delinquency in impoverished communities was the lack of legitimate opportunities available to area youth. In the absence of such incentives to conform, youth would therefore be more inclined to seek out illegitimate means to material acquisition and social status. This is basically the same model of the causes of juvenile delinquency deployed previously in New Haven's Community Progress, Inc., and even earlier in the influential Mobilization for Youth project on Manhattan's Lower East Side.[39]

Most of the solutions outlined in the SAY action proposal were also very similar to those of its community action program precursors. They consisted primarily of a comprehensive range of social services built largely around employment and education programs. All of those projects also had a community organizing component that, relative to the total program budget, tended to be rather small. At the time SAY's action grant was being prepared, it was clear that the federal government was shifting its resources from antijuvenile delinquency to antipoverty programs in anticipation of President Johnson's War on Poverty. Therefore, PCJD encouraged the SAY planners to focus more on poverty and less on juvenile delinquency with the expectation that the project would soon be transferred to that new source of government funding as a War on Poverty community action program.[40] But what made SAY different from most of the other PCJD projects was that, although all of those projects were controlled by elite professionals, SAY took the participation of the poor seriously—even though much of that participation would come later, with pressure from the civil rights movement, after the project was designed and implemented.

The proposal's major element of subversive intent was inserted with the urging of project consultant Warren Haggstrom. The Saul Alinsky–modeled scheme was to turn over SAY's community organization operations to indigenous leadership as soon as possible so that it could escape control of the project's federal and urban racial state sponsors.

The Proposal's Community Development Section

Chapter 7 of the SAY action proposal—a chapter titled "Community Services" written by a three-member team chaired by Betty Baer—contained the insurgent "Community Development" section that encompassed the community organization ideas of Saul Alinsky and Warren Haggstrom. Antecedent to that section of the chapter, a "Rationale" section explained that education and employment programs were not enough because such programs did nothing to address the social disorganization of the focus-area neighborhoods and the sense of powerlessness and distrust that it bred. The proposal noted the difficulty its planners had recruiting SAY project-area residents to serve on its community development task force to provide input for that chapter to make its case about their "distrust of the larger community," "lack of access to people who make many of the decisions that effect [sic] their lives," and "lack of interaction . . . around issues of common concern." Because that community development task force was a likely source of African American insurgency, its report—which was inconspicuously placed in the appendix of that chapter—merits a brief examination.[41]

The "Report of the Community Development Task Force" began with the following summation of the determined voices of SAY project-area residents: "We are more than statistics, cases, numbers, or pins in the Urban Relocation Office. Yes—some of us have been relocated, or uprooted while still others of us spin in bewilderment at the rapid changes occurring in our neighborhood. The social conditions and the problems, you (others of the Commission) explore—we experience."[42]

The task force report then went on to provide the input of neighborhood residents on the area's problems of education, employment, housing, public welfare, and community services. And in its closing statement, the fifteen-member community development task force stressed that neighborhood residents had no intention of being treated as passive recipients of program services. "We dislike the term 'target areas.' . . . [T]argets are usually immobile and are acted upon by outsiders who actively 'shoot arrows,' in this case, of services that they hope will penetrate or change a passive target. We plan not to be an idle target. We need the kind of help the broader community can offer but we must use the skills, talents and resources of the people in the neighborhood."[43]

The experiences of both the Community Services writing team and the Community Development task force may have been significantly shaped by gender. All of the members of the writing team were women, as were fourteen of the nineteen members of the Community Development task force, including eleven task force members listed as "civic workers" in the SAY action proposal.[44] Ironically, their gender (combined with their relatively low racial and class status) may have not only made those task force members more inclined to challenge Syracuse's affluent "white," male-dominated power structure but might have also resulted in their subversive actions being less likely to be detected by powerful individuals and institutions that were accustomed to ignoring such women whose activities were generally considered to be unimportant.

Of course, we should be careful not to uncritically accept the official SAY line on the influence of area residents on project planning because a major function the Community Development task force served for the proposal's professional planners was to legitimize the project as an initiative that reflected the will of the area residents to be served. As you have seen, the essential contours of the community development program had already been drawn by elite program planners and consultants. Moreover, in his unpublished notes on the history of the SAY planning process, Daniel Knapp concludes that "the CD task force was more or less handpicked" and the social structure and neighborhood participation-focused "point of view" of the SAY project was "considerably stronger in the abstract than in its concrete expressions in terms of proposed programs." For example, Knapp observes that with the exception of the Community Development section the SAY project's proposal "placed a heavy emphasis on professionalism and direct service." Finally, Knapp points out that the SAY professionals chose to ignore some of the more controversial suggestions of area residents, such as one that might have posed a challenge to the authority of the local public school system through the establishment of sub-boards and another that called for reform efforts that would go way beyond community action within the ghetto by fighting racial discrimination in housing.[45]

Not surprisingly, the impact of the Community Development task force was most evident in the "Community Services" chapter of the SAY proposal, which stressed not only the need for "action area" residents to be involved in the planning of initiatives like SAY but the importance of their being able to maintain their autonomy in deciding what happens in their own neighborhoods. "Our major emphasis is on a community development approach so that the action residents themselves become the chief agents for changing the character of their neighborhoods. In order that the residents of the action area can, indeed, begin to think and act for themselves, and to assume responsibility for their actions, emphasis will be placed on a high degree of autonomy so that unnecessary restraint is avoided."[46]

Let's take a closer look at this subversive emphasis on neighborhood autonomy. The "Community Development" section of that chapter begins with the following call for participatory democracy: "All citizens have a right to participate in the planning and decision-making activities which effect [sic] their lives and those of their children." However, the nomenclature of that rallying cry "to develop the competence of action area residents to deal with the problems of their neighborhood and community" was phrased in such a way that it fit the culture-of-poverty and "community competence" ideas popular with powerful social science gatekeepers to PCJD funding like Lloyd Ohlin and Leonard Cottrell. Although SAY's community development plan was marketed with conservative-sounding community organizing terminology, the real aim of Baer, Zimmerman, and their Syracuse University–based Youth Development Center consultants was to plant the seeds of the more militant Saul Alinsky–style of community organizing.[47]

The community development program component of SAY was designed to be implemented in three phases with the program becoming progressively more independent during each phase. In phase one, community organizers would be hired, a facility would be found for a Neighborhood Development Center, and its staff would work with area residents to identify community issues and leadership.[48] The primary focus of phase two was the recruitment and development of a cadre of neighborhood workers. These neighborhood workers would organize individuals and groups in their respective "districts" to address community concerns and develop indigenous leadership. Finally, in the third and final phase, SAY's community development program would "begin to function as an autonomous unit," the Action Area Neighborhood Association. Although the Mayor's Commission would "continue to sponsor the organization," it would "determine its own policies and action."[49] With this new, autonomous, spin-off community development organization, SAY's planners thought they had solved the democratic conundrum of whether it was really possible to use federal government funds to sponsor social protest that challenged city hall and other components of the local white power structure.[50]

In the epigraph to this chapter, Betty Baer, the planning director for the SAY proposal, referred to a scheme she and her project-planning co-conspirators hatched to create a spin-off organization that would act as a second (i.e., challenging) force in militantly pushing for change while SAY could then play a much safer role as a third-force mediator of conflict between that organization of area residents and the first (i.e., dominant) force of the local white power structure. Baer was inclined to engage in this sleight of hand because she believed that their "social action" plans "to change the world" were being blocked by the fact that the project was "very much controlled by 'the establishment.'" This is what Betty Baer recalled about their scheme:

> So we hatched this thing that would bring in Alinsky—for that whole piece of the project. . . . The game plan was that [Fred Ross] would come to Syracuse and begin to raise private money, which he did—from the Presbyterians

and the Catholics, and others. He would go after private money. And then it would spin off in the Crusade into a totally separate organization.[51]

As you will see later, that plan did eventually materialize into an organization known as the Syracuse Community Development Association (SCDA). What Baer and her associates did not count on, however, was that SCDA would bite the hands of those who originally conceived it and would not allow SAY (now Crusade for Opportunity) to play its third-force mediator role. Here is how Baer continued her account of SCDA's origin and evolution:

> Of course, the thing that happened was that Fred Ross and company then began to attack the Crusade. Now, that we never imagined. All right, that was a real jolt. Because they saw us—the Crusade—as in the way of getting at the establishment. So we had no credibility with Fred Ross and company either. We were just the do-good, social-work, liberal types who were simply in the way. Alinsky would have said we just gave out sops and stuff to the folk, rather than the real social action community organization activity.[52]

Although the community development component of the SAY project proposal did not turn out as its planners had hoped, it was still a bold initiative relative to other PCJD project proposals, one that Daniel Knapp and Kenneth Polk described as "defining the limits" of community action. The limits pushed included not only the involvement of focus-area residents in project planning but, as I noted earlier, SAY's bold plan to spin off its community-organization component into an entity that would be free of government control as it deployed social protest in challenges to the local white power structure.[53]

The PCJD was well aware that the SAY proposal was intended to push the limits of community action. The minutes of a PCJD review panel chaired by Cottrell indicate that the panel was impressed with both the SAY proposal planners' efforts to involve project focus-area residents in the planning process and the implications of the proposal's "Community Development" section:

> The project staff recognize the problems in the community development approach, and the fact that there may be a series of unexpected consequences. The community development approach is "seeding." They will have to deal with issues as they come up, and recognize they are now past the point of no return. Some testing of consequences and implications of the action program has already taken place with Mayor, e.g., criticisms of police, welfare department, segregation etc.

Those minutes also make clear the program priority of the SAY project planners: "If they are unable to fund the entire program, the community development piece is the one they would want 'to go strong.'"[54]

Whereas the mid-level PCJD bureaucrats were aware of the trouble-making potential of the "Community Development" section of the SAY's action proposal, the local URS administration clearly was not. As I noted earlier, Mayor Walsh was not involved with the details of the SAY planning. It is unlikely that Walsh read the six-hundred-page proposal,[55] and the "Community Development" section of the proposal, which was placed among more traditional community services, seemed to have escaped the eyes of the more conservative Mayor's Commission appointees Mayor Walsh would have trusted most to represent his views and interests.[56]

By October of 1964 the Mayor's Commission for Youth, with its name changed to Crusade for Opportunity, was delegated as the entity in charge of Syracuse's War on Poverty effort. Various reasons have been given for that name change in different accounts of the origins of the project. One explanation mentioned is that the change of name represented a broadening of focus away from the juvenile-delinquency emphasis of the President's Committee on Juvenile Delinquency and Youth Crime toward the larger goal of the War on Poverty community action programs.[57] Another reason suggested is that the mayor was so distrusted among poor people of color that it was thought a name change was needed if there was going to be community support for the project.[58] Yet a third explanation given for the name change from the Mayor's Commission for Youth to Crusade for Opportunity was that due to an early controversy over voter registration Mayor Walsh no longer wanted to have his name associated with the project.[59]

CFO's Voter Registration Drive

Mayor Walsh may have soon come to regret his lack of oversight in the planning of what became Crusade for Opportunity. After veteran community organizer and Alinsky associate Fred Ross was hired as the director of the project's community development program, one of the first assignments he gave its staff was the organization of a voter registration drive. Although that drive was in keeping with CFO's community organization goal of reducing the alienation, isolation, and powerlessness of project focus-area residents, it provoked intense controversy that reverberated nationally. The conflict was rooted in the basic facts of political life in Syracuse at the time—that is, the mayor was a Republican, and most of those registered by the program were from the socially and economically downtrodden groups (including impoverished African Americans) that tended to register and vote Democrat.[60] Consequently, "the voter registration component of the proposal represented a distinct threat to a carefully maintained Republican political plurality" and ultimately to the Walsh administration.[61] As I noted earlier, the "Community Development" section of the SAY action proposal would also provide an important link to the more controversial Syracuse University–based Community Action Training Center (CATC) project of Warren Haggstrom.

THE ORIGINS OF THE COMMUNITY ACTION TRAINING CENTER

As noted, Professor Haggstrom of the Syracuse University–based Youth Development Center helped craft the "Community Development" section of the SAY project action proposal. But he was not content to serve as a project consultant for SAY. Haggstrom wanted his own Saul Alinsky–style community development program, which like the SAY plan he helped hatch would contain a spin-off organization of the poor, and he wanted Fred Ross to be its field director. This ambition, combined with the lack of respect Haggstrom had for the overall SAY plan, placed him on a collision course with what soon became the city's War on Poverty community action program, Crusade for Opportunity.[62]

That crash would not go unnoticed. It occurred under the glaring spotlights of the nation's influential politicians at their various levels of government, elite poverty-policy experts and program administrators, and controversy-driven commercial media. More than any other War on Poverty community action program, Haggstrom's Syracuse University–based Community Action Training Center promised to push community action and its "maximum feasible participation of the poor" mandate to their limits, and as a result it became an early and frequent target of white racial backlash. This was indeed ironic because, as you will see, in both its planning and its implementation CATC had very little involvement of poor people. Participation of the poor was but one of two controversial components of the more activist community action programs of the War on Poverty. That other part—the sponsoring of social protest[63]—was the main reason for CATC's existence.

The CATC Proposal

CATC's grant proposal for Office of Economic Opportunity funding begins with the following assertion of Haggstrom's basic assumption about the poor and the major problems they face: "the central problem of the poor is their dependency, their powerlessness, the fact that their lives are controlled by persons and forces outside themselves." Its next page asserts that a community development solution to that powerlessness and dependency and to the apathy and lack of confidence they breed was the "creation of effective democratic organizations through which the poor can exercise power to an extent comparable with other citizens."[64]

The CATC proposal identifies three major components of the project: demonstration, training, and evaluation and research. The project's demonstration component entailed proving the viability of Alinsky-style community organizing. That organizing included the development of neighborhood councils for areas that lacked organizations, strengthening already-existing but weak organizations, coordinating the efforts of existing and viable organizations, and bringing all of these organizational resources together as one powerful area-wide, Alinsky-style umbrella organization. One of the first power-building actions to be undertaken by the neighborhood councils was the organization of "an intensive voter registration drive," something the authors of the CATC proposal must have known would be controversial based on Mayor Walsh's intense reaction to the earlier Crusade for Opportunity voter registration drive. Another part of the proposal that would come back to haunt Professor Haggstrom was a statement, which would later make its way into a controversial CATC brochure, that the project's "trainees should be committed to help people who are grappling with apparently overwhelming problems and have a controlled but intense anger about injustice."[65]

In the next section, I examine how CFO's failed voter registration drive contributed to another important project failure that helped shape the development of CATC.

CFO's Stalled Community Development Program Plans

As I noted earlier, it was Warren Haggstrom who, while serving as a consultant to the planners of the SAY proposal, pushed for the inclusion of an Alinsky-style community development program that would be spun off from the Crusade for Opportunity project and into the hands of the indigenous leadership of project focus-area residents. I also mentioned that once CFO was established it was Professor Haggstrom who was instrumental in that project's hiring of Alinsky associate Fred Ross to head its community development program component. Haggstrom soon became frustrated both with the slow pace of the implementation of CFO's community development program and by that project's plan to grant the program only limited autonomy while it remained under its auspices.[66]

Indeed, after CFO faced an intense backlash from Mayor Walsh over its voter registration drive, which was well known to involve the work of an organizer who had been very active with CORE, there was some doubt as to whether it was prepared to follow through with its own community development program plans. Not surprisingly, Republican Mayor Walsh saw that drive, which was successful in registering low-income voters of color who were inclined to affiliate as Democrats, as an intolerable federally funded threat to his regime. As the CATC project historian recalled, "under the withering blows of the Mayor, they had folded during the voter registration drive of the previous summer." As a part of that capitulation, Haggstrom was fired as a CFO consultant and the project was placed under surveillance. The mayor's swift and intense reaction in asserting his control over CFO made its administrators feel anxious about the future of the project's community development component. That anxiety, which was compounded by the fact of CFO's many "pipelines to city hall," caused both Haggstrom and Ross to lose any confidence they might have had in the project's ability "to withstand political pressure."[67] This realization, in turn, made the two men leery of the use of federal government funds to challenge city hall and other components of the local power structure.

The significance of the Community Action Training Center and its social protest strategy of community reform was both reflected in and enhanced by the fact that Haggstrom's own community development initiative was the first War on Poverty community action program to be funded. On December 16, 1964, the OEO announced that it was awarding a $314,329, nine-month, renewable grant to Syracuse University to train sixteen organizers.[68] Haggstrom would be in charge of the project's research and training components, and he would soon hire Fred Ross to run the actual community-organizing piece of the project. Finally, Saul Alinsky was to be brought on board as a consultant and lecturer who would help train CATC organizers.[69] It should come as no surprise that it did not take long for the social-protest-centered CATC to become embroiled in numerous local conflicts.

CATC CONFLICTS

Attacks by Syracuse Newspapers

One of the first attacks the Community Action Training Center endured was from Syracuse's conservative and jointly owned morning newspaper, the *Syracuse Post-Standard*; its afternoon daily, the *Syracuse Herald-Journal*; and its Sunday weekly, the *Syracuse Herald American*.[70] The earliest broadsides against CATC ranged from accusations about its wasteful and misdirected spending[71] to the question as to whether the project was "designed, truly, to help the helpless of this community" or instead "to initiate and incite a type of insurgency."[72] These were just the opening salvos initiated by Harold E. Addington, a member of the Mayor's Commission for Youth and the *Herald-Journal*'s chief editorial writer. To African Americans like the editor of *The Challenger*, a newspaper with a readership of African Americans in western New York State, that attack was indicative of how the *Herald-Journal* "and the people in the power structure who control it have

[been] pushing the poor around and trying to run their lives for years." As a case in point, the editor recalls how Syracuse's white power structure had successfully squelched the recent CFO voter registration drive.[73]

Conflict between CATC and CFO

The Community Action Training Center's first big controversy grew out of an attempt by Office of Economy Opportunity official Sanford Kravitz to defend the project against attacks by the Syracuse newspapers by claiming that Crusade for Opportunity had given its approval of the CATC proposal prior to the OEO's funding of the CATC project. A February 21, 1965, *Herald American* editorial reported that its examination of CFO records found no minutes to support Kravitz's claim. Although that paper's investigation did find that the CFO staff had discussed the Syracuse University plans, project staff members reported they had no power to block it, and no formal approval was given by the CFO board. The *Herald American* editorial also complained that the proposal was written in a hurry in Washington, DC, and that the OEO pressured CFO to "assent" to the CATC proposal or risk the lost of future OEO funding.[74]

Another hidden source of conflict was the split within CFO regarding social action programs like CATC. As I noted earlier, it was CFO's key planners and administrators Betty Baer and Ben Zimmerman who, with Haggstrom's help, planted the seeds of community-development subversion within the Crusade for Opportunity proposal. That disagreement was exacerbated by the fact that those two CFO administrators were caught between the rock of their hope that CFO could serve as the third (i.e., mediation) force for the reform they felt was sorely needed in Syracuse and the hard place of opposition to social action from influential representatives of the local social work establishment who held powerful positions on CFO's board.[75] That opposition made it unlikely that the board would have approved the Community Action Training Center plan even if Zimmerman had managed to get the time he needed to take it to that body.[76]

CFO's top administrative leadership would not survive long after that dispute. In an oral history interview, Zimmerman indicated he wasn't sure Mayor Walsh believed him when he said he hadn't seen the CATC proposal. Zimmerman and Baer would resign rather than be subjected to an investigation Zimmerman thought may have had something to do with suspicion that they were working with Haggstrom and his CATC associates.

CATC's Conflict with Neighborhood Residents on the CFO Board

An increase in the number of poor people of color on the CFO board added a new racial twist to the conflict between Crusade for Opportunity and the Community Action Training Center over which organization met the OEO's "maximum feasible participation of the poor" mandate. Such tension could be seen in the misguided and hypocritical attempt of CATC and Syracuse Community Development Association leaders to portray CFO as a project that had little representation of poor people of color and that was little more than a tool of the mayor.

The neighborhood representation issue came to a head during the controversy over whether SCDA should be required as instructed by the OEO to apply for its funding through CFO, the city's official community action program umbrella organization. Less than a month after the CFO underwent a crucial board expansion that did not elect any African Americans or low-income individuals, a local newspaper article quoted Warren Haggstrom as referring to CFO as the "official city hall blessed organization that operates with a slate of officers excluding poor people, Negroes and including representatives of the white power structure."[77] Also that day the "strategy council," which represented nine neighborhood organizations, issued a statement saying, "Crusade is a fake controlled by City Hall."[78] And less than a week later, Edward McGuire, SCDA's head, was quoted as saying that his organization would not apply for funds through CFO "because it is controlled by City Hall and does not have representatives of the poor on its governing boards."[79]

Both Haggstrom's and McGuire's comments had some merit, but what those CFO critics missed was the change in the overall composition of the board that gave CFO's focus-area residents control of the organization if and when they decided to take it. When a newspaper reporter asked a board member from a CFO project-area neighborhood to explain those election results, an outcome that seemed to indicate "the poor passed up their first opportunity to take control," she initially responded with the complaint that "the trouble with Negroes is that they don't pull together." But then she went into a more detailed and more optimistic assessment, stressing that "there is going to be a next time for elections" and "we've got to go slow until we are sure of ourselves."[80]

A statement by three CFO neighborhood boards in response to comments by Haggstrom and others illustrates how quickly CFO's new board members were developing as a sophisticated force that was determined to carve out its own political landscape congruent with what it perceived to be its own interests. "We take issue with statements reportedly made by Dr. Warren Haggstrom and others implying that we are a tool of City Hall. The neighborhood boards were elected by their neighbors in an open election. . . . [I]n CFO . . . we are entitled to, and we get recognition of our strength." Those CFO board members concluded with this revealing glimpse into how they had come to see CATC and its SCDA offspring at that time of civil rights movement–driven African American solidarity:

"Dr. Haggstrom's statements serve no useful purpose except to try to divide the people in our neighborhoods. We have no quarrel with our neighbors."[81]

Ironically, because of the expansion of the Crusade for Opportunity board to include large numbers of the project's focus-area residents, the Community Action Training Center and Syracuse Community Development Association should have been able to count on greater support in their battle with the OEO and Mayor Walsh. Indeed, Clifford Winters—the Syracuse University dean to whom Haggstrom reported and a member of the CFO board—argued that had SCDA applied for funding through CFO there was a good chance that it would have gotten it because CFO neighborhood board members would not have been inclined to vote against a program that was supported by their friends and neighbors.[82] And of course, had CATC and SCDA had more neighborhood representation, they may have been more inclined to seek such a compromise, if for no other reason than to maintain solidarity among neighbors.

Dean Winters's position was supported by an investigation by an associate editor for the *Washington Post* that found that city umbrella agencies in other cities had, indeed, funded "philosophically hostile" projects. Moreover, consistent with the third-force mediating role CFO planners and administrators had envisioned for the project, that reporter noted "the CFO has some stake in the SCDA's continued existence" because "it makes the CFO look 'moderate' and tends to help it with concessions from City Hall that it might not otherwise receive."[83]

*Conflict over the OEO's Decision that
SCDA Must Apply to CFO for Funding*

By late 1965 the Community Action Training Center and the Syracuse Community Development Association had created so much controversy that both the Office of Economic Opportunity and Syracuse University had become skittish in their sponsorship of them. Under growing pressure from mayors, on November 30 the OEO notified SCDA and Syracuse University that future funding for SCDA must be submitted through Crusade for Opportunity, the city's official antipoverty agency for the receipt of federal funds. Soon afterward the OEO announced it would provide a three-month extension for CATC rather then what project administrators had hoped would be a pro forma renewal they needed for the completion of its mission.[84]

As I noted earlier, the success or failure of the Community Action Training Center was no mere local matter. Not only was CATC the first War on Poverty community action program; it was the one designed to test the spirit of the Office of Economic Opportunity's "maximum feasible participation of the poor" mandate by determining how far such projects, funded independent of mayors' approval, could go nationally in helping the poor fight city hall and local social work establishments. For a while, the federal and urban racial states were at odds—until the mayors organized to impress the Johnson administration with their intense opposition to programs like CATC. Those efforts included a vote by the U.S. Conference of Mayors in June of 1965 that established a committee chaired by the powerful Mayor Daley of Chicago, with Mayor Walsh as a member, to seek clarification as to the role of local government in the administration of antipoverty programs. Such efforts were so successful that in August, when Vice President Humphrey spoke before the National League of Cities, he identified himself as their "special agent."[85] Now those two levels of the racial state were once again in sync. The War on Poverty community action programs had found their limits. With the executive branch of the urban racial state governmental core firmly in charge, they would not be allowed to challenge local white power structures in any serious way.[86]

This convergence of the federal and local racial states was evident on December 8, when the People's War Council Against Poverty, a delegation of Syracuse Community Development Association supporters who had traveled to Washington, DC, while engaged in what was "believed to be the first major face-to-face confrontation Shriver has had with a protest group of the poor that was open to the press,"[87] accused Crusade for Opportunity of being controlled by Mayor Walsh. SCDA would soon reject the idea of seeking funding from CFO, and a few days after that Syracuse University announced its decision not to renew Saul Alinsky's contract as a CATC consultant. SCDA continued with private funding for a time after Syracuse University discontinued its involvement with the program but would ultimately reorganize as an organization of organizations that lacked the resources for actual organizing.[88] These developments had a powerful racial impact by increasing the importance of Crusade for Opportunity and of James Tillman, who would replace Ben Zimmerman as its executive director that following year. That racial conflict over the control of CFO was preceded by racial tensions within CATC.

Racial Conflict within CATC

The burdens CATC carried as it unsuccessfully struggled to survive as a federal government funded challenge to city hall were not limited to the fact that under Haggstrom's leadership the project found itself facing external criticism from both the local power structure and the very types of people it was assumed it was there to assist, people who were disproportionately low-income African Americans. It shouldered the additional heavy weight of growing conflict within CATC, some of which was racial. The earliest racial anxiety seemed to have reflected the divergent strategies and tactics of the old racism-blind Alinsky approach to community organizing and the racism-centered approach of the younger civil rights movement activists Haggstrom had recruited into CATC. This included, for example, the failure of Fred Ross in his organizing strategy to accommodate the very different backgrounds and experiences of both African American and European American students who had worked in the South with organizations like the Southern Christian Leadership Council and the Student Non-Violent Coordinating Committee (SNCC).[89] This tension was representative of the conflict that arose in the 1960s between the class-centered Old Left and the more issues-diverse New Left. Another source of racial tension in the mid- and late 1960s was the shift in the civil rights movement from the nonviolent, integration-focused approach of Reverend Martin Luther King Jr. to the more militant, black-power-centered strategy that would radically transform organizations like SNCC and CORE.

Both differences were likely to have created tension between Warren Haggstrom and CATC's African American associate director and Crusade for Opportunity's future executive director, James Tillman, who as you will see was no fan of Alinsky or King. As CATC historian Robert Pickett remembered about Tillman's arrival,

> This was where the emergence of black power came into the works. And so there was some conflict, and argument, and uncertainty, unease, and some weird acts of one kind or another. Weird telephone calls, and things of that nature, that were kind of like harassment . . . an attitude . . . the kind of roiling-below-the-surface attitude that took away the attention to organizing the people out there, in the community. . . . The staff became more interested in the politics of the organization, rather than the politics of the community.[90]

Dean Winters, Haggstrom's administrative superior at Syracuse University who believed that through the power of his personality Tillman in effect seized control of CATC from Haggstrom, saw the political chasm separating the two men as follows: "I think Warren Haggstrom basically believed that both blacks and whites ought to be able to solve problems. And I think Tillman took a harder racial line on this thing. It was the blacks against those whites that are controlling it."[91]

Unlike what was likely the case for Haggstrom, as I noted earlier, Tillman was no fan of the philosophies, strategies, and tactics of Saul Alinsky or of those of Martin Luther King Jr. When asked, "What did your husband think about Saul Alinsky? How did they get along?" Mary

Tillman answered, "They didn't. My husband was absolutely opposed to the Saul Alinsky approach. Without trepidation, without apology, he was quite straightforward with Haggstrom and Alinsky, about his opposition to that kind of approach to the problem." And when she was asked, "Why was he opposed to the Saul Alinsky approach?" she responded,

> The Alinsky approach . . . was one which required people to place themselves in a conflictual situation. . . . That is, such as marching, or maybe putting garbage cans in front of somebody's house, or being confrontive [sic] in that manner. My husband . . . thought that was counter-productive. He thought it was demeaning to the people. He thought it was an insult to the people's intelligence.[92]

As I mentioned earlier, James Tillman was also no fan of the nonviolent, direct-action approach to civil rights of Martin Luther King Jr. Mary Norman Tillman recalled that her husband, who "came from the other side of the spectrum," was "not too happy with King's approach." James Tillman's experience working in the area of fair housing in Minneapolis, as the head of a program that stressed racial integration as the ideal, helped forge his political worldview. And that experience struck the Tillmans personally when they were "met by a mob" as they attempted to move into a "white" neighborhood. Such experiences, as remembered by Mary Tillman, were emblematic of an attitude change many other African Americans underwent as the civil rights movement goals like ending housing discrimination proved so elusive that militant community action to improve living conditions within existing ghettos seemed the only plausible option. Mary's Tillman's painful memory of those events and the lessons they brought was that "at the same time Martin Luther King was using the approach of appealing to the goodness of the white psyche, we were . . . actually experiencing the fact that the white liberal—so-called liberal, the northern psyche—was quite deeply racist, which was really shocking and disappointing."[93]

Finally, Mary Tillman recalled that it was her husband's strong rejection of the Alinsky approach of the Community Action Training Center that led him to resign his position with the project, place their house on the market for sale, and prepare to leave the city. However, an opportunity to implement his philosophy in Syracuse would soon open for Tillman. For with the expansion of the CFO board, pushed by the increasing call for the maximum feasible participation of the poor in the operation of the community action programs serving their neighborhoods and the growing militancy of the civil rights movement, Tillman's views proved attractive to many of the CFO project focus-area residents who were added to the board as new members and who proved decisive in the hiring of Tillman as its new director.[94]

CONCLUSION

In this chapter my examination of the links between the civil rights movement, the War on Poverty, and conflict over the use of community action programs in New Haven and Syracuse reveal how the northward spread and increasing militancy of the civil rights movement sparked conflict over the deployment of the community action programs of the racially ameliorative URS as instruments of either African American co-optation or insurgency. For example, it reveals both similarities and differences in how that conflict manifested itself in New Haven and Syracuse.

Both cities had to respond to the rapidly shifting community action program policies and practices of the federal racial state. In this struggle for control of the War on Poverty community action programs, those URS administrations deployed the ideology of a consensus-based, single-public-interest, top-down philosophy of city government common in the 1950s. In contrast, the reformers used the "maximum feasible participation of the poor" ideology and the mandate provided them by the federal racial state to push for a more participatory URS, one which was more responsive to the needs of low-income residents of color.

The New Haven and Syracuse URS mayors differed, however, in both the level of control they exercised over the community action programs that operated within their political jurisdictions and in their racial use of those programs. Not only did the New Haven URS administration retain tight control of Community Progress, Inc., but it used that project as a first force to stifle African American insurgency. In stark contrast, in Syracuse, where the URS administration at least temporarily lost control of that city's community action programs, they were allowed to act as second- (CATC and SCDA) and third-force (CFO) agents of reform.

In chapter 4, I explore in greater depth that shift in Syracuse to a battle over control of community action over the next two years (1966 and 1967) as maximum feasible participation of the poor met black power and white racial backlash. As you will see, one of the consequences of that conflict was the movement of both the federal racial state and local URS administration from racially ameliorative to racially repressive modes and the subsequent suppression of activist community action. As will become clear in the next chapter, even with the federal and urban racial states once again acting in concert in response to a white racial backlash to restrict community action that relied heavily on the participation of the poor and on social protest, in Syracuse and other cities there would soon emerge another type of struggle—racial battles over who controlled local community action programs, and for what purpose.

4

Maximum Feasible Participation Meets "Black Power" and the White Backlash: The Struggle over Community Action in Syracuse

> Systematically, he moved . . . [Crusade] to an organization which was challenging the white power structure. . . . Probably it was the first time in OEO history that had been taken so far in a community, where there was an actual attempt to eliminate all the white influence in the project to make it . . . a completely black project. That led to a rather bloody showdown in Syracuse . . . where they actually did end up shutting down the whole program.
>
> —Frank Woolever, Community Action Training Center Trainee[1]

At the core of the history of the United States are white racial dominance and the numerous challenges to that oppression by African Americans and other people of color. This was certainly the case with the emergence of the black power phase of the civil rights movement during the middle and late 1960s. In Syracuse and other cities, struggles over racial power often played themselves out in battles for control of the War on Poverty community action programs (CAPs). Of course, as is clear by the very definition of the words *racially oppressed*, the odds were clearly stacked against them. As you will see in this chapter, when African Americans gained control of Syracuse's Crusade for Opportunity (CFO) community action program, the federal and urban racial states shifted to their racially repressive mode of operation as they joined other national and local components of the white racial backlash to successfully suppress that challenge to the white power structure. However, as we will also see, that defeat was not enough to stop the larger changes in race relations and urban politics of which that battle was a part.

UNDERSTANDING THE RISE AND FALL OF CRUSADE FOR OPPORTUNITY AS AN AGENT OF AFRICAN AMERICAN INSURGENCY

In chapter 1 of this book, I rooted my conceptualization of the urban racial state (URS), in part, in what Joe Feagin aptly referred to as the new urban paradigm.[2] Of particular relevance to this chapter are (1) the important contributions Manuel Castells has made to that emergent power-and-conflict-focused view of urban phenomena, including his insightful work on urban social movements,[3] (2) Carter A. Wilson's ideas about the indeterminate and paradoxical nature of the operation of racial states,[4] and (3) Aldon Morris, Naomi Braine, and Jane Mansbridge's scholarship on cultural sites of social protest.[5] That is, we can view activist War on Poverty community action programs like Crusade for Opportunity[6] as cultural sites of social protest[7] that supported progressive urban social movements, but for only as long as they were allowed to do so by their federal and urban racial state sponsors.

This chapter examines the rise and fall of CFO as an agent of African American insurgency in Syracuse during the late 1960s as it unfolds in three acts: Changing Race Relations, the Federal Racial State, and Maximum Feasible Participation of the Poor; African Americans Capture Crusade for Opportunity; and the Federal and Urban Racial States Strike Back.

ACT ONE: CHANGING RACE RELATIONS, THE FEDERAL RACIAL STATE, AND MAXIMUM FEASIBLE PARTICIPATION OF THE POOR

The Expansion and Contraction of Community Action

As you may recall, the main argument of the New Haven and Syracuse case histories of this book is that the urban racial state's executive branch governmental core used CAPs to balance African Americans aspirations against white racial resentment (figure 1.1). This was often done by its expansion of community action program policies and practices that encouraged social protest and participation of area residents in response to African American protest and its later contraction of such policies and practices in reaction to white racial backlash (figure 1.2). I also noted that in shifting its CAP and other responses to accommodate the demands of these two racial constituent groups, a mayoral administration, in its URS capacity, moved to one of three modes of operation: the racially oblivious, the racially ameliorative, and the racially repressive (figure 1.3). Finally, I mentioned that the same types of action were possible at the federal and individual racial state levels and that different branches of the federal, individual, state, and urban racial state might act in sync or in opposition in their choices of particular lines of racially targeted action at a particular point in time (table 1.1).

In my previous book, *Impossible Democracy*, I found that "in response to the white backlash to the increasingly militant protests of African Americans—which included widespread civil unrest—the federal government in its racial state capacity contracted its community action policies in order to restrict CAP-based challenges to local white power structures."[8] In chapter 3, I showed how influential the controversies provoked by the Community Action Training Center (CATC) and its Syracuse Community Development Association (SCDA) offspring were in that shift. In this chapter I examine how Crusade for Opportunity's pushing of the "maximum feasible participation of the poor" envelope provoked not only additional but lethal reaction from the federal racial state.

This CAP contraction process was evident in 1966 when the Johnson administration capitulated not only to a general white backlash but more specifically to the pressure from mayors like William Walsh of Syracuse and from Congress to reduce the participation of the poor in the governance of the community action programs serving their neighborhoods. In January Sargent Shriver and his Office of Economic Opportunity (OEO) calmed the mayors' angst when the OEO "quietly shifted its stand" on maximum feasibility of the poor by now requiring "that 'indigenous representatives' make up only one-fourth, rather than one-third of policy making boards." And from then on representatives of the poor need not themselves be poor.[9]

But that was not enough. For Congresswoman Edith Green and some of her other colleagues charged with congressional oversight of the War on Poverty and its CAPs, the experiment with maximum feasible participation of the poor had gone too far. Following a long hot summer of urban unrest, in mid-October Rep. Green successfully pushed for an amendment to the 1967 bill that reauthorized the Economic Opportunity Act and the funding of its War on Poverty community action programs. The Green Amendment is best known for its requirement that community action agencies be run by state or local governments or their designated agencies. It was, however, one of the bill's lesser-known provisions that was probably more important: the mandate that a third of community action agency board seats go to public officials, with representatives of the poor holding another third of those seats, and the remaining third being allocated to various social service agencies and other representatives of the private sector. This was most likely more important in its impact than the largely symbolic mandate that placed community action agencies firmly under the control of local or state governments because for political reasons most mayors were reluctant to be seen running those projects in an obviously heavy-handed manner.[10] For example, in newspaper and other records of controversies involving who should control CFO's board of directors, Mayor Walsh's name is rarely mentioned.

As you will see, battles over the meaning and proper implementation of the War on Poverty community action programs' "maximum feasible participation of the poor" mandate in Syracuse and elsewhere helped shift many of the CAP conflicts from social protest targeted at the local power structure to internal struggles for control of community action program boards. In Syracuse the importance of that struggle was also magnified by the decline of the civil rights movement as a voice for poor people of color. As I noted in the previous chapter, the Congress of Racial Equality (CORE) no longer had a strong presence in Syracuse. This decline was exacerbated by racial tension within the organization and by the hiring of CORE activists into area CAPs like the Community Action Training Center, the Syracuse Community Development Association, and Crusade for Opportunity.[11] That leadership vacuum made the city more vulnerable to the civil unrest it would experience in mid-August 1967,[12] a time when Crusade for Opportunity was in near disarray.

With the decline and demise of CATC and SCDA, there was a further depletion of the requisite organizational resources for social protest by Syracuse's low-income African Americans. As those organizations were phased out, their university and federal funding and other support were gradually withdrawn.[13] With the CATC's demise, the importance of Crusade for Opportunity as an arsenal for African American insurgency greatly increased and was further amplified by the legacy CATC left of high expectations for organizing the poor. It is within this context that we can appreciate the significance of James Tillman's plans for CFO, plans that were deeply rooted in his views of racism, poverty, and urban politics.

James Tillman's Views on Racism, Poverty, and Urban Politics

In the previous chapter, I discussed James Tillman's role, when he served as CATC's assistant director, in the highly racialized dispute over funding of the Syracuse Community Development Association. In that battle, Tillman sided squarely with those neighborhood residents who wanted SCDA to seek funding through CFO, an action that, contributed to his decision to leave CATC.[14] And it was with the support of those CFO action-area residents, who were heavily represented on the project's board, that in June

1966 Tillman was selected from a pool of twenty-nine applicants to replace Ben Zimmerman as its executive director.[15]

To understand Tillman's politics, it is necessary to go beyond stereotypical images of who he was and what he was about. James Tillman was clearly no black nationalist or revolutionary. The roots of his militancy went much deeper into the fabric of American history and ideals than did recent cries of black power or racial insurgency. They tapped into his insistence that all people, regardless of their color or class, had a right to full and dignified participation in the American mainstream.[16] In a nutshell, Tillman's goal was "full citizenship," not racial separatism or revolution.[17] To comprehend the real James Tillman, critics who labeled and dismissed him as simply an angry race man who schemed for black power needed to go deeper, much deeper.

Tillman's Views on Racism and Poverty

Based on his own account of his Crusade for Opportunity goals and activities, Tillman's primary mission was to challenge class relations in Syracuse, not race relations. He made this clear in a book he wrote with the assistance of his wife, Mary, after he left CFO. In *Why America Needs Racism and Poverty*, the Tillmans explained what they referred to as the "exclusivity compulsion" in the United States by identifying gender, "race," and socioeconomic status as the three criteria by which Americans define themselves and their relationships. According to the Tillmans, the struggle over control of the CFO board was part of their larger goal of helping the poor develop a collective consciousness of their status and needs, what Karl Marx referred to as class consciousness, or as Morris and Braine and Mansbridge might put it, class-based oppositional consciousness. With such an understanding, Syracuse's poor would be able to go beyond what the Tillmans concluded was the too-limited goal of seeking *"individual social mobility"* and instead "elevate the lower class *as a group* to a level of relative parity with the middle class." Finally, Tillman and his wife attributed the failure of that effort to "the reactions of the middle-class, as it sought to maintain and reinforce its group exclusivity."[18]

To refute the claim that with the annual meeting election of 1967, which placed CFO under the solid control of neighborhood residents, the project had become a "black power outfit," the Tillmans presented a table for the years 1965–1966 and 1966–1967 titled "Ethnicity of Individuals Using Crusade for Opportunity Neighborhood Centers." The table shows that the most active form of involvement-neighborhood residents "who attended at least one meeting" as members of program committees, neighborhood boards, or task forces had increased for European Americans from 1 percent in 1965–1966 to 18 percent in 1966–1967, while such involvement for African Americans during that period actually declined from 98 to 71 percent. To further make their class-centered argument, James and Mary Tillman also maintained that middle-class African Americans were hostile to the improvement of the conditions of the poor in Syracuse at that time.[19]

Unlike Warren Haggstrom's conflict-based, social-protest strategy for increasing the confidence of the poor, who in Syracuse as in other American cities tended to be disproportionately African American, the Tillmans' strategy was education-centered. But that education was not targeted solely at preparing area residents for full participation in civic affairs. Its main focus was on changing the attitudes of the dominant group. For such change was needed if they were "to ever impute to American minorities that elementary humanity which must be the foundation on which the majority group and minorities can begin to build *together* a new and different urban community."[20] What is evident from the preceding quote is the fact that whether they were naïve or true believers in the American dream, or both, despite some of their system-challenging rhetoric, the Tillmans' approach was built solidly on the values of community consensus and social integration.

As I noted earlier, however, this was not how James Tillman's critics perceived him. Although such confusion about Tillman's complexity may have been exacerbated by racial fear and stereotyping, another related factor that also probably clouded his critics' vision was their inability to see an essential side of the man, his strong commitment to American democracy. In addition, their view of Tillman was clouded by the fact that his largest and most visible base of support was low-income African Americans and that most of the "maximum feasible participation" militancy of that time was fueled by the rising expectations of the increasingly militant civil rights movement. Yet another factor that may have made it difficult for his critics to get a clear sense of Tillman was that his role and actions were largely invisible. That invisibility was due primarily to Tillman's goal of empowering community residents to develop and assert their own indigenous leadership, not to depend on the leadership of local elites like himself. As you will see, it was that process of what we would today refer to as community empowerment that was more important to Tillman than any other goal.

From what I have discussed so far, I think it is reasonable for me to conclude that despite the fact that James Tillman may have represented the battle for control of the CFO board as largely a class struggle, in that intensely racial environment of black protest and white backlash in the late 1960s his critics were also right in viewing it as entailing for all practical purposes a racial battle for control of the project. It was both. Although Tillman's opponents may have chosen not to see the class-focused component of that struggle, as will become evident as I examine those events, its more visible racial side was no illusion.

Tillman's Vision of Urban Politics and the Challenges Facing Its Urban Racial State

Of particular relevance to this study is the fact that the Tillmans' book offered much more than a theory of racism and poverty. The Tillmans articulated nothing less than an alternative vision of urban politics and its urban racial state, one which called for greatly expanded citizen participation congruent with the emergence of our current, more participatory, era of urban politics.

In their book James and Mary Tillman critiqued what they saw as the limits of both conservative and liberal approaches to racism and poverty—both of which assumed that "the existing system is essentially sound and must be preserved" through various forms of positive or negative manipulations of token "have nots." From that critique they concluded that there was a need for a new, emergent approach to urban reform that placed the problem of racism at its center and in other ways challenged the fundamental assumptions of the dominant elitist and consensus-seeking urban politics of that time.[21]

The Tillmans coined the phrase "new urban necessitarians" to refer to the proponents of this approach, "the thoughtful Americans" who dared to venture beyond the racism-blind liberalism and paternalism that would have likely included Warren Haggstrom and some of the more establishment-oriented but relatively progressive members of Crusade for Opportunity's board of directors. They argued that to ensure the survival of American cities, reformers must go beyond the "black uplift" focus of "white liberals" to an acknowledgment that because "racism is a white illness" that cannot be resolved through tokenism there is, instead, a need to "develop programs which alter relationships between whites and blacks as *groups*."[22] In brief, because their "traditional programs of pacification" will no longer work, the federal and urban racial states must realign themselves both philosophically and programmatically to fit the changing times and the challenges they bring.[23] In the next section, I examine James Tillman's failed attempt to force those two levels of racial state government to do just that.

ACT TWO: AFRICAN AMERICANS CAPTURE CRUSADE FOR OPPORTUNITY

As I previously mentioned, the 1966 Amendment to the Economic Act of 1964 reserved a minimum of one-third of the board seats of projects like

CFO for representatives of the poor.[24] But perhaps even more important for James Tillman and other CAP insurgents was the federal racial state's promotion of the ideology of maximum feasible participation of the poor. Under that ideological banner, Tillman and CFO action-area residents marched into new participation territory with the bold interpretation of the one-third rule of maximum feasible participation as a "base" as opposed to what would become the Office of Economic Opportunity's stance that, indeed, it was actually a "ceiling."[25] Tillman's audacious attempts to push the public-policy envelope would be tolerated for a while as the federal racial state's catch-up game of attempting to soothe rising African American aspirations became more urgent in response to the growing militancy of the civil rights movement. However, it was ultimately doomed to failure by the hardening of racial attitudes that accompanied the shift of the movement from the goal of racial integration to that of black power and by the spread of civil unrest to many American cities.

James Tillman's Plans for the Realization of Resident Participation

In *Why America Needs Racism and Poverty*, James and Mary Tillman maintained that due to the lack of "realistic" and "effective steps" for their realization, prior to his tenure as executive director beginning in July 1966, the various commitments to the participation of neighborhood residents in the governance of CFO remained largely verbal. Of course, it was not just Tillman's efforts that would make CFO more participatory. Tillman had the huge benefit of being able to ride not only the national crest of the civil rights movement but the local currents of his former project, the Community Action Training Center. A report on human rights in Syracuse from 1963 to 1983 concluded that CATC's "short lived" organizational successes must be taken into account in explaining how it was that CFO "began as a mainly all white establishment representing city hall and ended as a mainly black organization representing neighborhood residents."[26] That succinct statement describes CATC's role in CFO's intriguing transformation from an appendage of Mayor Walsh's URS administration to one of its chief challengers. For better or worse when it came to community action resources, CFO was nearly all that people of color now had to satisfy their greatly raised expectations.

This was the environment in which James Tillman carefully laid out his plan to shift control of the CFO board to the hands of the neighborhood residents who had supported his being hired as the project's executive director.[27] Tillman's plan was executed in two stages during his first, and what turned out to be only, fiscal year as CFO head (July 1966 to June 1967). During the first stage, Mr. Tillman initiated efforts "to educate the action area residents in the use of the legitimate constitutional processes open to them in the formulation, implementation and evaluation of program services." Such education was deemed necessary if community action programs like CFO were to achieve their goal of serving as "the *vehicles* and *instruments* through which poverty populations can organize themselves, thus enabling them to develop effective *independent* decision-making." During that first six months, efforts were made to increase the influence of area residents in the project's *"program development, implementation and evaluation"* at the board level by having CFO's Neighborhood Center Boards include them on various program committees (e.g., "education, housing, employment").[28] In the second phase of Tillman's plan, those project-area residents would employ their newly acquired political skills to battle for control of the CFO board.

As I noted earlier, in retrospect at least, Tillman came to see that conflict as a class struggle between middle-class and low-income board members. With the representatives of the poor constituting only a third of the board, they were badly outnumbered by the two other major board components of a third "community-at-large" and another third "social welfare executives" and other institutional representatives, who collectively composed a two-thirds middle-class majority.[29] In explaining why there would inevitably be conflict between those two groups, the Tillmans portrayed the middle class as a reactionary force that was inclined to oppose any real change. Its members' commitment to maintaining the status quo was rooted in their role as "the social system's implementing technicians." That is, their job was to serve the interests of the city's political and economic elite. For example, from their ranks would come the watchdogs of Mayor Walsh's URS administration. Their actions would be guided by what the Tillmans referred to as their *"middle-class conventional wisdom* concerning the poor"—that "the poor must *not* be permitted to organize and adopt their own positions around poverty issues *before* dialoging with the non-poor; the non-poor must 'help' the poor adopt the policy positions of the poor so these policy positions will be 'realistic'; and the poor are not yet ready to have real power in a poverty agency." Other key assumptions of this middle-class view of the poor are that they should have an uncritical acceptance of the operation of "free enterprise," with a limited role for government; that they should not seek "political power" but instead content themselves with the pursuit of self-improvement by "getting jobs and securing better education"; and that they "must not engage in confrontation with the non-poor."[30]

Apparently, Syracuse's white power structure knew little about Tillman, his beliefs, and his plans. This oversight may have been facilitated by a false sense of security it deduced from Tillman's very dignified manner, consummate professionalism, and previous actions at CATC. In an oral history interview, Mary Tillman indicated that her husband surprised the Syracuse power structure by taking the OEO's "maximum feasible participation of the poor" mandate seriously and by aligning himself with the poor. She had this to say about the views of the mainstream media, federal government officials, and CFO board members:

> They all asserted that Tillman didn't understand that the mandates were really *not* meant to be operationalized.... One of his board people, who happened to be a white middle-class person, said in a meeting, "We thought when we hired Tillman that he was a *responsible* Negro" [laughs]—because we lived on the Hill, we were highly educated and Jim had an air and attitude of self-assurance. "It was just assumed that he would be one of us, you know." It was not thought that he would align himself with the poor people.[31]

Yet another reason why Tillman's subversive plans and actions caught many of those who would soon become his opponents off guard was that they seemed to have underestimated the ability of Tillman to work with low-income people and their capacity to not become distracted by superficial appearances. This is what Mary Tillman recalled about how CFO action–area residents responded to what she described as one of the attempts by "middle-class people . . . to drive a wedge between the poor black and white poor people and the Tillmans," in this instance by making an issue of Tillman's proper way of speaking. "'If you can't understand what Mr. Tillman's talking 'bout, just come to us and we'll translate it for ya. We likes the way he talks.' And they went on to say, 'Because he talks to us just the way he talks to the people downtown. He don't talk down to us.'"[32]

Neighborhood Residents Seize Control of the Crusade for Opportunity Board

As I noted earlier, the first phase of James Tillman's plan to have CFO's action-area residents take control of the project's board of directors was executed largely within its own walls and involved mainly civic education and program planning. The second and last phase would be acted out primarily in the very public arena of the project's January 25, 1967, annual meeting of its then 160 "corporation" members, ninety of whom were representatives of CFO's three neighborhood boards. The main item on the agenda of that meeting was the election of board members and officers.[33]

Two days prior to that meeting, a *Syracuse Post-Standard* headline succinctly exposed Tillman's scheme, "Poor Seek Control: CFO Board Choices Challenged." Neighborhood residents were to gain control of CFO in two ways. First, the Neighborhood Boards representatives would reject the slate of candidates nominated by the establishment- and URS-administration-aligned CFO board nominating committee in favor of its own, more neighborhood-representative slate. Second, representatives of the Neighborhood Boards proposed changes to the composition of the CFO board that included an expansion of its size by adding representatives of an additional neighborhood board that would soon be established. If CFO's corporation members approved all of the changes proposed by the Neighborhood Boards, most of the members (i.e., nineteen) of the smaller but now expanded Crusade for Opportunity thirty-six member board of directors would be representatives of the poor, compared to their premeeting holding of only twelve out of thirty-two CFO board seats.[34]

Syracuse's two conservative dailies had generally been supportive of CFO as Mayor Walsh's program, and one of those co-owned newspapers, the *Syracuse Herald-Journal*, had an editor on the CFO board. Their attitude toward CFO changed quickly now that, like CATC had done earlier, CFO challenged the city's power structure.[35] The day prior to the meeting, the *Syracuse Post-Standard* made it own stance clear that the "Poor Must Be Heard. But CFO Takeover Is Unwise." In its editorial, that newspaper also gave voice to the position of Syracuse's URS administration and its other more conservative, community-wide supporters on the CFO board. Reflecting perhaps the growing momentum nationally of the "maximum feasible participation of the poor" movement, the reform legacy of CATC, and its attempt to appear to be a voice of reason, the *Post-Standard* supported the project's annual report in which it advocated greater participation of the poor. But the newspaper drew a clear line between participation of the poor in CFO decision making and their actual control of the project through its warning that "members of the Neighborhood Boards . . . are doing themselves a grave disservice in their current effort to 'take over' the Crusade board of directors and community leadership at the annual meeting tomorrow night." And consistent with the Tillmans' framing of that conflict as essentially a class struggle, the *Post-Standard* cautioned that such a move would raise "an artificial and harmful barrier between 'the haves and the have-nots' in the community." The *Syracuse Herald-Journal* also identified the dispute as being "between some neighborhood people who are seeking to take over control of the federally-supported agency and some board members from the community at large who feel the neighborhood people are not ready for such a step."[36]

Ready or not, Tillman and the Neighborhood Boards scored a huge victory in their successful effort to shift control of the CFO board from its more conservative and Walsh-administration-aligned, social-welfare-agency establishment and community-at-large members to those representing the Neighborhood Boards. Neighborhood residents rallied to the "standing room only" meeting to vote in favor of the alternative officers' slate and other changes intended to tip the balance of board power to the poor. In the aftermath of various parliamentary maneuvers (like the suspension of the project's bylaws to dramatically expand the number of neighborhood representatives who could vote and to allow nominations to be made from the floor) and votes, Mayor Walsh's firm control of the CFO board was severed with three former board chairs now reduced primarily to the status of corporation members who met once a year at the project's annual meeting.[37] Once that battle was won by project-area residents, it didn't take long for elements of Syracuse's white power structure to openly frame the battle for control of the CFO board in racial terms.

Was the Conflict Racial?

Although two days after the CFO annual meeting, the *Syracuse Herald-Journal* continued to hold to a nonracial, "sin of exclusivity" explanation of the conflict, it also reported a racial-conflict-centered accusation about the recent CFO elections. According to that account of what happened, "the white community and the Negro community confronted each other during this Crusade election," as evidenced by "the words that were spoken, the parliamentary procedures that were employed," and "the final selection of nominees."[38] In their recollection of that article, the Tillmans charged that the *Syracuse Herald-Journal* intended to do much more than to report on how some people had framed the issue as being racial. "In its attempt to destroy the Crusade . . . the afternoon paper introduced the 'race issue' into the discussion."[39] As the Tillmans continued, they made an observation that helped explain why neither the newspapers nor they themselves were inclined to acknowledge the controversy's obvious racial undercurrents: "The reader should be reminded that *race* is still an emotional flag which opinion manipulators use to divide the black and white poor and to create suspicion among both black and white poor."[40]

Then and now, the dominant group response to the existence of racial problems in highly racialized societies like the United States is an emotionally intense denial.[41] Consequently, in such environments the denial of racial conflict may be fueled by fear that even one's acknowledgment of the issue is enough to risk being labeled as a racial instigator or even a bigot. So when racial conflict is recognized, it is likely to be assigned as the opinion or manipulations of others. In addition, that quotation from the Tillmans suggests that the very acknowledgment of the existence of racial issues could divide a movement involving an interracial alliance built upon the assumption that "race" does not or should not matter. In brief, such racism blindness may have been the price the Tillmans, who as I discussed earlier, were intensely concerned about racism as a social problem, had to pay to keep low-income European Americans, if not on board as strong allies, at least not mobilized against them as formidable opponents.

Not surprisingly, both the Tillmans and the *Syracuse Herald-Journal* made it clear that it was not their intention to racialize a conflict they felt should not be racialized. But their intentions and wishes about what *should have been* seem unconnected to what *actually was*. In a city where Africans Americans were as oppressed and locked out of the local power structure as was clearly the case in Syracuse, the actions of an African American executive director and overwhelmingly African American participants at CFO's annual meeting to push through changes intended to elect an African American board chair and increase the board representation of disproportionately African American project action-area residents clearly posed a challenge to Syracuse's racial order. This fact was graphically clear in the newspaper photographs of the conflict's key participants and the text accounts of which side of the issue they stood. In the highly racialized environment of the late 1960s, such a picture would indeed be, as the expressions goes, worth a thousand words. Although the struggle for control of the Crusade for Opportunity board was clearly racial, accounts like the one articulated in this chapter's epigraph that portray Tillman as little more than a "race" man who wanted to transform CFO into an "all black project" widely missed the mark. It is likely that such simplistic thinking had at least some of its roots in suspicions that arose about Tillman when he was the associate director of the Community Action Training Center. That particular charge was made by former CATC trainee Frank Woolever. And this is what Clifford Winters, a Crusade for Opportunity board member and the Syracuse University dean to whom CATC's executive director answered, had to say in his more nuanced account of the night in which the poor won control of the CFO board

> There must have been twelve hundred people there. I would guess Tillman had brought in—I remember I must have been one of no more than six white people in what must have been eleven hundred there, at this mass meeting. It was certainly over-balanced by black people. That's one of the times I felt most uncomfortable. Now this was, I think, an effort by Tillman to take the program out of the control of what he considered to be middle-class board members, like me [laughs]. Yes, I think there were some racial overtones to it, yes.[42]

Here is another account that also includes racial conflict in an explanation of that controversy without excluding other relevant factors. In his oral history reflections on that conflict decades later, Norman Hill, who was elected CFO board chairperson at the meeting, made the following observation as he acknowledged that racial division was a source of the conflict, in addition to the division between community-wide and neighborhood-resident board members: "Race was always an undercurrent. It was never in the forefront. The inferences were always there, that the neighborhood folk, who, for the most part, were black, were incapable of carrying forth the programs and making decisions involving large sums of money. So it was never said that it was black people, but it was always positioned as 'you neighborhood people.' . . . It all meant the same."[43]

Through his observation that "quite honestly, color was something that was rarely discussed as an issue" Hill helps explain why at that time he and other African Americans involved in the CFO board takeover did not frame their actions racially even though "the neighborhood people . . . were primarily black" and the successful implementation of their plans "would have resulted in a color change on the board." And congruent with Tillman's work-inside-the-system mode of reform (as opposed to social protest), Hill recalled, "We weren't militant in that regard—not racially militant."[44]

Even the most obvious racial components of the CFO board conflict did not fall neatly along racially "black" and "white" lines. For example, as I mentioned earlier, War on Poverty community action programs like CFO were criticized by the left-leaning Syracuse CORE chapter for hiring away its leaders. Under Tillman and Hill, the project would also come under a more serious attack from its political right by the city's NAACP chapter president. Among Mrs. Shelton's accusations was that the neighborhood residents' takeover of the CFO board was illegal and that the project's administrators distributed reading material on topics including "slavery, the American Revolution, and union organizing" and deployed other inflammatory methods as part of "destructive training . . . geared to rioting . . . in preparation for war." These charges were followed by her demand "that Tillman be fired 'in the interests of the Negro community in particular and the total community in general.'" For this the NAACP president was said to have been called a "house nigger" by some Tillman supporters, a term popularized by Malcolm X to refer to an African American who betrayed the interests of fellow African Americans in favor of personal benefits derived from serving the white power structure.[45]

Both the salience and the complexities of the racial component of that dispute were apparent as it reached its climax.

The Crusade for Opportunity Board Suspensions and Resignations

As part of the power struggle for control of the Crusade for Opportunity board, the project's young and inexperienced new board chair, Norman Hill,[46] found his leadership and that of James Tillman under attack from the deposed community-at-large/institutional-representative faction that tended to be closely aligned with Mayor Walsh and the URS administration he headed. Over the next few months the CFO leadership faced not only criticism for its policies but charges of project mismanagement and misappropriation of funds. There was a further escalation of the conflict when Hill was said to have responded to these criticisms by scheduling only "special meetings" with agendas that were both "predetermined" and "unchangeable," and his CFO board opponents in turn reacted by taking their complaints public. That conflict reached its very public climax with the suspensions and resignations of CFO board members opposed to the Neighborhood Boards takeover of the project.

The escalation of the conflict was soon followed by a vote by the CFO corporate body, which was loyal to Hill and Tillman, that nine of Hill's critics be investigated for public comments it deemed as being damaging to the project. And on May 11, 1967, Norman Hill suspended eight of those dissidents.[47] By that time the anti-Hill-and-Tillman faction had grown to include previous supporters of the CFO board takeover. Indeed, one of those suspended was Reverend Emory C. Proctor, a Methodist minister of a church in the CFO project focus area. Reverend Proctor charged that the suspensions were in response to the plans of those dissident CFO board members to push for an investigation of the project and that the CFO leadership had a racial agenda of "fostering Black Power, not in the sense of something helpful and uplifting, but as an instrument of destruction."[48]

The conflict reached its climax on June 14 when twenty-one board members resigned in protest over the way the project was being run. At that meeting Hill ordered four of the board members he had previously suspended to leave the meeting. It was reported that when Dean Winters asked Hill what was being done in response to the Office of Economic Opportunity's recommendation that the suspended board members be reinstated Hill's response was "Let's be adult." And when a dissident board member remarked, "Yes, let's be adult," Hill's reply was "Shut up." But as undemocratic and shocking as Hill's comments were, they appear to have been little more than a visually powerful pretext for the walkout protest of eleven board members, which was reported to have been planned in advance of the meeting. While in a corridor outside of the meeting area, they announced not only their own resignations but those of ten other board members. Ultimately, twenty-two board members resigned, leaving only two who were not representatives of the poor. The powerful impact of these resignations was much more than a symbolic protest. It signaled nothing less than the death of Crusade for Opportunity. In a newspaper article published the very next day, the federal government's Office of Economic Opportunity indicated that with those board resignations Crusade for Opportunity was now ineligible to receive community action agency funding.[49] With that announcement, the federal and local urban racial states' backlash against CFO shifted into high gear.

ACT THREE: THE FEDERAL AND URBAN RACIAL STATES STRIKE BACK

> It was not organized primarily for grassroots people to become such powerful people. And when they became as powerful as they did, then that's when the problem started. It would have been okay as long as the grassroots people kind of went along with the program. But when they started demanding things, based upon what the philosophy of the agency was . . . then they became bad people.[50]

With the mass resignations from the Crusade for Opportunity board, the community-wide and institutional-representatives faction—which included those board members most closely aligned with Mayor Walsh's URS administration—brought to a screeching halt the Tillman-and-Hill-led insurrection. Mindful of the OEO policy mandate that community action agency boards be composed of a third community-wide representatives, a third institutional representatives, and a third representatives of the poor, the community-wide and institutional-representatives faction knew that with this backing from the federal racial state they possessed a clear, although drastic, alternative to losing control. By simply withdrawing their participation from CFO's board, they set into motion actions by the federal racial state that would either restore their power and the mayor's influence or shut the project down. This attitude was consistent with a position that Mayor Walsh articulated in congressional hearings a few months prior to the passage of the Economic Opportunity Act of 1964 when he made it clear that, without "direct control" of the War on Poverty community action programs proposed for their cities, the mayors did not want them.[51] It also fit his later successful efforts as the vice president of the U.S. Conference of Mayors to pressure the Johnson administration to bring the War on Poverty community action programs under the strong control of the nation's mayors.[52]

The Office of Economic Opportunity had already positioned itself to either rein in or terminate Crusade for Opportunity. Not only had it been monitoring the situation in Syracuse, but as I noted earlier, it advised CFO board chair Norman Hill to reinstate the board members he had suspended. That agency appendage of the executive branch governmental core of the federal racial state warned Norman Hill that it would stop its funding of CFO on June 30, 1967, unless he made sure that there would be regularly scheduled board meetings, with open agendas, and representatives from all segments of the city.[53] This federal government crackdown was, of course, much larger than Syracuse. Nationwide, Congress and the Johnson administration found themselves scrambling to adjust OEO policies and practices in response to a growing white backlash against the War on Poverty community action programs as resources for African American insurgency.[54] As I noted earlier, however, because Syracuse served as a national laboratory for how far maximum feasible participation of the poor would be allowed to go, what happened in that city was clearly beyond the ordinary in its importance. That was the case for CATC in terms of its use of federal government funds to promote social protest, as it was true now for Crusade for Opportunity in how far the federal racial state would allow the envelope to be pushed regarding participation of the poor. The experiment was over. The CFO leaders had crossed the line drawn by this new white-backlash-fashioned racial and political reality.

When the Office of Economic Opportunity's June 30 ultimatum deadline passed without the changes, it appointed a three-person trusteeship known locally as "the three wise men" as its conduit for funds to Crusade for Opportunity.[55] Within little more than a couple weeks both Tillman and Hill had resigned, and Reverend Ernest Boston was appointed as the project's new executive director. But conflict remained over the control of the project, with some neighborhood board members continuing the fight begun by Tillman and Hill. OEO funds were withdrawn from the project about two months before the Green Amendment to the Economic Opportunity Act placed the CAPs firmly under the control of urban racial state mayors. Earlier the following year, a new antipoverty agency would be established in Syracuse that was designed to be in compliance with the Green Amendment and to place the project securely under Mayor Walsh's control. Unlike the Community Action Training Center and Crusade for Opportunity, the focus of that project would be limited to social services, and there would be no attempt to push the envelope either in the direction of social protest or resident participation. As a clear signal that such insurgent ideas had been soundly defeated in Syracuse, the name of that organization was People's Equal Action and Community Effort, or simply, PEACE.[56]

The nationwide implications of what happened in Syracuse were not lost on the national media. An article titled "Syracuse: What Happens When the Poor Take Over" depicted the Syracuse events as a case in point of the failure of robust implementation of the "maximum feasible participation of the poor" mandate following the initial excitement among OEO officials about Syracuse serving as a prototype for increasing the participation of the poor. What that reporter portrayed as the fact that "the poor overplayed their hand" was deemed to be a motivating factor behind the Green Amendment. "Thus what happened in Syracuse is not apt to be repeated." Both in Syracuse and nationally, the nation's experiment with the concept of maximum feasible participation of the poor was now essentially over. Both the federal and urban racial states had had enough.[57]

CONCLUSION

In this chapter I examined the rise and fall of Crusade for Opportunity as an agent of African American insurgency in Syracuse within the sociohistorical context of changes in the civil rights movement and U.S. race relations. As the struggle intensified, spread north, and increasingly focused on economic justice issues, it emboldened African Americans in Syracuse and other cities to push the War on Poverty's mandate for the maximum feasible participation of the poor to its limits and beyond.

The highly racialized struggle for the control of Syracuse's Crusade for Opportunity community action program offers revealing insights into how the federal and urban racial states managed race relations through community action. As I noted earlier, those racial states expanded CAP participation by the poor in response to the demands of increasingly militant African American social protest and then later contracted such involvement in reaction to the ensuing white racial backlash. In Syracuse, when African Americans managed to briefly gain control of the CFO board, dissident board members supportive of the local urban racial state asserted themselves to regain power with the backing of a national and local white racial backlash and the assistance of the federal racial state. These events demonstrate how, as I have argued, the federal and the urban racial states shifted from their racially ameliorative to their racially repressive mode of racial management.

In the next chapter, I examine a very different use of a War on Poverty community action program in New Haven during the same time period. In that city, in its URS capacity, the liberal Lee administration deployed Community Progress, Inc., to co-opt and otherwise suppress indigenous African American leadership and insurgency. But, as you will see, those efforts ultimately proved unsuccessful. As was true in Syracuse, the URS in New Haven could not buck national trends that forced transformations in both local community action programs and the larger urban politics of which they were a part.

5

Black Rebellion, White Repression, and the Transformation of Community Progress, Inc., and Urban Politics in New Haven

> August 20 '67
> Mayor Richard C. Lee
> City Hall
>
> Dear Mr. Lee
>
> Now our welfare city of the generous welfare State of Connecticut has racial violence and destruction!
>   The summer grants allowed to the Hill section was a waste of money!.... It boils down to one thing they are still savages! What shall we give them next?
>   How about a free trip to Africa? for all dissatisfied people. I'll bet they won't go for that either! Maybe they won't be happy until they run everything!
>   Lets stop appeasing that never got us anywhere, at home or abroad. Its time for action!
>   Election time will be here soon and I'm advocating voting o-u-t spenders and appeasers!
>
> Respectfully yours,
an Irate citizen.[1]

Popular admonitions against opening "that can of worms" or letting "the cat out of the bag" aptly describe the fact that once certain changes occur things may never be the same. This is often true for race relations when, even though a particular revolt is successfully repressed, its spirit lives on in ways that are of much greater significance than the original battle. That was certainly the case in the 1960s for the highly racialized conflicts over control of local community action programs. Such struggles were part of a larger movement for community control of African American communities and the institutions that served them. Those battles and that movement also contributed to the transformation of urban politics. As a representative case, in this chapter I examine African American challenges for control of New Haven's Community Progress, Inc., project.

COMMUNITY ACTION AND THE COMING OF A NEW, MORE PARTICIPATORY, AND RACISM-COGNIZANT ERA OF URBAN POLITICS

In the previous chapter, I examined how African American insurgents in Syracuse attempted to wrest control of that city's remaining War on Poverty community action program (CAP) from the conservative urban racial state (URS) administration of Mayor William Walsh. In this chapter, I explore how, in its URS capacity, New Haven's liberal Lee administration unsuccessfully deployed its community action program and police department to respectively co-opt and suppress African American leadership, and how ultimately that leadership forced reforms in Community Progress, Inc., (CPI) and city government. In both cities those clashes between African American aspirations and white racial resentment were fueled by and in turn helped propel a shift in urban politics that required changes in how their URSs managed race relations (see again figures 1.1 and 1.3).

In *Urban Policy and Politics in a Bureaucratic Age*, Clarence Stone, Robert Whelan, and William Murin articulate a provocative theory of that shift in urban politics in post–World War II America, one that highlights the role of factors relevant to this study, like changing race relations and community action programs. That transformation was from what was largely a *machine politics* era that persisted into the 1940s and 1950s and a *reform politics* period of politically progressive cities like Philadelphia and New Haven in the late 1950s and early 1960s, to the *post-reform politics* era of urban politics, which became commonplace in the middle and late 1960s and persists today.[2] As you will see, however, this brief summary, like the figures I present in chapter 1, simplifies a more complicated phenomenon. For example, there are no rigid dates for when one period ended and another began, and some cities—including New Haven—possessed characteristics of more than one era type. In this chapter I examine the difficult period of transition for Mayor Lee from his preferred top-down reform governance style, with its convenient remnants of machine-style political patronage, to a more participatory, post-reform era that was driven by the major racial and other social transformations that occurred in the 1960s and was both opposed and supported by the mayor's community action program, Community Progress, Inc.

Not only did reform politics challenge the so-called good government era notion of "a single overarching community interest best served by technical experts and highly trained professionals"; it dragged racial and class conflict to the center of public-policy discourse. The one-common-public-interest and conflict-avoidance ideology of reform government you saw articulated in the epigraph to chapter 2 by CPI's deputy director Howard Hallman was soon challenged by a very different premise of urban governance, one that reflected the rising aspirations of African Americans, which were driven by an increasingly militant civil rights movement as it entered into its black-power phase. According to Stone et al., it was that black-power ideology that challenged the basic principles of "good government" reform as it "rejected the idea that problem solving could be neutral," "embraced a conflict strategy," and "explicitly repudiated the unitary conception of the public interest."[3] You saw the influence of that post-reform era ideology in the previous chapter in James Tillman's advocacy of a new urban necessitarian vision of reform, one that placed the issues of racism and poverty at the center of its policy discourse. One of the ways the Lee administration responded to this challenge was through the use of CPI to continue its practice of co-opting African American leadership.

COMMUNITY PROGRESS, INC., AND THE CO-OPTATION OF NEW HAVEN'S AFRICAN AMERICAN LEADERSHIP

Both the Ford Foundation and the governmental core of the federal racial state were more mindful of the nation's changing political and racial currents, which called for greater participation of project-area residents, than was the Lee administration. This is not surprising since at the root of their reform efforts was making city government and the social work establishment more responsive to the needs of ghetto residents, a goal that was more in sync with the demands of the emergent post-reform era of urban politics the Lee administration resisted.

An example of the Ford Foundation's concern that CPI's strong executive-centered leadership had not proven itself up to that task was a June 15, 1966, letter from one of its consultants, Clifford Campbell, to Paul Ylvisaker, the director of the foundation's public affairs program.

In that report on his recent visit to New Haven, Campbell noted how the city's grassroots and middle-class African American leadership were being co-opted by CPI. To make this point, Campbell reported that a group of "angry young men," whom he later identified as being involved with the Hill Parents Association (HPA), saw CPI as functioning merely "as a holding operation" and pointed out their belief "that most of those representing the opposition are enticed to accept positions in the CPI operation, are silenced and follow the bidding of the institution." Campbell also mentioned that they "know that the present president of NAACP is head of the counseling service for CPI" and added that "NAACP activities in the city of New Haven are minimal" and that "they now follow the moderate line and the program rarely functions in a manner to challenge the status quo." Campbell also mentioned that the "angry young men" he talked to were "aware that representatives of CORE [the Congress of Racial Equality] and SNCC [the Student Non-Violent Coordinating Committee] have been engaged in semi-professional roles as neighborhood workers, counselors, etc." and that those young men questioned where these former activists might find comparable employment if CPI should close. Based on these and other observations, Campbell concluded that "the critics are correct in saying that the potential Negro leadership in the city of New Haven is concentrated in CPI."[4]

Although the War on Poverty community action program's siphoning off and co-opting of indigenous and civil rights leadership was certainly not limited to New Haven's Community Progress, Inc., as you have seen, the Lee administration, in its URS capacity, had an especially notorious history of undermining local African American leadership. In oral histories conducted decades after these 1960s events, African American leaders on either side of the Lee administration agreed that, indeed, CPI had a negative impact on local African American leadership. For example, attorney Earl Williams, an NAACP activist who became the organization's president, stressed that "the empowerment of the black community . . . was not the object of the program here, in New Haven" and surmised that as "the whites saw it—if you use this money to empower black people, that would change the status quo."[5] And here is how Reverend Edwin Edmonds, an original CPI board member who later became its president, put it: "You see, it was eat at the trough. But we controlled the food that goes into the trough. And we can control you by cutting it off, or reducing its quantity. . . . We maintain the power."[6]

In New Haven this view was not held only by African Americans. It was also a conclusion drawn by some of the city's progressive European American leaders. Another member of the executive branch of Mayor Lee's URS governmental core who had misgivings about what he saw as Lee's use of CPI to co-opt leadership among the city's poor people was Attorney

Richard Belford, director of the city's Commission on Equal Opportunities (CEO), an agency that handled discrimination complaints. He recalled that CPI chose to align itself with the mayor rather than neighborhood people. "Invariably ... although they spoke the language of participatory democracy and having the people develop and run the programs, in my opinion, they were working to co-opt the people, and to get them to be working for what the mayor considered to be in his best interests, as distinguished from the best interests of the people involved. It got down to a question, I think, of control of the programs, and ultimately, control of the people."[7] Such control was increasingly needed by the Lee URS administration as it faced an upsurge in African American rebellion.

AFRICAN AMERICAN REBELLION IN NEW HAVEN

In the late 1960s, urban rebellion involving African Americans against local white power structures included both the social protest and other challenges of militant grassroots organizations and the less organized and more destructive violent civil disorders. In this section I examine how each of these manifested itself in New Haven, and with what consequences. A good place to begin is with the Hill Parents Association.

The Hill Parents Association Flexes Its Muscles

In chapter 3, I discussed the emergence of the Hill Parents Association as a grassroots challenge to the Lee administration, a regime that, as you have seen, skillfully hid elements of old-style patronage politics behind a facade of "good government" reforms. In New Haven, as was true elsewhere, African Americans remained highly marginalized under both machine politics, which rewarded residents of white ethnic neighborhoods for their votes, and reform government, which, while ostensibly now serving the public interest of the entire city, kept both people of color and also white ethnics on its margins of political input and accountability. The rise of HPA in the Hill, the city's largest low-income neighborhood and a dumping ground for those dislocated by Mayor Lee's major reform effort of urban renewal,[8] signaled the demise of what Stone et al. deemed the reform era of urban politics and the coming of the post-reform period. For Community Progress, Inc., specifically, with the organization of its neighborhood boards, this required a shift from, to borrow the words of CPI board member Edwin Edmonds and others, a "do for" project to what would ultimately become a "do with" project.

I began discussing the origins and significance of the Hill Parents Association in chapter 3 when I placed its emergence in 1965 within the context of the African American leadership vacuum left in the wake of Mayor Lee's effective co-optation and marginalization of the city's two major civil rights organizations. I also noted that HPA quickly found itself at odds with CPI, an organization that not only held a radically different view of the nature and role of indigenous African American leadership but that HPA leaders believed actively worked to subvert their organizing efforts of Hill area residents. Because of their diametrically opposed views of indigenous leadership and organization, these two organizations could not simply leave one another alone. Those fundamental differences made it impossible for them to peacefully coexist.

The Hill Parents Association gained the attention of Community Progress, Inc., and city hall after its successful protest for changes at the Prince Street Elementary School, which among other changes resulted in the replacement of its principal with an African American.[9] HPA was now ready to flex its muscles as it not only pushed to reform CPI but pressured the Lee administration to accept the newly emerging post-reform urban politics. As one scholar of New Haven during that time period put it, the emergence of HPA represented nothing less for the city's repressed African American leadership than "a new day in Babylon." HPA symbolized the coming of a new day because of its independence from CPI and city hall.[10] That new day in New Haven was but one manifestation of the nascent black power phase of the civil rights movement and its demand that African Americans operate their own organizations independent of white control. Fred Harris stated that what distinguished HPA from the local chapters of the National Association for the Advancement of Colored People and the Congress of Racial Equality, which by then had "sort of petered out," was that although HPA had European Americans working with it, unlike the NAACP and CORE they operated under African American leadership and therefore did not dominate the organization.[11]

The Hill Parents Association was also different from the local chapters of the NAACP and CORE in that its issues, membership, and leadership all accrued from one neighborhood. As a neighborhood organization, HPA was also free of control from a national office that might be more accommodating in its dealing with the nationally well-connected Mayor Lee. And because the Hill was so overwhelmingly a low-income area, there would be little influence from the middle class and affluent people who tended to dominate the leadership of the NAACP and CORE.[12]

HPA had no shortage of issues important to Hill residents through which it could demonstrate its prowess. Once it demonstrated its ability to win significant concessions regarding the operation of a neighborhood school, it would then prove itself adept at helping Hill residents deal with the local welfare system and with the major dislocations caused by the city's urban renewal projects.[13] The Hill Parents Association soon added to its duties the responsibility of applying grassroots pressure to ensure that Community Progress, Inc., lived up to the Office of Economic Opportunity's "maximum feasible participation of the poor" mandate for its federally funded War on Poverty community action programs. Under this pressure, CPI was forced to enlarge the size of its board and to include more representatives from the low-income neighborhoods it served.[14] Next, HPA decided to seek a summer programs grant from CPI, a choice that contributed both to the demise of HPA and to the rise of a movement to decentralize CPI and turn over most of its program operations to neighborhood corporations.

HPA Seeks a Summer Grant from CPI: Co-optation vs. Self-Determination

Aside from the fulfillment of its role as a neighborhood watchdog to make sure that Community Progress, Inc., was faithful to the federal "maximum feasible participation of the poor" mandate, there were still other reasons why the Hill Parents Association sought a summer grant from CPI, including the bad social conditions in the Hill, the rising militancy of New Haven's progressive grassroots organizations, and their relatively few concrete gains from the Lee administration.[15] As Raymond Wolfinger put it in his study of New Haven politics, "militants found few promising avenues of political action" and were frustrated by the fact that "for years various groups of discontented citizens had asked unsuccessfully for an equal voice in planning and executing policy in renewal, anti-poverty, and school programs."[16]

But those reasons do not fully explain why HPA would risk both embarrassment if its proposal was rejected and, even if it was funded, the possibility of co-optation by CPI. As I noted earlier, a key motive behind many of HPA's actions was its resolve to remain true to the issue that was rooted to its very reason for being: community self-determination, which of course included control of CPI's operations in the Hill. Fred Harris recalled: "We talked for a long time with them about direct funding. It bugged us that they should get all the money and then administer it. We told them at a meeting that we weren't children and they didn't have to take care of money for us. . . . People in the Hill certainly weren't getting the money, and an awful lot of it never seemed to leave downtown."[17]

Although the Lee URS administration recognized the urgency of establishing a working relationship with the Hill Parents Association, it was also reluctant to do so. One reason was that the organization was a very independent group that touted its autonomy in both the planning of its summer programs proposal and its plans for administering it. The other reason was both race- and class-related. Fred Harris was neither understood nor appreciated by most of the city's European American residents who Mayor Lee was careful not to upset.[18] However, this was a time when mayors were being pressured from a variety of sources, including the federal government, private foundations, and local activists, to appear to be more responsive to the demands of local indigenous leadership. The symbolic significance of program funding for grassroots leaders was matched by the more practical concerns of Lee and the other mayors that if more was not done programmatically they might face a long, hot summer of civil unrest.

It was in this ambivalent environment of both high expectations and equally high trepidation that the Hill Parents Association submitted a summer grant proposal to Community Progress, Inc. Not surprisingly, both sides proceeded cautiously. For example, as Fred Harris recalled, "I don't know if they thought we were going to take them up on it or not."[19]

Clearly, Community Progress, Inc., and the Hill Parents Association had not only very different but perhaps diametrically opposed goals when it came to HPA applying for a summer programs grant. For CPI it was an opportunity to engage, and possibly co-opt HPA's radical[20] grassroots leaders, whereas for HPA it was a chance for Hill residents to express self-determination by gaining control of CPI programs in their area. An early indication of the danger of grants to a militant grassroots organization like HPA was the large amount of time the preparation of a fundable grant proposal took, time that could have otherwise been spent on organizing and challenging the Lee administration and other components of New Haven's local white power structure.[21] In the next section, I examine another, much larger, controversy involving HPA's acceptance of a summer programs grant from CPI.

Program Extortion? Racial Co-optation? or Both?

When its proposal was completed, the Hill Parents Association requested $34,000 for a set of five summer programs that were designed to address complaints the organization's leaders had received from area residents. In addition to a program known as Operation Breakthrough to provide summer jobs, the HPA proposal requested funds for a neighborhood park, silk screening, adult education, and a summer camp. HPA's members became angry when CPI appeared to drag its feet on their request, then offered them a grant of only $6,000, and later refused to reconsider its decision. That anger was reported to have been especially intense among some of the neighborhood men who had looked forward to having summer jobs.[22] Things then happened very quickly. This is what Fred Harris had to say about the events of June 14 that caused the Lee administration, in its URS capacity, to override CPI's decision the following day and grant HPA the full amount it had requested.[23] "We kept saying things. The people are getting tired of this, and the police were brutalizing people in the community, and all kinds of stuff. . . . We weren't getting any justice. So one night, all the poverty offices caught on fire. So then, the next day, the Mayor called me downtown, and gave me the money for the proposal."[24]

The "Deal": A $34,000 Misunderstanding

Here is how Fred Harris saw the "deal" he made with Mayor Lee. Note that Mayor Lee's understanding of what could and would happen as a result of the Hill Parents Association getting its full summer programs grant request seemed to be quite different from that of Harris. Indeed, they appeared to have agreed to different deals.

> The mayor ran the meeting. I guess from what he said they never caught the people who did the firebombing. Maybe they did and weren't saying who they were. But for whatever reason, he wanted to make a sort of deal. He told us he'd found the $34,000 for us. He said that in return for it we should make sure that there was no trouble this summer. I know it sounds crazy, but that is what the man said. We weren't going to tell him we didn't control people in the entire city and didn't even control people in the Hill. I don't know what he thought. So we told him we didn't think there was going to be trouble. We weren't going to cause any, but we couldn't speak for everyone.[25]

It would not be long before the precise meaning of that agreement would be put to the test.

The Deal Breaker: Civil Disorder in New Haven during the Summer of 1967

What may have been Mayor Lee's worst nightmare materialized on August 19, 1967, when despite the summer programs insurance policy he thought he had purchased from HPA, violent unrest broke out in the Hill section of the city after a European American restaurant owner shot and wounded a Puerto Rican youth. For three nights African American, Puerto Ricans, and European Americans—mostly youth—"broke windows, looted shops, and started fires." With that "riot," which the police, the media, and the general public viewed largely through a racial lens,[26] Mayor Lee's carefully constructed image of New Haven as the nation's model city literally went up in flames. New Haven was now clearly no better than the scores of other American cities that experienced civil unrest that summer.

As is often the case when racial politics are involved, accounts of what happened that summer, who was involved, and why vary widely. Even the terminology used to describe the phenomenon—e.g., riots, violent outbreaks, civil disorders, civil disturbances, or urban rebellions—reveal as much about the racial and political outlook of the commentator or analyst as the reality of what occurred.[27]

Divergent Accounts of Civil Unrest

The Kerner Commission Report

Lyndon Baines Johnson was so troubled about the civil disturbances that erupted in the nation's black ghettos during the summer of 1967 that he appointed a presidential commission to examine their causes and to make recommendations to prevent their reoccurrence. By placing white racism generally and the housing discrimination that caused and maintained racial ghettos more specifically at the center of its discourse, what became known as the Kerner Commission Report went way beyond the racism-evasive intellectual and political foundations upon which the War on Poverty community action programs and their project precursors like Community Progress, Inc., were built.

After examining whether local community action programs had fulfilled the Office of Economic Opportunity's "maximum feasible participation" mandate, the Kerner Commission concluded that because "ghetto residents increasingly believe that they are excluded from the decision-making process which affects their lives and community" they share a "feeling of exclusion" that "has engendered a deep seated hostility toward the institutions of government."[28]

The Kerner Commission Report singled out Detroit and Mayor Lee's model city of New Haven as examples for the lesson they offered that "well intentioned programs designed to respond to the needs of ghetto residents were not worked out and implemented sufficiently in cooperation with the intended beneficiaries." And in its criticism of New Haven, the report did not limit itself to CPI; it also criticized both the inadequate protection and the misconduct of its repressive state apparatus unit, the police.[29]

The Kerner Commission was certainly not the only component of the federal racial state that was worried about the racial unrest in New Haven and other cities in the United States. Congressman Giaimo, a vocal critic of CPI, also let his views be known.

Congressman Giaimo Places His Views on "Jungle Law" into the Congressional Record

Unlike Mayor Lee, after New Haven's summer of civil unrest, Congressman Robert Giaimo of Connecticut was willing to openly acknowledge that the city was facing a racial crisis. Giaimo elaborated on his views about the nature of that crisis, its causes, and its remedies in comments he placed in the *Congressional Record* in January 1968 along with a copy of an investigation he and his staff conducted not long after that summer's civil unrest. Early in that commentary and report, which were also summarized in an article in a local newspaper, Rep. Giaimo made it clear where he stood in regard to the proper balance of African American aspirations and European American resentment in the wake of that violence. After briefly stating his concern about the importance of addressing "the plight of the unemployed Negro," he quickly let it be known that "most important of all" was "the growing disregard for law and order." Congressman Giaimo then went on to use a highly racialized "jungle-law"[30] metaphor to make clear his rejection of the view articulated by the Kerner Commission and others who rooted the unrest that engulfed much of the United States that summer in white racism and other sources of social deprivation.

> I am disturbed by those misguided persons who claim to support law and order but who really excuse every violation of law and order by stating that "injustices which victimize the people of the inner city are equally reprehensible and must be equally prohibited." In short, by equating the two propositions they justify disregard for law and order. Certainly injustices exist and must be prohibited. But first and foremost we must have law and order or we will not have any society at all. We will revert to jungle law.[31]

Just as the various components of the federal racial state differed in their responses to the urban rebellions of the summer of 1967, the same would be expected at the level of the urban racial state, and it could be anticipated that even within the mayor's executive branch of the URS governmental core there might be conflicting and competing interests and perspectives. Let's take a closer look at another divergent perspective from within Mayor Lee's URS administration that was far to the left of the mayor's office.

The Report of the New Haven Commission on Equal Opportunities

That conflicting perspective was expressed in the account of the city's civil disturbances presented in a report by the New Haven Commission on Equal Opportunities (CEO), a city agency component of the URS administration that had supported HPA's request of CPI funds for summer programs and had since December of the previous year urged the mayor to recognize the potential for civil unrest in the city.[32]

In the introduction, Richard Belford—CEO's executive director—was careful to include the disclaimer that the agency "does not purport to represent the viewpoint of the City Administration."[33] Before becoming head of CEO, Belford had been supportive of HPA activities in various ways, and after he assumed the leadership of that agency he "took the position that the goals of the Commission on Equal Opportunities coincided . . . in many respects—with that of the Hill Parents Association."[34]

Belford's sympathetic portrayal of the role Fred Harris, Ronald Johnson, and other members of HPA played as they "walked the streets in the Hill area for the purpose of calming people down and minimizing the breaking of windows and looting" was out of step with the disappointed and angry reaction of Mayor Lee. The CEO narrative stressed that not only did the HPA try to stop the violence, but it persisted in that effort despite interference from the police. For example, the report told of an agreement between HPA and the Lee administration that its public works department would deliver large brooms to the Hill the same night the disturbances began for residents to use to begin cleaning up the area. The brooms never arrived because the police did not allow the public works truck loaded with them to enter the area. The report also recounted that there was an incident that resulted in Fred Harris being arrested and maced before ultimately being released on his own recognizance.[35]

A day after the disturbances began, delegates from HPA, the president of the local NAACP chapter, and a national officer of that organization met with Mayor Lee and worked out an agreement that entailed, among other things, a minimum police presence in the Hill with no rifles or shotguns and an understanding that HPA would keep order.[36] According to the Commission on Equal Opportunities report, that night a key provision of that agreement was broken when Mayor Lee announced a curfew for the area and the state police entered the Hill with rifles and shotguns. Fred Harris's wife and other HPA representatives faced numerous hurdles as they attempted to schedule a meeting with Mayor Lee, and when they were finally able to do so he informed them that the situation was out of his hands and under the control of the state police.[37]

The fact that the state of affairs in the Hill had reached a new crisis point was evident to Richard Belford later that night when he received a call from the Council of Churches to inform him that the police were using tear gas in a neighborhood housing project. At that point, according to the CEO report, Belford and area mental health professionals called a meeting "to analyze the situation and to attempt to reopen lines of communication and rapport between the Mayor and the black community."[38] They managed to schedule a meeting with the mayor the following day in which they worked out a six-point agreement. First, Mayor Lee and the police chief were to issue a statement of appreciation for the helpful efforts of HPA and its leaders, Fred Harris and Ronald Johnson. Second, the mayor and police chief would make it clear that HPA was assisting the police and should not be interfered with. Third, the organization was to recruit Hill area people to help calm the situation. Fourth, bail would be lowered for the people arrested. Fifth, Mayor Lee was to minimize the visible police force in the area. And sixth, a doctor would be allowed to assist those in jail.[39]

According to the CEO report, this agreement failed with the Hill Parents Association claiming that they did not receive the city ID badges they needed and the Lee administration blaming that failure on what it said was HPA's decision not to use them. Tensions persisted and were exacerbated by rumors that there would be more violence, including the burning of Hill area homes. On Tuesday afternoon, after a meeting with a group of mostly area clergy members, Mayor Lee issued a press release that indicated that not only hadn't the efforts of the New Haven police and his seeking the support of citizens calmed the unrest, but the number of fires that previous night actually increased. While promising to continue to keep lines of communications open with community groups, Lee indicated more was needed in the way of a strong police presence and that he had made arrangements to have fifty cars of state policemen sent into the Hill.[40]

That following month Belford resigned as CEO's executive director as Mayor Lee apparently moved to regain control of the agency and enforce upon it his edict of the avoidance of controversy that CPI had accepted from its inception. Belford left the Lee URS administration after he concluded not only that the mayor wouldn't tolerate dissent within his administration and that Lee intended CEO to have as its main goal the furtherance of his positive image, but that the agency would not get the support it needed from Mayor Lee as long as Belford remained its executive director.[41] As you will see later, Belford's criticism of the Lee administration had just begun.

The Color-Blind Account of the Lee Administration and Community Progress, Inc.

Of course, Mayor Lee and CPI had their own spin on the civil disturbances that so badly tarnished both of their images that summer. Consistent with Lee's reform-government philosophy and the history of their racism-blind approach to urban reform, the public message was that, because the unrest was not really racial, it did not reflect negatively on race relations in the city or on CPI and other Lee administration reform efforts.[42]

Privately, however, Mayor Lee's position was more similar to what he told me in an oral history interview about how difficult he found Fred Harris and fellow CPI leader Ronald Johnson to deal with. As he recalled, "when a riot hit in 1967, they were involved in that up to their eyeballs."[43] In brief, Mayor Lee believed that not only didn't the HPA leadership keep its part of what he saw as the bargain to guarantee racial peace in the city that summer, but they were actually implicated in the occurrence of that "riot."

The 1967 Community Progress, Inc., annual report, which on its cover page had the mayor's name followed by that of CPI board president Reuben Holden and, finally, CPI executive director Lawrence Spitz, reflected the mayor's official line that the disturbances in the city that summer were not racial in nature and in no way reflected negatively on CPI or the mayor's other reform efforts. This point was made in the document's preface:

> To some it was a rebellion; with most others, the violence reflected more of a thirst for revelry than a social protest. The rebels made up only a tiny fraction of the Inner City population. Much of their following comprised teenaged hooligans more bent on "fun" and vandalism than possessed of a cause. . . . Few if any of the incidents of the four days bespoke any widespread discontent. There is no basis for reading into the four-day flare-up (as a few have done) an Inner City-wide indictment of the physical and human-renewal efforts of 14 years.[44]

After absolving the Lee administration and its urban renewal and CPI programs of any responsibility for the civil disturbances, the report then went on to try to restore New Haven's tarnished reputation as a model city by reclaiming the city's advanced position "along the road to human and social progress" relative to "the vast majority of communities." It then made the case in bold print that CPI was indeed an effective instrument of racial control. "Had there not been a CPI (and its partner agencies in New Haven's human-resource effort), the August violence could quite conceivably have flared into a Newark or Detroit."[45]

No mention was made of the Hill Parents Association, its summer programs grant, and the efforts of HPA's leaders to stop the violence. Instead, perhaps getting more than a bit carried away in touting its own virtues, the CPI report went so far as to designate the Lee administration and CPI as "the chief militants in the Inner City crisis" with its "large number of action programs, militantly conceived and militantly executed."[46] Here the Lee administration sounded like a drum major in the march toward a new post-reform era of urban politics. But that was just one perspective.

The View from Below: The Hill Parents Association

Based on what you have already learned about the relationship between HPA and the Lee administration, it should not be surprising that Fred and Rose Harris, Ronald Johnson, Willie Counsel, and other leaders of the Hill Parents Association had a very different take on the dispute over the summer programs grant and the civil disturbances in the Hill during the summer of 1967 than did Mayor Lee and Community Progress,

Inc. In making his point that the civil disturbances had roots that went well beyond the shooting of a Puerto Rican man that day, Curtis Belton, who ran HPA's Operation Breakthrough summer employment program, concluded that that incident provided Hill residents an opportunity "to express their feelings about where they live." To sum up that attitude, Belton said, in an obvious challenge to the Lee administration's liberal and reform reputation, "We know this ain't no model city."[47]

As I noted earlier, from the perspective of the leaders of the Hill Parents Association, the mayor's assumption that he had an agreement with them wherein in exchange for a summer programs grant they would ensure no violent outbreaks in the city, or even the Hill, was not only unrealistic but was just plain strange. Nevertheless, they consented to do what they could do. To Lee, however, a deal was a deal, and the deal was simple: by accepting the grant from Community Progress, Inc., the Hill Parents Association had promised to keep the peace. When it did not, Mayor Lee acted as if their agreement had been broken by HPA. Fred Harris recalled what he saw as a dramatic change in Lee's behavior when they "went downtown to see the Mayor" after the violence began. "It was like he just freaked out. He couldn't even function. . . . That cut off the communication between us . . . from that point on."[48]

In a one page statement HPA released on August 24, 1967, the organization expressed its dismay at what it saw as the change of Mayor Lee's position toward HPA: "why has an organization that has tried to maintain a public service for all, constantly come under fire from our city fathers?" With that query HPA portrayed itself as being reasonable in its efforts to keep open channels of communication with Mayor Lee and as seeking help with its peace-keeping efforts, "only to be confronted with, 'We don't need your help,' and have guns stuck in their faces and told, 'This is the only help.'"[49]

From Fred Harris's view of things, Mayor Lee had very little understanding of the workings of ghetto communities, which the mayor apparently thought functioned like ward politics in his well-oiled political machinery, such that their insurgent residents could be rapidly contained to guarantee racial peace. Fred Harris and his HPA associates found the simplicity of Mayor Lee's thinking to be shocking. Moreover, they believed that once the civil unrest began there were still things the mayor could have done to diffuse the situation by working with HPA and other organizations.[50]

From HPA's point of view, Richard Lee was not only out of touch with reality he was incompetent, manipulative, and vindictive. The Hill Parents Association believed that the mayor relinquished control from the moment he declared a curfew and allowed the state police to enter the Hill.[51] At that point Mayor Lee seemed to have either decided or acquiesced to the belief that with the failure of community action it was now time to rely on police action to repress the racial insurgency threat HPA's leadership posed to his administration.

FROM COMMUNITY ACTION TO POLICE ACTION

You may recall that the epigraph for this chapter is a racist letter to Mayor Lee from a constituent complaining about what that person saw as the mayor's coddling of the city's African Americans. But that "irate citizen" did not stop there. The letter concluded with a call for "action." It is probably safe to say that what was being demanded was not additional community action, but more police action. Here is an excerpt from another angry letter calling for action: "Well Mr. Mayor: What do you think now of your niggers? You've been favoring them over white people ever since you are in office."[52] The letter also challenged Lee's account of the city's civil disturbances: "What are you trying to do? Exonerate t e [sic] colored people of their crimes? You want to blame the white people for it? Why? Do you want more colored votes next election, or do you want t [sic] just save your neck." The irate letter writer then made it clear that Mayor Lee's apparent attempt to balance African American protest and white racial backlash was doomed to fail: "You are mistaken Mr. Lee, the colored people are going to get you anyway, and if the colored people don't get you the white people will." That warning was followed by a demand for racial action when the mayor was reminded that it was his URS obligation to "white people . . . to put te [sic] blacks in their place now."[53]

Unleashing the Repressive State Apparatus of New Haven's URS

In New Haven and elsewhere, a major contributing factor to the hardening of racial attitudes on both sides of the racial divide in the late 1960s was a change in racial power relations. New Haven's civil disturbances upset the balance of power between Mayor Lee and the Hill Parents Association leadership. Now Lee's image and that of his "model city" administration were tarnished while the stature of Fred Harris and his HPA associates as legitimate spokespersons for the city's grassroots African Americans was greatly enhanced.[54]

That summer the conflict between HPA and the Lee administration intensified. Harris attended an "Angry Young Black Men's" rally of six hundred people who shouted, "Spitz has got to go. Spitz has got to go." And that was not all. A photograph of Harris at the podium appeared on the front page of the *New Haven Journal-Courier* above a caption that read, "Fred Harris Urges End of CPI."[55] For Mayor Lee, who now perceived the HPA leadership to be his mortal enemy, simply ignoring them was no longer an option. Harris's death wish for Community Progress, Inc., was consistent with his belief that the project was yet another weapon Mayor Lee deployed in his attack on the Hill Parents Association. In an oral history interview, Harris went on to assert that such repression was not limited to "strong-arm bullshit like in the gangster movies. There are more subtle ways and they knew them all."[56] The withdrawal of Community Progress, Inc., support was one of those ways.

CPI as an Example of a More Subtle Form of Suppression of HPA

In that same oral history interview, Harris recalled that after its falling out with the mayor not only did HPA not receive the funding it had been encouraged to apply for for year-round programs, but CPI took a harder line on the need for neighborhood groups to demonstrate their ability to manage programs, and the potential funding from foundations that had previously expressed interest also dried up. This inability to get program jobs for Hill-area residents in turn reduced HPA's organizational capability.[57] It was not enough to freeze the HPA out of community action resources; however, they would be the targets of repressive police action.

Police Action as Part of the Repressive State Apparatus of New Haven's URS

Although, as Antonio Gramsci has noted, oppression is normally maintained through hegemonic ideas (or ideology), the ultimate defense of oppressive systems is force, as institutionalized in the military, the police, courts, and other components of a state's repressive apparatus. In New Haven the police and other parts of the URS's repressive state apparatus exacerbated racial tensions in three major ways in the late 1960s. First, their long history of bad behavior toward ghetto residents was a significant factor that helped ignite the conflagration during the summer of 1967.[58] Second, both the New Haven and the state police played a major role in suppressing African American insurgency during that civil unrest.[59] And finally, after the rebellion, it was the local police, with the help of the courts, that seemed to exact white racial revenge against HPA and other insurgent African Americans.

Two and a half months after New Haven's civil disturbances, a "Coalition of Concerned Citizens," released its "Report of the Committee to Enumerate Harassment and Repression." That committee, which consisted of local ministers and other professionals, including Richard Belford—the former director of New Haven's Commission on Equal Opportunities—warned that "there exists in the City of New Haven a system of harassment and repression being exerted against the black community and its outspoken leadership" that "threatens to stifle those who wish to express dissenting opinions."[60]

The report listed the following repressive activities targeted against African Americans deemed as insurgent: "questionable use of legal process," "public unsubstantiated accusations by police against black leadership," "personal degradation, indignity, and humiliation," "intimidation," "broken promises," "alienation," and "forced isolation from the decision-making process of government." Most of those seven categories of repressive actions involved the Hill Parents Association leadership as targets of the police or courts while another focused specifically on the behavior of Community Progress, Inc.[61]

The first case in point detailed the recent arrest of Hill Parents Association vice president Willie Counsel on robbery and violence charges, only to have the charges dropped a few days later. The second of a total of eleven examples cited involved members of the New Haven Police Department (NHPD) making public statements to the media that charged HPA president Fred Harris with criminal acts, including extortion. No arrests were made, and after hearing government evidence a federal grand jury made no indictments. Another illustration was that during a federal grand jury investigation of Fred Harris and others for extortion, an attorney who had been subpoenaed to testify was asked to reveal the legal advice she gave them as their attorney. Still another case example cited was the October 26 police raid of Fred Harris's home during which Harris's wife was said to have been forced to put her clothes on in a room with male police officers present, despite the availability of a female officer in an adjacent room of the apartment.[62]

The arrest of Fred Harris for possession of heroin and stolen property merits closer scrutiny because Harris's supporters believed he was set up. For example, they argued that since the typewriter was given to him at his birthday party, he could have received it from anyone there, including someone who was trying to frame him. Harris maintained that heroin was planted inside a basketball trophy by a police informant he had grown up with and played Little League baseball with, the same person who gave him the stolen typewriter.[63] It was no secret in New Haven that Fred Harris was a long-time heroin addict, including of course when he worked closely with the Lee administration.[64] So it is very unlikely that the police and Mayor Lee would have suddenly discovered Harris's addiction after the civil disturbances in the summer of 1967 and his break with the Lee administration.

These and other relentless attacks by New Haven URS's repressive state apparatus proved fatal to HPA. "Within a year of the riots, the only organization that had provided leadership and grassroots community programs for the black people of the Hill was essentially 'destroyed.'"[65] But before its demise HPA had exposed the failure of the Lee administration as a liberal reform government, pushed CPI to take the federal government's "maximum feasible participation of the poor" mandate seriously, and emboldened other African American organizations to follow its own lead in pushing for a new, more accountable, era of urban politics. After the challenges of the Hill Parents Association, neither Community Progress, Inc., nor New Haven politics would be the same.

THE COMING OF THE POST–REFORM ERA OF URBAN POLITICS TO THE MODEL CITY AND ITS PRESSURE TO REFORM CPI

The urban rebellion in New Haven's poverty-plagued Hill section that summer of 1967 signaled the death of Mayor Lee's carefully constructed myth of New Haven as a model city and exposed for all to see the ugly political machine foundation upon which his regime's good government facade was built. During much of his sixteen years as mayor (1954–70),[66] Richard Lee had managed to project a national image as one of the nation's most progressive and effective urban reformers while he skillfully co-opted and otherwise contained potentially insurgent African American leadership. The changing times finally caught up with Mayor Lee as what might be described as his hybrid machine/reform city government was no longer able to function effectively in its URS capacity as either a well-oiled political machine or an instrument of good-government reforms. Under neither regime modality did the Lee administration prove itself capable of balancing African American aspirations against European American resentment and of meeting the other demands of the emergent post-reform era of urban politics. With the birth and development of the Hill Parents Association, it became increasingly clear that Richard Lee's racially paternalistic brand of city politics was on its last leg.

Around the time Richard Lee announced he would not seek a ninth two-year term as mayor, thus bringing to a close his more than a decade and a half rule, he had come to realize the awesome power of the winds of change. For example, a November 1969 *Harper's* magazine article reported that Mayor Lee faced a violent confrontation by mostly African American young militants as he addressed the Democratic Town Committee at a meeting where the party's new mayoral candidate was to be chosen. Their angry shouts included "the people want to be heard!" as they demanded to address the delegates about lead paint and other housing code enforcement matters. After the police stepped forward with mace and arrests to block the advance of those fist-clenching activists, Mayor Lee was hurried to his limousine where he was asked to comment on the reception he had just received. Lee reportedly smiled as he responded, "I can adapt." But could he?[67]

Pressure to Reform Community Progress, Inc.

In New Haven in the late 1960s, there was probably no better sign of the coming of a new, more racism-cognizant, conflicting-group-interests encompassing, and participation-focused era of urban politics then the pressure to reform Community Progress, Inc. This reform movement is especially noteworthy given the political and administrative philosophies under which CPI operated from its inception and throughout its formative years, programmatic guideposts that were diametrically opposed to the core ideological tenets of the post-reform era of urban politics. Indeed, the changes CPI would be forced to make to remain relevant to the nation's and New Haven's dramatically changing racial order were so large that at times they appeared to take on more of the trappings of a revolution than of a reform movement.

The Community Progress, Inc., reform, which placed the agency in sync with the coming of the post-reform era of urban politics to New Haven, was driven primarily by three forces. As I have already discussed, from the bottom came demands from the Hill Parents Association as a representative of the Hill's grassroots of low-income African Americans.[68] From the top there was pressure from one of CPI's major funding sources, the Ford Foundation, and to a lesser extent from the federal government's Office of Economic Opportunity. And from the middle would now come increasing pressure from New Haven's middle-class African Americans.

In a statement that reads as if it could have been written by James Tillman as a challenge to inspire his new urban necessitarians, in its 1967 annual report CPI concluded that "the crisis that spawned violence in August and could do so again is, above all, a crisis of the comfortable middle-class—white and Negro."[69] Before I examine the response of middle-class African Americans in New Haven, let's take a closer look at how that crisis was seen by the professionals employed by the Ford Foundation to monitor CPI's various community-action-related issues and controversies.

Criticism of CPI from the Ford Foundation

Ford Foundation consultant Clifford Campbell returned to New Haven in June of 1967 as chair of a nine-member review team to conduct "the Foundation's first extensive look behind the national reputation to scrutinize CPI operations." Although the review team expressed concern that CPI fell behind its earlier levels of innovation and had not sufficiently advanced in the areas of research and resident participation, it expressed optimism about the "able and dedicated leadership" of both Reuben Holden as CPI's president and Lawrence Spitz as the project's new executive director.[70]

Both that report and the fact that it was not released to the public became the subjects of the following headlines in the conservative *New Haven Register* eight months later: "Ford Report on CPI Asks Stronger Effort, Resident Involvement" and "Ford and CPI Sit on a Report." The paper charged that "typical of the Ford Foundation's own cool isolation and of CPI's ingrained arrogance" the report that noted CPI's problems was not made available "to the community for evaluation," and instead, those two "big-brother" organizations tried "to hush-up any notion of waste or weakness and to settle things quietly between themselves." And in its left-handed jab at Community Progress, Inc., the *New Haven Register* charged the Ford Foundation with engaging in hypocrisy for not releasing the "concealed report," given that it "makes much of 'resident participation,' speaks out in praise of 'dissenting voices,' [and] has good words for 'independence and militancy.'"[71]

The author of the other newspaper article noted that although the critical Ford Foundation report was written prior to the outbreak of the city's civil uprisings, which began August 19, it was not "submitted" until August 20, after the violence began. With its emphasis on the "national climate of racial tension," the report made clear that the foundation was attempting to push the project in a direction that better fit the emergent post-reform era of urban politics. "The team found that CPI's program, as the agency itself, was created in the image of an 'executive-centered coalition' which 'assumed that power plus planning, without the ingredient of 'community participation' would lead to success—an assumption more valid five years ago then today.'"[72] Not surprisingly, and consistent with what you have already seen about the conservative impact of the determination of CPI's leaders not to threaten that coalition, the Ford Foundation review team also charged CPI with avoiding controversial issues like housing integration and police harassment.

The foundation's need to accommodate to the nation's rapidly changing race relations was evident in the fact that the longest part of the report was titled, "resident participation in the neighborhood." Here the Ford Foundation, which had previously noted the success of the Hill Parents Association in addressing problems with an area school, cautioned that although CPI should support neighborhood organizations, that must be done in such a way as to not reduce their militancy. The report lamented, however, that at present, "CPI seems to be cast in the mode of doing FOR rather than WITH people, and is having a most difficult time in breaking out of this mode."[73]

As I noted earlier, one of the key features of the shift from the reform to the post-reform era of urban politics was the increasing salience of racial conflict and the need to deal with it explicitly. The foundation's shift was most evident in the report's human relations section, where it cited both the "national climate of racial tension" and the city's "two minor racial disturbances in 1968" to make its case that "CPI should give more attention to human relations," its "most pressing problem." Comments like that make it clear that the words *human relations* were used as a euphemism for race relations.[74]

In brief, using the stealth, racism-evasive, language of "human relations," the Ford Foundation pressured CPI to move more overtly into the area of race-relations management. This would include even racism-specific actions like the agency "joining with the city's human rights commission to develop programs for producing equal opportunity in jobs, housing and living conditions." And in a recommendation that CPI do more in the area of human relations, particular attention was given to the project addressing what I noted earlier is the ultimate cause of ghettoization by "fostering housing integration."[75] In brief, the normally racism-evasive Ford Foundation appeared to have, at least for a moment, undergone a transformation in its approach to racial issues and was now insisting that CPI follow suit.

The final of the report's twelve recommendations was "that the new executive director be given support and encouragement by the Ford Foundation and top leadership in New Haven."[76] But what a difference six months would make. In a January 4, 1968, memorandum, Clifford J. Campbell reported on his most recent visit to CPI, during which he found a low level of staff morale that was "quite alarming," an amount that was, indeed, lower than what he had seen at any of the foundation's other projects. Campbell placed the blame squarely on the shoulders of CPI director Lawrence Spitz, who he concluded was "the focus of 95 percent of the criticism" of CPI, from both outside the agency and inside its own ranks. Spitz was said to have done poorly in all areas of "interpersonal relationships." Campbell found that because Spitz persistently exhibited "a special brand of paternalism toward staff," and especially the agency's African American employees, and had poor relationships with Mayor Lee and other local government officials who were feeling pressure from a white backlash, he had failed to balance the rising demands of African Americans against the often-divergent wishes of the mayor.[77]

Although Campbell's memorandum did mention that New Haven was "a tinderbox and highly explosive" as evidenced by "recent events in the school system and in the 'Hill district,'" consistent with the Ford Foundation's aversion to dealing directly and explicitly with racial issues, he made no attempt to place Lawrence Spitz's difficulties within the context of the dramatic national and local changes in race relations driven by rising African American aspirations and a growing white racial backlash that were not nearly as intense during his predecessor's tenure as CPI head. Given that tumultuous racial climate and the mounting African American demands for control of their communities and the programs operating within them, a reasonable question is, could Mitchell Sviridoff have done any better? Indeed, during that time and in that racial environment of African American pride and self-determination, wouldn't almost any European American director have become the target of resentment simply because the position was not held by an African American? Moreover, there was no acknowledgment of Richard Lee's failure to deal effectively with these changes, aside from a brief observation that the mayor's illness had contributed to "unsettled political conditions" in the city. And, of course, there was no recognition of the Ford's Foundation's own failures in meeting such challenges in its own program efforts.[78]

With the convenient omission of these and other contextual facts to help explain what was happening with CPI at that time other than what was deemed to be Spitz's terrible interpersonal skills, Campbell's memo provided the Ford Foundation with a convenient scapegoat for the foundation's own poor choices of program focus areas and strategies, project leadership like Sviridoff, preferred working relationship with local political leaders like Mayor Lee, and difficulties in adjusting itself to the demands by poor people of color for greater project decision making.

Not surprisingly, in his oral history interview with me, Lawrence Spitz gave a very different account of the Ford Foundation's role in CPI's problems. When I asked Spitz if there was anything he would do differently with CPI if he had an opportunity to do it again, he had this to say regarding what he saw as the Ford Foundation and the Office of Economic Opportunity's negative reaction to his plans to decentralize CPI in such a way that its programs would be operated by neighborhood boards:

> I would have done one thing differently. I would have told both Ford and the OEO to go jump in the lake, and insisted that they do not delay, or seek to delay, under the guise of the slow process of developing responsible neighborhood personnel to carry out programs.... Because there's no sense in spinning off a program and saying, "You're responsible for that program," unless you give them full responsibility, and that includes the financial responsibility.[79]

Pressure on CPI from New Haven's Middle-Class African Americans

As I noted earlier, one consequence of the Lee administration's success in the co-optation or marginalization of New Haven's largely middle-class African American leadership was the huge leadership vacuum that left for the emergence of the Hill Parents Association to fill. In its well-publicized and sometimes successful challenges to the Lee URS administration, which included Community Progress, Inc., HPA provided a model of militant African American insurgency that the city's largely ignored middle-class African American leaders would now tap into in the wake of the recent civil disturbances the Lee administration and HPA had failed to prevent. That crisis provided the city's middle-class African American leadership an opportunity to assert itself consistent with the good cop/bad cop racial negotiations game that was then playing out in communities nationwide, as the white power structure would be given the choice of dealing with the bad cop of *militant* grassroots leadership or the good cop of *responsible* middle-class African American leaders. But of course, as was true in the police work tactic well known in black ghettos at that time, both "cops" would actually be working together on the same team, toward the same ultimate goal. In this racially united front, the city's militant indigenous African American leadership gained an ally at a time when it was coming under increasing attack from the Lee administration's repressive URS police and court apparatus.

But this association with the city's African American masses is only part of the story. As we will see, its ultimate power linkage was along class lines with various European American professionals who helped manage the city's white power structure. Not surprisingly, with such divided loyalties, New Haven's middle-class African American leaders were at best ambivalent agents of change.[80] This ambivalence was also due to the fact that these leaders were not firmly located in any one particular era of urban politics. While keeping the stiff upper lip of professionals associated with a progressive reform government, they stretched one foot forward into the race-conscious post-reform era of politics as they dragged the other behind in a slightly updated version of machine politics, one in which some African Americans were now allowed access to old-style political patronage. In his study of New Haven politics, for example, Raymond Wolfinger suggests that black power could be viewed as "a continuation of ethnic politics" in that it provided a mechanism "to bring black leaders into the political mainstream by giving them a stake in the system." But that was not all: "this form of black power" promised to "have important benefits for whites" as it diverted "black demands for social justice into the same concern for patronage and recognition that absorbed nationality groups."[81]

One of the earliest African American middle-class critiques of CPI came in the form of a report written by a former CPI staff member, Janette Parker, which was given to a team of Ford Foundation investigators. In her critique Parker pursued a middle-class African American agenda. Indeed, one of the reasons she gave for her resignation from CPI a year earlier was its failure to involve "the staple black community institutions and concerned black middle class in a mutually helpful relationship with the black disadvantaged." Parker's most damning criticism of Community Progress, Inc., focused on its employment practices and what she saw as the punitive way the project's leaders treated its outspoken employees. She complained that hiring practices "were so unfair toward the Negro employees at CPI that we organized to see if we could bring some solutions to our plight."[82]

In another New Haven newspaper article, Parker was said to be critical of CPI's "white paternalism" and its failure to address the "root causes of problems in the black community." Parker also saw African Americans as being shut out of opportunities to work as consultants for the project. She complained that despite the fact that they were supposed to possess expertise on the "Black Poor," "99 per cent of the consultants were white." There was no mention in that article, however, of her expressing any reservations about the ability of middle-class African American consultants to bridge the class gap between themselves and the city's African American poor, and indeed one of her complaints was that CPI hired too many "non-professionals."[83]

In that article Parker was linked to Community Progress, Inc., board member Edwin Edmonds through her echoing of his earlier criticism of what they both saw as discrimination against African Americans in the hiring of people to fill top level CPI positions.[84] In his oral history interview with me, Edmonds indicated that although he didn't remember her report he agreed with Parker's criticism of CPI as being racially paternalistic, stifling dissent, and being community disempowering. When I mentioned Parker's concern that CPI hired too many nonprofessionals, Edmonds extended such class-based criticism to include Mitchell Sviridoff, CPI's first executive director, and his boss, Mayor Lee, both of whom had earned only a high school diploma. Reverend Edmonds stressed that when it came to job qualifications he was "opposed to shortcutting the process for blacks or whites."[85]

Janette Parker's husband, Henry, headed a middle-class-dominated alliance of African American organizations known as the Black Coalition. That umbrella organization was comprised of a wide array of sixteen organizations ranging from the grassroots and relatively radical HPA to the politically middle-of-the-road and very middle-class local chapter of the National Urban League.[86] With the establishment of the Black Coalition, which had among its goals the prevention of a repeat of civil disturbances in the city, the white power structure had a group it thought was both respected and politically moderate enough to work with.[87]

In New Haven the real power behind the throne resided not in city hall but in the ivy-covered gothic halls of Yale University. Yale University president Kingston Brewer not only lent the fledgling Black Coalition the prestige of his meeting with their representatives; he provided them funding. As HPA president Fred Harris recalled, in the Black Coalition, under the moderate leadership of Henry Parker, Yale found an organization with "a lot of virtues." Chief among them was that it was "more responsible and less militant than we were supposed to be."[88]

Despite those "virtues" and the coalition's strong support from Yale and other components of the private sector, the Lee administration would have little to do with the Black Coalition.[89] Indeed, CPI executive director Lawrence Spitz seemed to view the organization with contempt. In a letter to Mitchell Sviridoff, who was now a Ford Foundation vice president, Spitz complained that "this community seems to have a penchant for anointing certain groups and creating additional problems." That letter was written less than a week after the outbreak of violence that followed the assassination of Martin Luther King Jr. in more than a hundred American cities, but not in Black Coalition–protected New Haven.[90] In his oral history interview with me decades later, Spitz went much farther when he dismissed the Black Coalition as "a self-selected group of middle-class blacks" that "was formed, and sponsored, and brought forth by Henry Parker, for his own political designs."[91]

The Black Coalition soon pushed the Lee administration and CPI to reform in ways that were consistent with the new struggles for African American self-determination and community control. For example, a Black Coalition document called for a shift from "the iron, one-man rule of Mayor Lee" to a time when "the era of the anti-poverty or urban renewal program designed and implemented by white planners yielded to that of black self-determination."[92]

A March 2, 1968, local newspaper story reported on a meeting between the Black Coalition and "some 15 representatives of agencies and institutions of the white community," including the Chamber of Commerce and the Council of Social Agencies, during which the Black Coalition announced its "proposal for an orderly 'phase out' of Community Progress, Inc." Parker made clear the middle-class bias of that proposal when he indicated that the new role of the restructured and downsized CPI would be funding, not programming, but to accomplish what CPI had failed to do, "involve the stable black institutions and the stable black middle class." For example, unlike HPA's summer programs, neighborhood programs would not be administered by grassroots people. Instead, their funding would be controlled by neighborhood corporations "consisting of neighborhood clergy, teachers and businessmen, etc."[93]

There would be still other challenges to CPI in which the city's middle-class African Americans played a prominent role. One of those battles involved an attempt by African Americans to place CPI's largest program, its Manpower employment program, under African American control. When Lawrence Spitz proposed placing CPI's Manpower program within a consortium, with the Chamber of Commerce as its "overseeing group," Je Royd Green, the then-president of the HPA's Operation Breakthrough jobs program, called for the removal of both Spitz and of CPI's Manpower program director and their replacement with African Americans.[94] Operation Breakthrough was joined a couple weeks later in a joint statement by five other organizations, including the city's Opportunities Industrialization Center and the New Haven chapter of the Urban League, which demanded that all Manpower program funds go to a consortium that included those African American organizations.[95] As you have seen, CPI was now under intense pressure to reform itself.

COMMUNITY PROGRESS, INC., TRIES TO REFORM ITSELF

I mentioned earlier that by the mid- to late 1960s the CPI leadership no longer enjoyed the previous period of relative African American quiescence during which it could impose its will through the executive-centered leadership style for which Mayor Lee and his first CPI executive director had become well known. Pushed by the increasingly militant civil rights and citizens-participation movements, both Mayor Lee and Mr. Spitz, the new head of Community Progress, Inc., were forced to adapt to the coming of the new, more participation- and conflict-centered era of urban politics. Spitz arrived at the beginning of a tumultuous turn in race relations where he would be stuck between the proverbial rock and a hard place of both growing African American protest and white racial backlash. While Spitz and Sviridoff shared similarities and differences in background, both were European American men who seemed to be severely limited in their ability to respond to the challenges for CPI to reform itself, whether such challenges came from the grassroots or from middle-class professionals.

CPI found its mission, organization, and decision-making processes upset by the civil unrest that rocked New Haven in three ways: its failed efforts to prevent such unrest, its unsuccessful attempts to contain that violence during its occurrence, and the project's need to reform itself to better fit the city's new post-civil-disturbances racial environment. Its predicament was now emblematic of a white power structure, which to ensure the racial peace must quickly reform itself. In that effort CPI got off to a slow start, with its immediate reaction fitting the pattern both it and the Lee administration had previously followed when their usual efforts at co-opting African American leadership failed. They would create new African American leadership to own. As Fred Powledge stated in his study of New Haven politics in the 1960s, "CPI's first post-riot actions in the direction of citizen participation had been to help organize its *own* 'militant' groups." For example, CPI's alternative to the truly indigenous Hill Parents Association was the Neighborhood Hill Action Group. And despite the fiasco that resulted from the Lee administration's decision to direct CPI funds to HPA in its attempt to buy racial peace, CPI met with residents of impoverished neighborhoods to ask them to submit program proposals for that following summer. But instead of this old co-optation strategy working once again to tamp down African American militancy, "CPI's new and somewhat conciliatory attitude toward the neighborhoods" seemed to spark instead "a demand for more power."[96] That demand also put the agency at cross currents with the antiparticipation politics of Mayor Lee and his efforts even prior to the civil disturbances to have his URS administration reign in its community action program in response to the growing white racial backlash.[97]

But the changes in Community Progress, Inc., would not be limited to an expansion of its policies and practices regarding the OEO's mandate for maximum feasible participation of the poor. One of the first CPI policies to fall was the very tight restriction Mitchell Sviridoff, the project's previous director, had placed on the organizing activities of neighborhood workers in order not to upset Mayor Lee's governing coalition. Barely a month after the eruption of the civil disturbances in August of 1967, Spitz acknowledged at a meeting of the CPI board of directors that some of the project's neighborhood workers could have been more effective in their efforts to curtail that violence if their role had been more clearly defined in such a way that encouraged them to go beyond that of being mere "enablers." To Spitz the term *enabler* was "an ambiguous word that has tended to inhibit some CPI workers, causing them to retreat from controversy." Rev. Edmonds brought in the racial angle of "divided loyalty" in articulating his view as to why CPI's African American neighborhood workers, who were "almost trying to serve two masters at one time," were often ineffective. Once again Edmonds pushed for a reform he thought was long overdue at CPI: the need for African Americans in top-level project positions.[98]

Edmonds and others who had intensified their pressure for African American management of CPI after the civil disturbances would have to wait another eight and a half months until Lawrence Spitz announced his resignation as the project's executive director. But before I discuss the appointment of African American leadership, I will examine in closer detail what Spitz left as his legacy to the project. The same newspaper article that announced Spitz's resignation also reported his recommendation, which was "unanimously endorsed" by the CPI board, that the project be essentially phased out, with most of its program funds being turned over to "neighborhood-controlled structures," and with the focus of what remained of CPI being limited to "planning and funding." But unlike Spitz's recollection that this was his plan from the very beginning of his tenure with CPI, the *New Haven Register* seemed to root that decision in external pressure when it noted that Spitz's recommendation was "basically along guidelines suggested in separate recommendations from the Ford Foundation and from New Haven's Black Coalition."[99] This was consistent with the view expressed later that year by Joseph Downey, CPI's new Community Services director, who stressed that "we have been forced to decentralize," as he put it, "to get out of the 'do for' business" because "the [neighborhood] people would [rather] have nothing, than be spoonfed."[100]

Both of those announcements, one that paved the way for African American leadership of the project and the other to turn over most of its operations to neighborhood control, seemed to be consistent with the shift toward the post-reform era of urban politics. But there was an ironic twist about the racial implications of the plan to turn over most of the Community Progress, Inc., functions to the neighborhoods it served that was similar to what happened when African Americans were finally elected, beginning in the mid-1960s, to head major American cities, which by then seemed to be only a shell of what they once were. By the time an African American would be hired to head CPI, there was already a commitment to eliminate much of its power.

But that shift in power would not happen right away. The Community Progress, Inc., plan to decentralize its operations became so bogged down that more than six months after it was approved and announced by the CPI board a reporter for a local newspaper estimated the process would take at least another two years.[101] Former CPI head Lawrence Spitz dismissed then-current CPI staff claims that the neighborhoods weren't ready to run programs as being reminiscent of "the British claim that the colonies were not ready for self-government."[102]

In his paper on the decentralization of social services in New Haven in the late 1960s, Jonathan Bunge observes that after the civil disturbances during the summer of 1967 what used to be a Community Progress, Inc., strength—the fact that it was highly centralized—now became a liability. An important factor that Bunge discusses that was not mentioned by Spitz was opposition from politicians who feared they would lose control of the political patronage that continued to flow at the city and state governments. For example, Bunge notes that with the decentralization of CPI, Mayor Lee would no longer be able to make appointments to its board. Bunge also mentions that a local state representative had complained that "we politicians don't have anything to give out anymore. We don't have patronage. We'd have to work with the corporations as a way of protecting ourselves." He expressed concern, for example, that the corporations might become a powerful political force that did things like registering the poor to vote.[103]

CPI's New African American Leaders

The appointment of African Americans to Community Progress, Inc., key leadership positions was the reform that was especially important to some of the city's most outspoken middle-class African American residents like CPI board member Edwin Edmonds. That change finally happened in the summer of 1968. It began with the selection of Harry D. Jefferys, the former president of the Neighborhood Hill Action Group, as president of the CPI board of directors. Milton Brown, an African American, was chosen as CPI executive director after a controversy over whether the new director should be selected by a vote of the CPI board or should, as the Black Coalition proposed, go through a "neighborhood screening process."[104] Brown was also attractive because he was a New Haven resident who had been employed with CPI since its inception, most recently as head of the project's Community Services program.[105] However, as I noted earlier, those victories for African American empowerment came only as CPI had already begun its decline and was headed toward its ultimate demise.

THE DEATH OF COMMUNITY PROGRESS, INC.

As you have seen, Community Progress, Inc., was born in politics when Mayor Lee envisioned it as a necessary public-relations complement to his massive urban redevelopment projects. Not surprisingly, its golden years occurred when it had the greatest mayoral support. The project experienced decline after African American militancy and push for control of local CAPs provoked a white backlash that manifested itself at both the level of the federal racial state with the election of Richard Nixon and locally in New Haven as Mayor Lee not only came to see the project as no longer useful to his political agenda but increasingly viewed it as a liability. And it would die—after the civil rights movement stalled—under the politics of one of his successors.

The project's luck in surviving without mayoral support officially ran out when on October 6, 1976, the *New Haven Register* announced that "Community Progress Inc., the nation's oldest anti-poverty agency, is dead." The reporter deduced that the crime for which the project received its death sentence "appears to be that CPI pushed too far in resisting the push by Mayor Frank Logue to seat his group of appointees as the local government representatives to the CPI board."[106]

CONCLUSION

In this chapter I examined how the dialectic between African American protest and white backlash helped shape the federal and urban racial states' use of community action to navigate the swift and rapidly changing currents of the more participatory, conflict-driven, and racism-cognizant post-reform era of urban politics in New Haven and in other cities throughout the United States.

For the Lee administration, managing race relations during that turbulent period of high African American aspirations and rising European American resistance was very much like being stuck between the proverbial rock and a hard place. It would have taken a nimble URS administration and community action program to negotiate such tension successfully. Unfortunately for Mayor Lee, his outdated executive-centered governing coalition philosophy and style of governance, inability to work effectively with independent African American leaders, and strong vestiges of machine politics made his URS administration and its CAP ideological state apparatus incapable of transitioning his administration into the post-reform era. Consequently, although the facade of Lee's city hall office was liberal and reform-oriented, its foundation would prove too politically and racially rigid to survive the racial earthquake the city experienced during the summer of 1967.

The cracks in the foundation of Lee's city hall became quite visible with its URS administration's shift from its racially ameliorative to its racially repressive mode when after the "carrot" of co-optation through the ideological state apparatus of community action failed to stop African American insurgency the Lee administration tried the "stick" of its repressive state apparatuses of the police and courts. Although the Hill Parents Association was destroyed after it failed to do the mayor's bidding in keeping the racial peace, its contagious spirit survived and spread as a coalition of organizations emerged to take its place. Soon it was evident that to stay relevant Community Progress, Inc., would need to break free of the mayor's tight control. Unfortunately for CPI, reforms like the turning over of the project program funds to neighborhood corporations and the appointment of African American leadership made the project more of a threat to Mayor Lee and his successors, under whose leadership New Haven's URS administration had returned largely to its racially oblivious mode, than a valuable resource of patronage and racial control. For this reason, Community Progress, Inc., did not survive to see the full emergence of the change of urban politics that it, despite the wishes of Mayor Lee and other members of his governing coalition, helped to initiate.

In the next chapter I demonstrate the relevance of the urban racial state concept for explaining more recent events that involve issues other than community action. I begin by applying the concept to analyses of the URS actions of the Mayor Giuliani administration concerning police misconduct against young men of color in New York City and of the Mayor Nagin administration in New Orleans in response to the flooding after the levees broke in the wake of Hurricane Katrina. Following those two case examples, I suggest still other examples of highly racialized urban politics and policies that can be examined in other cities through the analytical lens of the urban racial state.

6

Recent Examples of the Urban Racial State

> Those who want to see this city rebuilt want to see it done in a completely different way: demographically, geographically and politically.
>
> —James Reiss, Mayor Ray Nagin's Bring New Orleans Back Commission[1]

An understanding of history is essential for anyone who would venture to comprehend contemporary social structures. This is not just because those who are ignorant of history may suffer the affliction of reliving horrific historical events. History is much more important than that. Indeed, for historical sociologists like myself, history is nothing less than the foundation of a two-story house where the main floor is the present and the second floor is our future. What is happening today and what will happen tomorrow are powerfully shaped by a society's highly institutionalized historical legacies. Social arrangements don't just disappear over time. Unless they are dismantled, they can be expected to persist, oftentimes with just the minimum adjustments needed to adapt to changes in their larger social environment. As you will see in this chapter, this is certainly the case for the existence and persistence of the urban racial state (URS).

In this chapter I demonstrate the contemporary relevance of the urban racial state concept by applying it to more recent case examples in New York City and New Orleans that do not involve community action programs, and by suggesting three additional research projects to which the concept can be applied. As usual I will begin by placing those events within the broader historical context of race relations in the United States.

FROM RICHARD NIXON TO BARACK OBAMA: POST-1960s RACE RELATIONS IN THE UNITED STATES

Unfortunately for African Americans and other people of color, the white racial backlash to the militant black-power phase of the civil rights movement was much more than a spike of angry reaction in race relations. Many decades later, that soon-to-be-politically-institutionalized legacy of the 1960s continues to shape American politics. Beginning with Richard Nixon's presidential campaign victory in 1968, the increasingly conservative Republican Party has harnessed and institutionalized white racial resentment to its advantage. In that campaign Nixon, following the lead of third-party presidential candidate and southern segregationist George Wallace, successfully deployed racialized code words like the need for "law and order" and opposition to forced "busing" to address de facto school segregation as part of his southern strategy to win the votes not only of southern segregationists but of racially resentful European Americans throughout the nation.[2]

Since the 1960s the Republican Party has staked its success on a steady flow of highly racialized issues that have helped make the white racial backlash of that decade a highly institutionalized and perhaps permanent feature of American politics. That long list of political "race card" issues includes various controversies involving the War on Poverty community action programs, urban unrest, busing, high rates of inner-city crime, opposition to affirmative action as "reverse discrimination" against European Americans, high taxes paid for social programs seen as benefiting lazy African Americans, welfare dependency among African Americans, and more recently racial profiling of Muslim Americans as potential terrorists and opposition to illegal immigration involving Latinos and other people of color.[3]

That strategy of stoking white racial resentment was not well disguised when of all of the places Ronald Reagan could have chosen to launch his 1980 presidential campaign he picked the otherwise obscure town of Philadelphia, Mississippi—the very place that was thrust into the national spotlight sixteen years earlier when three civil rights workers were murdered there with the aid of the local police. If that was not enough, the subject of Reagan's talk was his support for "states rights," the precise term southern segregationists deployed to justify their opposition to federal government protection for civil rights workers and other challenges to their terror-based system or racial apartheid. And as if to prove that his appearance and stance in Philadelphia, Mississippi, four years earlier was no fluke, Reagan returned there during his 1984 presidential reelection campaign and boldly rallied the crowd with the neo-Confederate battle cry of "The South Shall Rise Again."[4]

Similarly, in 1988 Republican candidate George H. W. Bush, was elected president in 1988 with the help of the highly racialized "Willie Horton" television commercial about a violent African American convicted murderer who raped a European American woman during a weekend prison furlough. In addition, George W. Bush's elections in both 2000 and 2004 would probably not have been possible without the widespread disenfranchisement of African American voters respectively in Florida, which included the hyperaggressive purging of the rolls of those listed, often incorrectly, as ex-felons, and in Ohio, where there were mass-scale failures of voting machines in largely African American inner-city neighborhoods.[5] In 2008, with the nation's economy in a free fall and widespread fear of another depression, the racial dynamics of American politics shifted dramatically as Barack Hussein Obama was elected the nation's first African American president. With the election of President Obama some social commentators actually proclaimed that we had indeed entered a post-racial society.

As we will see, in New York City from 1994 through 2001 and in New Orleans from 2002 through 2010, the white racial resentment that had shaped federal racial state policies during much of that period was also reflected at the local level. In his analysis of race relations in the United States during the 1990s, Manning Marable identifies racism within the criminal justice system as the major civil rights issue facing African Americans. This repression included an "epidemic of cases of police excessive force and violence against black citizens." Nowhere was the racial conflict over such abuse of power more intense than in the nation's largest city.[6]

RACIALLY-TARGETED POLICE MISCONDUCT IN NEW YORK CITY UNDER THE GIULIANI ADMINISTRATION

Americans who thought that the African American struggle for civil rights ended successfully in the 1960s may have been surprised decades later when they turned on the nightly television news and saw shocking police violence and mass protests and arrests in the nation's largest city as mostly African American city residents rallied against what they saw as essentially the police state of Republican Mayor Rudolph Giuliani. There is perhaps no better recent example in the United States of an urban racial state relying almost exclusively on the powers of its repressive state apparatus to maintain the racial control it deemed necessary to serve its own political interests then the eight years of the Giuliani administration. Clearly, the problem of what W. E. B. Du Bois so aptly described in 1903 as the "color line" would not be limited to the twentieth century.[7] It was obvious from the very beginning of the Giuliani administration that it would make no attempt to balance African American aspirations and white racial resentment. Instead, the Giuliani URS placed all of its political eggs in the basket of the brute expression of white power.

The Giuliani URS Administration and Its Repressive State Apparatus

Despite assurances Mayor Giuliani gave to African Americans in Harlem shortly after his victory in a highly racialized campaign over David Dinkins—the African American incumbent—that he was mindful of the fact that he was elected with only 51 percent of the vote, and that he had no intention of putting "together a government of all one group," that promise went unfulfilled. During his first month in office, Mayor Giuliani's URS administration threw out the affirmative-action plan initiated by Mayor Dinkins, stopped advertising city job openings in African American newspapers, ignored the city charter mandate that in hiring the city should consult with the Equal Employment Practices Commission, and announced his decision to abolish the city minority-contracting program.[8]

Giuliani's office made no real attempt to engage African Americans to bring them on board as part of his political constituency ideologically, programmatically, or even through the co-optation of their leaders. In brief, there was no carrot of ideological state apparatus (like ethnically targeted patronage through jobs and social programs) the Giuliani administration would use to balance rising African American aspirations against potential white racial backlash, as was usually the case in racially ameliorative URSs. The best that African Americans would get from Mayor Giuliani, if they were racially well behaved, was being ignored as his administration's URS rested firmly in its racially oblivious mode. If, however, African Americans asserted themselves through criticism and protest, they would be subjected to a strong racial crackdown by the racially repressive URS through harsh political rhetoric and its New York Police Department (NYPD) as the Giuliani administration relied heavily on its repressive state apparatus.

The workings of that repressive state apparatus were soon evident in the treatment of the city's African American and Latino American citizens by the NYPD. Although Mayor Giuliani seemed to have had a more favored relationship with Latino/a Americans, who voted for him in greater numbers than did African Americans,[9] Latino/a Americans were also the recipients of some very highly publicized killings by the police.

As I will show, the attitudes and tactics of the police were indeed sanctioned by or actually originated in city hall. This included support for officers who engaged in behavior that an increasingly large percentage of New Yorkers would come to see as indefensible. Moreover, in most of these cases the criminal court division of the judicial branch governmental core of the urban racial state also condoned those police actions through its tendency not to convict the police of wrongdoing no matter how outrageous their actions. In addition, as you will also see later, in most of these high-profile cases, the police officers involved had work histories that should have sounded an alarm about the danger of their continued employment on the force. Not surprisingly, it was a common practice for the city to either settle or lose the civil suit brought against it and thus pay out millions of dollars to the families of those killed. This pattern suggests that the problem was systemic, and not one that could be reduced to the misbehavior of just a few rotten apples on the force. The contour of police misconduct under the Giuliani URS administration began to come into focus with the killing of Anthony Baez.

Anthony Baez

The killing of Anthony Baez in December 1994 was one of the first examples of the workings of the repressive state apparatus under the Giuliani URS administration. This high-profile police killing of an unarmed young man of color revealed the attitudes of a police department and mayor who seemed to condone such behavior. Baez was a twenty-nine-year-old Latino American who was unfortunate enough to have his football strike a police car. Despite Baez's father's pleas that his son was asthmatic, Frank Livoti, a police officer whose precinct commander had previously tried to remove him from street duty, killed Baez when he placed him in an illegal chokehold, pinned him down to the ground for ten minutes, and then pulled him to his police cruiser without attempting to revive him. Once again, Livoti's commander was unsuccessful in having him removed from street duty. His attempt to assign Livoti to a desk job was overruled by Lou Anemone, the NYPD's highest ranking uniformed officer, a man who had a very close relationship with Mayor Giuliani and who rejected the requested transfer as not being "practical" because Livoti was a Police Benevolence Association delegate with close ties to that organization's head, a powerful union figure who supported Giuliani during his mayoral campaign. Anemone went so far as to praise Livoti for having "a distinguished career of service to the community" and for "doing the kind of work that the citizenry of the city and certainly this country are looking for."[10] As is typically the case for criminal cases involving police misconduct in the United States, Officer Livoti was acquitted—in this case of the charge of criminal neglect. However, Livoti did not fare as well in his dealings with the judicial branch governmental core of the federal racial state and in the wrongful death civil suit brought by Baez's family. Officer Livoti received a seven-and-a-half-year prison sentence in 1998 for violating Baez's civil rights, and the Giuliani administration settled with Baez's family for three million dollars.[11]

Abner Louima

Three years later the entire nation was shocked by an incident of police brutality that was so savage that it seemed incomprehensible. That event and its aftermath put many levels and branches of the racial state governmental core on notice that the URS in New York City may be out of control. The case was the sodomization of Haitian immigrant Abner Louima in the bathroom of a Brooklyn police station by NYPD officer Justine Volpe. The incident that provoked that awful act began on August 9, 1997, when Officer Volpe was punched in the head as he tried to break up a fight outside a bar that was frequented by Haitian immigrants. Volpe, who mistakenly concluded that it was Louima who struck him, arrested Louima for assault and disorderly conduct. He and other police officers then drove Louima to a secluded area where they took turns beating him. That was not enough revenge for Volpe, however, who beat Louima some more in his police precinct bathroom, sodomized him with a broken broomstick, stuck that end of the stick in Louima's mouth, and, as he paraded Louima out of the bathroom, bragged to other officers in the precinct that "I just broke a man down."[12]

The Louima case is important not just because it showed how outrageous police misconduct had become under Giuliani's rule, but because of what it demonstrated about how effectively Mayor Giuliani could act to diffuse such a situation when it suited his political purposes and how quickly he could reverse course again as soon as he was no longer politically vulnerable. Prior to the Louima case, Giuliani's modus operandi for handling incidents involving complaints against the police was to insist that the public not rush to judgment, while doing whatever he could to discredit the character of the victim, and later—backed by the usual pro-police verdict by a local court—coming out in support of the accused police officer. In this case, however, Giuliani was up for reelection amid widespread and growing outrage that the New York Police Department was engaging in a pattern of harassment against people of color as indicated by the increasing number of complaints of police brutality filed with the city's Civilian Complaint Review Board.[13] Under pressure from one of his most important political supporters—Ray Harding, the head of the city's Liberal Party—Giuliani took decisive action. He quickly denounced the alleged crime as being "reprehensible" and visited Louima in the hospital with Howard Safir, his police chief, at his side. Soon the two men announced a shake-up at the precinct where Louima was sodomized that included removal of the precinct captain, the transfer of the station's second in command, the suspension of the desk sergeant who was on duty that night, and the reassignment of ten of those precinct officers to desk duty. Further, by threatening to fire any member of the force who did not come forward with information about what happened that night, the mayor made it clear that he would not tolerate the code of silence commonly used to protect fellow officers who faced criminal charges.[14] Finally, Giuliani established a twenty-eight-member Task Force on Police-Community Relations, which included some of his most outspoken critics.[15]

Even with those quick and decisive damage-control actions, the Louima incident fed the image of the Giuliani administration as deploying essentially a police state that unleashed police thugs to harass young African American and Puerto Rican men. Although Louima later admitted that he lied when he said that Officer Volpe shouted, "This is Giuliani time. It is not Dinkins time," as he assaulted him, for many who had grown tired of police harassment of young people in their communities, the words "Giuliani time" epitomized a profound racial truth far deeper than the actual words Abner Louima may or may not have heard that night.[16]

In the end, because of his glib and arrogant response to the findings of his own Task Force on Police-Community Relations, Mayor Giuliani would lose much of the goodwill he had earned. Giuliani's ridicule of the one-hundred-and-fifty-page report and dismissal of nearly all of its recommendations reinforced the belief held by many of his critics that the panel was simply a public relations ploy to diffuse the mayor's racial problem during his mayoral campaign.[17] The impact of the Louima controversy was not limited to the ratcheting up of already strong antipolice and anti-Giuliani sentiment among African Americans and low-income Puerto Ricans. It sparked a backlash against the mayor and his city by a large and growing segment of city residents.[18] And as was often the case, city government would need to resolve the civil case brought against it through a large financial settlement. In this instance the Giuliani administration and the police union settled the civil suit by paying Louima close to nine million dollars.[19]

Antoine Reid

The belief that there had been a "Giuliani time"–type shift in law enforcement attitudes that was condoned by the mayor and thereby embedded in the structure and operations of his URS administration was further supported by the mayor's reaction to the shooting of an unarmed "squeegee man" by an off-duty police officer less than a year after the sodomization of Abner Louima. In mid-June of 1998, NYPD officer Michael Meyer shot Antoine Reid in the chest during an altercation after Reed attempted to solicit money by washing his car windshield.[20] As was true in the Louima case and in many other incidents involving accusations of misconduct against members of the NYPD, Meyer was no stranger to controversy. At the time of his shooting of the "squeegee man," he had been the subject of seven civilian complaints, most of which alleged excessive force, and had been removed from street duty earlier that year and reassigned to work maintaining a police precinct building. But this still did not stop the Giuliani administration from coming to Meyer's defense. The NYPD released Reid's "rap sheet," which showed nine arrests, all of which according to his lawyer were reduced to misdemeanors, and none of which involved violence.[21]

In the criminal trial nearly a year after the shooting, a state supreme court judge dismissed charges of attempted murder against Officer Meyer and acquitted him of the remaining charges of assault and reckless abandonment.[22] A few months later, Mayor Giuliani's publicly expressed impatience with "squeegee" and other homeless men he deemed to be public nuisances and it was presented as evidence by the defense in the police department's administrative hearing to determine if Meyer should be dismissed from the force. Giuliani's reaction to the "squeegee man" shooting is especially noteworthy for what it reveals about the mayor's strategy of cracking down on any public-nuisance behavior as his centerpiece for reducing street crime. It justified a heavy and oftentimes heavy-handed police presence in the city generally and especially in those high-poverty and largely African American and Puerto Rican neighborhoods where crime rates were the highest. Other cases would also shine a bright light on the link between police behavior in the streets and the mayor's highly racialized crime-fighting attitudes and policies. These included a killing that brought international embarrassment to the United States and its principal city.

Amadou Diallo

Less than eight months after the shooting of Antoine Reed, Mayor Giuliani's police department—the main component of his executive branch URS governmental core—faced a controversy that would make even the headlines-grabbing Abner Louima case look small by comparison. Shortly after midnight on February 4, 1999, four members of the NYPD's cocky Street Crime Unit, whose macho motto was "We own the night," fired forty-one shots at Amadou Diallo—a West African street vendor—as he stood in front of the door to his apartment in the Bronx with his black wallet in his hand, which they mistook for a gun. Nineteen of those bullets found their mark and killed Diallo.[23]

Once again, the real problem Giuliani's URS administration faced was not simply the behavior of the particular officers involved but the floodlight of scrutiny this new calamity brought to the doorstep of the entire NYPD. The magnitude of the Diallo controversy was due not just to how inconceivable that act was to people around the world but to the frequency and cumulative impact of such events involving the NYPD and to the department's apparent inability to reform itself. At this point even some of Giuliani's allies and former supporters had begun to express their doubts about the appropriateness of common police practices in the city. In brief, there was growing sentiment among many segments of New York City residents that with the NYPD attitudes, policies, and practices Mayor Giuliani put into place, or at least seemed to endorse, such unimaginable atrocities were not only inevitable but likely to be repeated. As protests grew, political and policy elites worried that if such high-profile killings continued the city could be ripped apart by racial strife.

To appreciate the magnitude and depth of that sentiment, it is useful to take a closer look at the elite unit of the NYPD, the four police officers who shot Amadou Diallo that fateful day and were assigned to the Street Crime Unit, and the crucial role it played in keeping the racial peace as the most aggressive component of Giuliani's URS administration. They were trained to be a quick strike force of plainclothes officers who rode in unmarked cars and either caught criminals in the act of a transgression or rounded them up before they could commit more crime. And as their "we own the night" slogan made clear, they were expected to project a cocky attitude that quickly earned them a reputation of toughness among those they stopped and others who observed their rough tactics.[24] The four members of the Street Crime Unit who shot and killed Amadou Diallo fit the widespread concern among people of color that their neighborhoods were often under siege by poorly trained and overly zealous cops. In stark contrast to the fact that at that time 90 percent of NYPD officers never fired their guns over their entire career, three of those four officers had been involved in previous shootings. Indeed, one of them—Kenneth Boss—was allowed to continue working on the streets even though he had killed a Brooklyn man several months earlier.[25]

Although the aim of the Street Crime Unit was to terrorize criminals, the massive scale of their "stop and frisk" actions, which seemed to target *all* young African American and Puerto Rican males both in high-crime areas and in neighborhoods where the officers deemed they did not belong, led many people of color to conclude that it was their youth and communities that were being racially profiled and terrorized.[26] The number of people stopped and frisked (i.e., detained and searched at the sole discretion of police officers) increased from just over 18,000 in 1997 to more than 27,000 in 1998. And of those, only one-fourth were arrested. That is, at least three-fourths had, in the judgment of the police who detained them, been found to have done nothing wrong. It was within this racially contentious environment that a group of African American NYPD officers proposed the disbandment of the Street Crime Unit.[27]

Indeed, racial profiling and harassment was so intense under Giuliani's URS administration that some of the mayor's relatively few African American supporters shared with him personal accounts of how members of the NYPD had mistreated them in their unsuccessful efforts to convince him that the problem was real. In a private meeting with Mayor Giuliani, Rev. Floyd Flake, a former congressman who as one of the mayor's few prominent African Americans supporters had endorsed Giuliani as a mayoral candidate, listened as Giuliani defended the conduct of the NYPD by citing statistics that he claimed showed that police shootings had actually declined during his administration. Hearing that Giuliani did not comprehend the seriousness of the problem, Flake shared an embarrassing incident in which as a congressman, with his wife in the car, he was stopped by a NYPD officer who said, "Nigger, didn't I tell you to stop that car?"[28]

Later, Rudy Washington, a deputy mayor and one of the highest-ranking African Americans in the Giuliani administration, arranged for a meeting with the mayor in his attempt to make the same point. During that meeting, Washington informed Mayor Giuliani of two encounters he had with NYPD officers. The first was when he was stopped as a passenger in a chauffeured city-administration car. The police officer insisted that Washington show his identification and explain "what are you doing with this car?" The officer, who initially did not accept Washington's explanation that he was a city commissioner, later tossed Washington's license and identification in his lap and left. In the second incident, while driving with his wife in a car, Washington was pulled over by a police officer who asked to see his license and registration. After Washington presented identification, which indicated that he was on the board of the Metropolitan Transportation Authority, the police officer told him to get out of the car, shoved him against that vehicle, frisked him, and informed him that he was taking him downtown to check his identification. Washington was saved from further abuse when a police supervisor who recognized the high-level city official happened to drive by. After he complained to the mayor's liaison to the NYPD about the incidents—in an unofficial acknowledgment of one URS manager that the repressive state apparatus arm of Mayor Giuliani's URS administration was engaging in racial profiling and harassment—Washington was given a police identification badge with his name on it and told he should keep it on his person at all times.[29]

Whereas the resolution of the Louima case brought about some racial healing in the city with thirty- and five-year prison sentences for two of the principals involved, in stark contrast the acquittal of the four police officers who killed Amadou Diallo left New York City in a state of intense racial division and for many African Americans and Puerto Ricans a condition of racial shock. That shock was exacerbated by an internal NYPD investigation that found that Diallo's killers had done nothing wrong because they acted within department guidelines. The city did, however, pay the Diallo family three million dollars to settle its wrongful death lawsuit.[30]

Public-opinion polls did not support Giuliani's claim that he had been vindicated by the not guilty jury verdict. They showed instead that most of the city's European Americans rejected the view that the police officers who shot Amadou Diallo nineteen times as he held his wallet in his hand in front of his own apartment had done nothing wrong.[31] Things were now getting politically more complicated for Mayor Giuliani and his URS administration. He could no longer simply pick the side of the majority racial group.

Patrick Dorismond

It didn't take long for the next incident to occur. And the way Mayor Giuliani and his top-level police officials handled that killing made it clear to both elite observers and ordinary city residents alike that police repression under Giuliani's URS administration had brought the city to the brink of racial warfare. Only three weeks after the four police officers who killed Amadou Diallo were found not guilty, NYPD undercover detective Anthony Vasquez fatally shot Patrick Dorismond, a Haitian immigrant like Abner Louima. Vasquez claimed to have killed Patrick Dorismond when a police officer's gun went off during an apparent scuffle over the weapon. That scuffle was part of a fight that broke out when Dorismond shouted at another plainclothes police officer who had targeted him for a drug buy "sting"[32] as he angrily rejected the officer's presumption that he was a drug dealer. Apparently not knowing that he had been set up for a sting operation, Dorismond, who worked as a security guard, actually threatened to call the police.[33] Because Dorismond's righteous indignation so powerfully captured the growing anger of many New York City residents of African descent over racial profiling, he quickly became a symbol of a proud black man who had the courage to face death by confronting such stereotyping and denigration.

As was his routine, while Mayor Giuliani pleaded with the public that the officers involved should be given the benefit of the doubt until the charges had been adjudicated in a court of law, he had his police commissioner release any records that might smear the reputation of the shooting victim.[34] Perhaps it was precisely because Dorismond's expression of moral indignation at being mistaken for a drug dealer left behind such a powerful martyr symbol for an insurgent movement that Giuliani and his police commissioner felt it was so important to work especially hard to destroy its potent image.

Giuliani's first step in his smear campaign against the memory of Dorismond was begun immediately after the shooting when he had Police Commissioner Safir release Dorismond's sealed juvenile arrest record.[35] Juvenile arrest records are normally kept "sealed" and are not made public because they involve a minor and document arrests only, not actual crimes that have been adjudicated by a court.[36] Mayor Giuliani then took his attacks against the deceased Dorismond on the road. In an interview for the ultra-right wing "Fox News Sunday," as he campaigned in upstate New York for a U.S. Senate seat against Hillary Clinton, Giuliani justified both his release of Dorismond's juvenile arrest record and Officer Vasquez's shooting of Dorismond by cautioning the news media that it "would not want a picture presented of an altar boy, when in fact, maybe it isn't an altar boy, it's some other situation that may justify, more closely, what the police officer did." Although, as it turned out, Patrick Dorismond had indeed been an altar boy, Mayor Giuliani did not stop there.[37] He also released the autopsy on Dorismond's body that found a trace of marijuana in his system, an amount so small that toxicology experts would later conclude that it could have come from the secondhand smoke in the bar where Dorismond had been before he was approached by the undercover police officer for the drug sting as he waited for a cab. And Giuliani would baffle many legal experts with his claim that Dorismond's right not to have his sealed juvenile arrest record released had not been violated because, indeed, as a dead man Dorismond had no legal rights.[38]

By that time many of the city's social, political, and economic elites had concluded that Mayor Giuliani was out of control. For example, in late March 2000 a *New York Times* editorial reminded its readers that the fatal shooting of Patrick Dorismond that previous week marked "the fourth time in little more than a year that the police have killed an unarmed black man in the street." The nation's most respected newspaper warned that "the outrage over Mr. Giuliani's smearing of the dead man began in the black community but has quickly spread, reaching Democrats and Republicans all over the state." The editorial concluded with the recommendation that Mayor Giuliani "diffuse" the situation and "allay doubts about his leadership by admitting that defaming the dead man—and failing to express sympathy to the Dorismond family—was a mistake."[39]

The *New York Times* was right in pointing out to Mayor Giuliani that concern about his behavior was no longer limited largely to African Americans, Democrats, or New York City residents. Less than two weeks later, Governor George Pataki, a Republican, said during his meeting with Dorismond's mother, which also included the mother of Amadou Diallo "and other relatives of victims of high-profile police shootings," "all New Yorkers owe you an apology and our efforts to make sure it doesn't happen again."[40] With these words and deeds, the head of the executive branch of New York state's racial state governmental core pressured Giuliani to get his URS administration house in order.[41]

The boiling over of the city's racial cauldron that the *New York Times* and other city and state elites feared would happen if Giuliani continued to stir that pot and turn up its flames with his continued attacks on the ghost of Patrick Dorismond happened at Dorismond's funeral when a melee broke out as some in the crowd of five thousand turned violent. Before order was restored, two dozen police officers had been injured and twenty-seven civilians were arrested.[42] A few weeks after that racial brawl, Giuliani's approval ratings dropped to fewer than a third of all New York City voters polled, with the number of African American voters who still approved of the way Giuliani ran the city being too small to be measured.[43] Although the police officer who shot and killed Dorismond was acquitted of charges brought against him, as had become a common practice, the city paid millions (in this case two and a quarter million dollars) to settle the civil suit brought by his family.[44]

That was not, however, the end of Rudy Giuliani's career. His stock as mayor was restored on September 11, 2001, after what was generally viewed as his adept handling of the city after it was thrown into a crisis when terrorists struck was followed by his being dubbed "America's mayor." With that national spotlight, it was widely believed that Giuliani would likely be the Republican nominee for president in 2008, and that his Democratic opponent would probably be none other than his U.S. Senate campaign foe Hillary Clinton. But that was not to be. Giuliani was beaten badly in the Republican primaries in 2008, ironically in large part because he was considered to be too liberal by the conservative Republican electoral base. Still, his style of leadership was admired in some quarters way beyond the boundaries of the nation's largest city. Indeed, as you will see in the next section, that influence was felt as far south as New Orleans.

THE POST–HURRICANE KATRINA LEVEE DISASTER IN NEW ORLEANS AND THE NAGIN URS ADMINISTRATION

Thus far, all three of the urban racial state cases discussed in this book have involved European American mayors. While the intense racial conflict inflamed by Mayor Giuliani's URS administration in New York City, which extended into the new millennium, made it clear that America's serious racial problems and the existence of the urban racial state did not end with the civil rights victories of the 1960s, the denial of the existence of systemic racism has continued under the conservative ideology that

America is a color-blind society. For example, as I mentioned earlier, with the election in 2008 of Barack Obama as president, there was whimsical speculation that the United States have become a postrace society. Indeed Rudolph Giuliani had this to say the night of Obama's victory: "[W]e've achieved history tonight and we've moved beyond . . . the whole idea of race and racial separation and unfairness."[45] Within the context of such strong and pervasive racism-evasive ideologies, many scholars and other social commentators may assume that with the election of African American and Latino American mayors the urban racial state would somehow simply wither away. I hope to demonstrate the absurdity of such an assumption through my next and final case example, which focuses on African American mayor C. Ray Nagin's disastrous and, as you will see, highly racialized mishandling of the post–Hurricane Katrina flooding catastrophe that destroyed much of New Orleans.

Why the Color of the Mayor May Not Matter for the Urban Racial State

By the 1980s the civil rights movement had lost momentum. Without the extraordinary alignment in the mid-1960s of the civil rights movement, the tipping of racial demographics in many cities toward an African American majority, and the election of the first African American mayor in many cities as a proud historic moment that mobilized a huge turnout of African American voters, urban politics for African Americans became less an extension of the civil rights movement and more and more just politics, and—as you will see—business, as usual.

In that political environment European American business elites came to play an increasingly large, if not dominant, role in the election of African American mayors. Although in cities like New Orleans, where racial demographics favor the election and reelection of African American mayors, *which* African American is elected mayor is mightily influenced by who can gain the substantial financial backing of the business-centered local white power structure. Increasingly, to get elected and reelected, and to govern, African American mayors must balance the needs and aspirations of low-income and working-class African Americans against those of their city's largely European American business leaders. Consequently, even when they have every intention to do so, African American mayors may find it impossible to simultaneously meet the demands of their voting base (e.g., for better schools and more social services) and those of their major financial backers (e.g., for lower taxes and various economic development incentives).[46]

This balancing act is in some ways similar to the one I illustrated in figure 1.1 when in the 1960s the European American mayors in cities like New Haven and Syracuse deployed their URS administrations and various organizational resources, like community action programs, to balance African American aspirations against white racial resentment. A significant difference is that many of today's African American and Latino American mayors are now balancing those ethnic aspirations against the demands of their cities' largely European American economic elite rather than that of the European American public in general. Another important difference is that other policy and program initiatives have replaced community action programs as the means through which a URS administration attempts to maintain a racial balance favorable to a mayor's political interests. For example, as you will see, after the flood waters subsided in New Orleans, that ideological state apparatus centered on the mayor's plans to rebuild the city.

As was true for the Giuliani URS administration, in its racial state capacity the Nagin administration made little attempt to balance African American aspirations and white racial resentment, and instead chose racial sides. But as you will see, unlike Mayor Giuliani, in exploiting the best possible path to electoral victory Mayor Nagin was as nimble as a racial chameleon as he switched sides from one election campaign to the next. And, unlike Giuliani, Nagin would not rely exclusively on his URS's repressive state apparatus.

Who Is Ray Nagin?

To understand C. Ray Nagin, it is important to begin with one fact that defines his political worldview. Above anything else (e.g., his racialized ethnicity and his humble beginnings), Nagin is a businessman, a former cable company executive[47] and current entrepreneur[48] whose conservative political and economic ideology is more akin to that of the Republicans he often supported politically and who dominated his governing coalition than the nominal Democratic Party affiliation he needed to achieve his political ambitions in heavily Democratic New Orleans. Like Rudolf Giuliani, whose book, *Leadership*, he was observed to have had on display near the conference table of his city hall office,[49] Ray Nagin—as he is more commonly known—is an opportunist, even more than is true of most politicians—a crafty entrepreneur who, also like Giuliani, has shamelessly played the race card as it has suited his political ambitions. In terms of the policies he has embraced as mayor, Nagin can best be described as a progrowth politician, one who in contrast with progressive politicians, who initiate redistributive policies intended to benefit the poor, mobilizes the resources of government to promote the economic growth agenda of the local business elite.[50]

With his probusiness, Republican-like platform, Nagin attracted the support of local business leaders, the city's major newspaper, the *Times-*

Picayune, and other conservative elements of New Orleans's white power structure. In addition, in a city of nearly a half million people whose residents were 68 percent African American, Nagin was also viewed as an African American who could be used to challenge the civil rights movement–influenced progressive leadership that had dominated New Orleans politics for decades. The city's conservative white power structure felt it could rely on a Nagin-administration-centered urban racial state to not only promote its economic agenda but ensure there would be the stable racial environment needed for it to thrive.[51]

With the overwhelming support of European American voters (85 percent), Nagin prevailed in a runoff against another African American candidate, the scandal-ridden former city police chief Richard Pennington. Unlike Nagin, Pennington had the backing of the African American political establishment. With its help he received the majority of the votes cast by African American voters, compared to just 35 percent for Nagin.[52]

Once elected, Mayor Nagin quickly began to repay his political debts as he shifted the city's URS administration from the racially ameliorative mode it had occupied under other African American mayors in that city back to its racially oblivious mode. He did this not only through his probusiness policies but with key appointments for his conservative European American and Republican supporters and, a year after his election, by endorsing Republican gubernatorial candidate Bobby Jindal over the eventual winner, Democrat Kathleen Blanco.[53] From that point on, Nagin and Blanco would have a bad relationship that served New Orleans poorly when close cooperation was needed between the city and the state to address the crisis after the levees broke the day after Hurricane Katrina struck New Orleans. Nagin's actions did not go unnoticed by his African American critics. A few months after Nagin's election, Bishop Paul Morton, a prominent New Orleans minister, dismissed Mayor Nagin as "a white man in black skin."[54] As you will see next, who Nagin was had a profound effect on his handling of the post-Katrina crisis.

The Nagin Administration before and during the Storm

Nagin's probusiness loyalties and lack of focus on the needs of the city's large number of poor people (in 2000 28 percent of the city's residents were poor compared to 12 percent nationally), who were overwhelmingly African American (35 percent of the city's "black" residents were poor compared to 11 percent of those identified in the census as being "white")[55] and most likely to live in the most flood-prone sections of the city, became evident in two ways when Hurricane Katrina entered into the Gulf of Mexico. First, Mayor Nagin had no plans to evacuate those residents who were without transportation despite the following: it had been predicted for years that New Orleans—a city below sea level that is nestled between a large lake and a huge river and protected by a system of poorly designed, built, and maintained levees, flood walls, canals, and pumps—would likely be hit by a hurricane that would have catastrophic consequences;[56] a large proportion of the city's residents were too poor to own cars; and the city's Comprehensive Management Plan specified that a seventy-two-hour notice was needed to evacuate an estimated one hundred thousand people who could not find private means of transportation to escape the city. Mayor Nagin would also fail to comply with the Louisiana state evacuation plan to use school and municipal buses to evacuate those lacking access to other transportation. According to a *Times-Picayune* reporter, what the mayor did have on his mind as the hurricane approached was the economic impact a mandatory evacuation would have on the city's hotel and tourism industry businesses. So as the storm moved closer toward the city, Nagin had his legal staff examine whether the city government would be financially liable if he mandated an evacuation that cost tourism-related businesses money. Consequently, despite an imminent threat of what was shaping up to be a national disaster of unparalleled proportions, Mayor Nagin waited until less than twenty-four hours before the large hurricane hit New Orleans to call for a mandatory evacuation of the city, an evaluation that made no provision for those without access to personal transportation.[57] A fifth of the city's residents—approximately 100,000—were still there when Katrina struck on August 29 and a day later when the levees broke and flooded 80 percent of the city. And as the television images of people waiting for days on roof tops for relief would make graphically clear to the world, those left behind were overwhelmingly African American and poor.[58]

When Mayor Nagin did act, he and other members of his administration hampered federal, state, and local rescue efforts by spreading racist stereotypes about dangerous evacuees. For example, on the Oprah Winfrey show Nagin fostered panic by asserting that "hundreds of armed gang members" were running wild as they killed and raped people at will in the Superdome, the city's major shelter for those who remained in New Orleans during the hurricane.[59] And New Orleans police commissioner Eddie Compass actually cried during a televised interview as he described "little babies being raped" there.[60] Those rumors, which turned out to be false,[61] fit easily with racist stereotypes pervasive in American society of African American males as violent, as criminals, and especially as rapists. The racial fears evoked in that way resulted in a further slowdown of already-sluggish rescue efforts and caused National Guard and law enforcement officials inside of New Orleans and in its surrounding towns and parishes[62] to treat innocent victims of Katrina as if they were dangerous criminals. In brief, by spreading such rumors the mayor and other members of his administration encouraged various levels and branches of racial state repressive status apparatuses to engage in crackdowns against those who remained in the city and were left homeless by the post-Katrina flood. But that was not all; those stereotypes of rapists, looters, and gangs of criminals shooting at helicopters also fueled growing highly racialized sentiment nationally that New Orleans should not be rebuilt, and locally that if it was rebuilt, it should be done in such a way as to contain fewer low-income African American residents, the types of people Nagin and Compass depicted as having terrorized the Superdome.[63]

As I stressed in earlier portions of this book, the urban racial state does not exist in isolation from other levels of the racial state. Let's take a closer look at how the racist stereotypes and fears generated by the Nagin URS administration impacted rescue and relief efforts at various levels of the governmental core of the racial state.

The Rescue and Relief Efforts of the Federal, Louisiana, and Local Racial States

President Bush's excruciatingly slow response to one of the worst disasters the United States has ever faced provoked intense negative emotions from African Americans nationwide. As Katrina hit, and for days afterward, President Bush remained on vacation, where a videotaped conference of him with the nation's top emergency relief officials suggested that he was both overconfident and disengaged. That was followed by a photo-opportunity flyover the Gulf Coast some three days later in the plush Marine One presidential helicopter that further reinforced the image of a president who was far removed from the suffering of the people below. President Bush added to his image of being out of touch with the realities on the ground when he told Michael Brown, the director of the Federal Emergency Management Agency (FEMA), "Brownie, you're doing a heck of a job," just as it was becoming increasingly clear that the agency had badly botched its early relief efforts.[64] Meanwhile, the media worldwide showed a continuous stream of live pictures of largely dark-skinned people trapped on rooftops with water all around them and little or no food to eat or clean water to drink.

Not surprisingly, for a highly racialized society like the United States, the Bush administration's early response to the crisis after the levees broke revealed a "stark racial divide," with six of ten "black" respondents to a Gallup poll concluding that "the fact that most hurricane victims were poor and black was one reason the federal government failed to come to the rescue more quickly," compared to nine out of ten "whites" who indicated that they were not factors. Not only did that survey find that "blacks" were "much more likely than 'whites'" to blame the federal government; "whites" were "much more likely to hold the residents responsible."[65] The African American outrage was succinctly articulated as "George Bush doesn't care about black people" by hip hop artist Kanye West during a nationally televised fundraiser for Katrina victims.[66] A little more than a month later, an NBC/*Wall Street Journal* poll found that President Bush's approval rating among African Americans had dropped to just 2 percent.[67]

Mayor Nagin's comments about roving gangs of outlaw evacuees who committed murder, rape, and other crimes in the Superdome not only helped justify the movement of his own URS administration into a racially repressive mode but also added fuel to the highly racialized response to the crisis at the state level of the racial state's repressive state apparatus. For example, in announcing the arrival of three hundred members of the Arkansas National Guard in New Orleans, Governor Blanco warned any looters and other wayward evacuees that those "battle tested" troops who were "fresh back from Iraq" "have M-16s" that are "locked and loaded" and that "they know how to shoot and kill" and "are more than willing to do so if necessary."[68]

The racial hysteria such statements fed also impacted how evacuees would be treated by other local racial states within Louisiana. The most dramatic example of that panic occurred when the Gretna police fired their guns over the heads of a crowd of hungry and thirsty evacuees to stop them as they attempted to cross a Mississippi River bridge into what they hoped would be a place where they could find relief. One Gretna police officer warned that "there would be no Superdomes in their city."[69] Other cities, towns, and parishes responded in a less dramatic but equally clear fashion. Melvin Holder, the African American mayor of Baton Rouge, publicly invoked racist stereotypes: "I want to make sure that some of these thugs and looters that are out shooting officers in New Orleans don't come here and do the same. I am not going to allow a New Orleans situation, shooting at people and looting, to happen here in Baton Rouge." The racist images of New Orleans evacuees that both Mayor Holder and Mayor Nagin helped promote were also likely to have had their impact at the parish level of government. Only ten of the state's sixty-four parishes allowed temporary trailers for Katrina evacuees. And half of the state's parishes actually banned them.[70] As you will see, the same types of racist stereotypes and racial fears soon captured the mayor's plans to rebuild the city.

Racism and Nagin's URS Administration in the Rebuilding of New Orleans

Mayor Nagin was not the only person from New Orleans to make statements that contributed to what at times seemed like a post-Katrina flood of racial panic. Especially revealing were the comments made in the *Wall Street Journal* by James Reiss, a "descendent of an old-line Uptown family," and a wealthy business and commercial real estate investor and chair of the Business Council of New Orleans, which was made up of the city's top sixty CEOs. The conservative and well-connected Reiss was appointed by Mayor Nagin as both the chair of the city's Regional Transit Authority—which failed to execute the state's emergency plan to use its buses to help evacuate stranded city residents before Hurricane Katrina hit—and later a member of the Bring New Orleans Back Commission (BNOB) Nagin designated to formulate plans to rebuild the city. Reiss stressed that his comments reflected not only his sentiments but those of about forty powerful New Orleanians, some of whom planned to join him that next day in Dallas to make their views known about how the city should be rebuilt to Mayor Nagin, who was now living there with his family. Through that interview Reiss made it clear that, as I included as the epigraph to this chapter, "those who want to see this city rebuilt want to see it done in a completely different way: demographically, geographically and politically." Reiss—a resident of the city's exclusive and gated Audubon Place neighborhood (which fared relatively well in the storm) who escaped Katrina and later returned by private helicopter—punctuated his group's demands for a new New Orleans with "better services and fewer poor people" with the following threat: "the way we've been living is not going to happen again, or we're out."[71]

Other members of the city's white power structure deployed language that actually evoked the image of "ethnic cleansing," a term that became infamous in the 1990s when it was used to justify the policy of forced expulsion and killings committed against persecuted ethnic groups in Bosnia and Croatia.[72] Usually, such comments were made privately. For example, a journalist for the *New Yorker* magazine reported that some of the people he talked to "passed along a bit of back-fence etymology, saying that the root of the word 'Katrina' is 'cleansing.'" But some of the area's elite openly embraced the city's new "cleansing" opportunity, like Donald "Boysie" Bollinger, a wealthy shipbuilder, prominent Republican fundraiser, past chair of the Business Council of New Orleans, and another member of Mayor Nagin's Bring New Orleans Back Commission, as well as Governor Blanco's Louisiana Recovery Authority.[73] After complaining about the drugs, crime, and poverty that were prevalent in some African American neighborhoods before the city's levees broke, Bollinger, who lost much of his African American workforce after Katrina's floodwaters forced them out of the city and complained to his friend, President Bush, that FEMA's $2,000 checks for families empowered evacuees not to return to work—actually referred to the disaster's "cleansing" effect. He promised a BBC correspondent that with the rebuilding of New Orleans "you're going to see a culture change," as he anticipated "a lot more Latin people here as permanent residents," who might be joined by Filipinos, Romanians, and other "people who are willing to work."[74]

In still other instances the comments were more subtle in their racial overtones but were still likely to be taken as a threat by low-income African Americans given the context of other less careful statements, and of the city's racist history. A case in point are the comments made by Joseph Canizaro, a local real estate developer who has been deemed New Orleans' Donald Trump, and who like Bollinger was a key Republican fundraiser who also described himself as a friend of George W. Bush and was a member of Nagin's Bring New Orleans Back Commission. Canizaro put a positive spin on the changes he expected to come with the rebuilding of New Orleans, but in doing so still used part of the word cleansing. Canizaro, who was generally regarded as the most powerful and influential member of Nagin's commission, framed the devastation caused by Katrina not only as a tragedy but as an opportunity that would provide the city with "a clean slate" in its attempts to overcome its serious problems, like a high crime rate, decrepit housing, and poor schools.[75]

These remarks were exacerbated by comments made by various Republicans from different branches of the governmental core of the federal racial state. For example, representing its executive branch, Housing and Urban Development secretary Alphonso Jackson, an African American and a federal government official with a major responsibility for rebuilding New Orleans, sparked controversy when he said in an interview with the *Houston Chronicle*, "New Orleans is not going to be as black as it was for a long time," and indicated that he had advised Mayor Nagin that "it would be a mistake to rebuild the 9th Ward,"[76] the flood-prone section of the city that contained its largest concentration of impoverished African Americans. House Speaker Dennis Hastert, a powerful Republican representative of the legislative branch of the governmental core of the federal racial state, suggested an even more radical and simple remedy: much of the city should be "bulldozed."[77] And another Republican representative, Louisiana congressman Richard Baker of Baton Rouge, celebrated what he saw as Katrina's divinely inspired good work when he proclaimed that "we finally cleaned up public housing in New Orleans. We couldn't do it, but God did."[78]

It was within this environment that a poll found a huge racial divide in opinions of New Orleans residents as to what the rebuilt New Orleans should look like, with "almost two-thirds of black citizens" indicating that it was important that the city regained the large African American majority it had before the flood while "only one in four whites" accepted that view and half of them "said it was 'not at all important.'"[79]

The city's rebuilding efforts and its politics would soon be profoundly affected by such public expressions and opinions that suggested that there were plans in the works to make New Orleans smaller, whiter, and wealthier.[80] To appreciate the impact of such assertions, it is important to understand that in New Orleans the volatile mixture of pervasive poverty and immense racism is very powerful. The impact of that incendiary combination could be seen in the rumors that circulated among impoverished African Americans that the Lower-Ninth Ward had once again been intentionally flooded to protect the whiter and more affluent areas of the city. That rumor was a repeat of a similar rumor of levees having been dynamited in 1965 to flood the Lower-Ninth Ward in order to divert the flood waters during Hurricane Betsy, and a still-earlier rumor about the blowing up of levees during the Great Mississippi Flood of 1927.[81] The pervasiveness and depth of those rumors among the city's African American poor reflected their personal and collective memories of a system of racial and economic exploitation so ruthless that almost anything was deemed plausible. The complex interplay of such racial dynamics with the economic interests of the city's business elite will become evident as I examine the rise and fall of Mayor Nagin's Bring New Orleans Back Commission as a major component of his URS administration's ideological state apparatus.

Mayor Nagin's Bring New Orleans Back Commission

The group Mayor Nagin commissioned to plan the rebuilding of New Orleans included some of the city's most powerful and most conservative business leaders. Indeed, while the main focus on the composition of Nagin's seventeen member Bring New Orleans Back Commission was the racialized ethnicity of its members, which was split evenly between African Americans and European Americans, with one Latino American member, the Commission was quietly set up in such a way that it would be dominated by the city's business elite. Politicians, community activists, and other civic leaders were grossly underrepresented.[82] And as you saw, at least three of the businesspeople on the Commission, James Reiss, Donald "Boysie" Bollinger, and Joseph Canizaro, had publicly articulated a reactionary social agenda in the rebuilding of the city that fueled speculation that there was a plan afoot by the local white power structure to cleanse the city of many of its least desirable elements by rebuilding New Orleans smaller, whiter, and wealthier. In addition to those prominent business leaders and the Commission's cochair, Mel Lagarde, who was the CEO of a regional health care corporation and a member of the executive committee of the New Orleans Business Council, there was a venture capitalist, the CEO of the city's largest African American bank, an African

American who was a former CEO of a utility company, and two African American entrepreneurs.[83]

As I mentioned earlier, the most influential member of that Commission was by far Joseph Canizaro. Indeed, his influence was so great that the BNOB Commission "came to be known as the Canizaro Commission."[84] Canizaro has been described in a *New York Times* article titled "A Mogul Who Would Rebuild New Orleans" as "perhaps the single most influential business executive from New Orleans." However, Canizaro's importance to Nagin's BNOB Commission may have rested more on his political clout than his business acumen. As I noted earlier, Canizaro was a prominent Republican fundraiser with close ties to President Bush. With that access, Canizaro served as a self-appointed commission liaison to the White House through his "conversations with people around the president, for guidance and direction and commitment and support."[85] Canizaro was also quite influential with Republicans at the state and local level. For example, Canizaro would cochair the Louisiana Committee for a Republican Majority with fellow BNOB Commission member Donald Bollinger.[86]

Canizaro worked closely with Mayor Nagin in setting up the Commission and played a major role in the selection of Commission members, especially those from the business community. It was also Canizaro who pushed for racial balance on the BNOB Commission while he countered potential opposition to that goal from other conservatives by citing support from President Bush.[87] As a member of the BNOB Commission, Canizaro also let his clout be felt as the chair of its most important subcommittee, the land-use subcommittee. It was that subcommittee that would make recommendations as to how the city should be rebuilt, including which neighborhoods, and according to what timetable. With his great wealth and connections, Canizaro brought extraordinary resources to that task, including those of the Urban Land Institute (ULI)[88]—a huge and influential nonprofit "research and education organization" that bills itself as the world's "preeminent, multidisciplinary real estate forum"[89]—to which he had very strong ties as a trustee and its former chair.[90]

Less than three months after Hurricane Katrina struck New Orleans and the levees broke, the Urban Land Institute released its recommendations for the rebuilding of the city. Its most controversial proposal was that because of the dramatic loss in population and the prohibitive cost of providing city services for the entire pre-Katrina city, there should be a shrinking of the city's footprint by not redeveloping the city's worst flooded, low-lying areas, and instead converting them to green spaces like public parks.[91]

Contrary to President Bush's bold color-blind pronouncement that "the storm didn't discriminate and neither will the recovery effort,"[92] Katrina did not dish out its pain haphazardly. As is true for cities in the United

States and other highly racialized and economically stratified societies, people in New Orleans do not reside randomly, independent of factors like racial segregation and their ability to pay. The city's low-lying areas like the Lower-Ninth Ward were the places low-income African Americans were allowed to live and could afford to reside,[93] and they certainly fared much worse, on average, than those who lived in higher places like James Reiss's Audubon Place.[94] The Urban Land Institute's smaller footprint plan confirmed for many that indeed the recovery effort, like the impact of the failed levees, would discriminate. Aware of the opposition the ULI plan would provoke, its designers also proposed the creation of a redevelopment corporation with the power of eminent domain and an oversight board with control of city finances, both of which had the power to override the wishes of the city's elected council.[95]

Given the long history of racial and class distrust in New Orleans, it was highly unlikely that such proposals from a group dominated largely by European American commercial real estate interests would be implemented as long as any semblance of democratic process survived. And at a time when Ray Nagin prepared himself for what promised to be a difficult reelection campaign, it was virtually impossible. It did not take long for Mayor Nagin to reject the Urban Land Institute plan. Just ten days after its release, the mayor announced his intentions to rebuild the *entire* city.[96] Although Mayor Nagin's Bring New Orleans Back Commission also backed away from some elements of the ULI plan, it proposed a smaller New Orleans strategy that would combine a moratorium on rebuilding in the most flood-damaged neighborhoods with a requirement that returning residents must first prove within a specified period of time the viability of rebuilding their neighborhoods (e.g., a sufficient number of people expressed their intent to return to support city services). Otherwise, the city's redevelopment agency could seize the properties within those neighborhoods.[97]

It didn't take long for city residents, including city council members—representing the legislative branch governmental core of the urban racial state—to make known their opposition to the BNOB Commission's proposed use of a building moratorium and eminent domain to rebuild New Orleans smaller. Indeed, five city council members held a press conference to denounce the BNOB plan, and later hundreds of city residents interrupted the presentation of that plan in a hotel ballroom. Angry residents denounced the plan before an open microphone as "'an academic exercise,' 'garbage,' [and] 'a no-good, rotten scheme.'"[98] Caroline Parker, a resident of the Lower-Ninth Ward warned "over my dead body" in response to the notion that her property might be seized, and Harvey Bender, a resident of the more affluent, but still low-lying New Orleans East section of the city, brought human agency to the forefront of the conflict by calling out the individual he and many others considered to be the real force behind the BNOB Commission: "Joe Canizaro, I don't know you, but I hate you," before threatening to "suit up like I'm going to Iraq and fight this."[99]

The opposition to the Urban Land Institute and Bring New Orleans Back Commission plans was so effective because it was not limited to the protests of the city's low-income African Americans. The moratorium would also affect other more affluent and racially diverse sections of the city like Gentilly and New Orleans East, as well as the wealthy and largely European American Lakeview section of the city.[100] With this politically powerful alliance, Nagin, who had initially indicated that he liked the proposal and thanked his commission members for "a job well done," also backed away from the BNOB Commission plan.[101]

It was within this racial and political environment that Mayor Nagin gave his notorious "Chocolate City" speech. Although those remarks were highly criticized as being both racially bigoted and ignorant, they should not be dismissed so easily. They epitomized the race card strategy the Nagin administration, in its URS capacity, successfully deployed as it shifted from its racially oblivious—and sometimes racially repressive—to its racially ameliorative mode. As Ray Nagin spoke to the largely African American audience that attended the city's annual Martin Luther King Jr. Day parade, he assured them that despite what they had heard about conspiracies and other plans to rebuild New Orleans smaller, whiter, and wealthier, the large number of African Americans who left the city to escape Hurricane Katrina or its floodwaters would return. Nagin took on his former white power structure allies like James Reiss almost directly when he promised, "I don't care what people are saying in Uptown or wherever they are. This city will be chocolate at the end of the day." Mayor Nagin said that God had ordained that "this city will be a majority African American city" and added his own commonsense logic that "you can't have it no other way. It wouldn't be New Orleans."[102] In response to the immense outrage expressed through the media regarding what many European Americans both in New Orleans and nationwide took to be an insult to the city's European American residents, Mayor Nagin soon apologized for his characterization of New Orleans as a "Chocolate City."[103]

Although his "Chocolate City" speech was widely condemned as idiotic and thoughtless comments that embarrassed New Orleans and threatened the national goodwill needed for the recovery effort, it was with those two words that Nagin adroitly made clear that in his campaign for reelection he would now be a Black mayor, with a capital B. As he succinctly put it in that presentation, "[W]e as black people . . . it's time for us to come together."[104] Politically, it turned out to be a brilliant move. In its urban racial state capacity, his administration had dramatically tipped its scales toward the African American voters he needed for reelection and away from European American voters he could now assume would abandon him in droves as his incompetence in handling the crisis after the levees failed and the city's dramatic drop in African American population offered the best opportunity in decades for the election of a European American mayor. As you have already seen, within this dramatically new political environment, Mayor Nagin had begun to publicly distance himself from his previously most powerful ally, the city's business establishment, and its plans for rebuilding New Orleans.[105]

The 2006 Mayoral Election and Beyond

Mayor Nagin was successful in reelection to his second and final term by exploiting the racial panic in the city—that, ironically, he and some of his conservative European American supporters in the 2002 election helped create—and with a major effort to ensure that as many displaced evacuees had a chance to vote as possible. In this way he seemed to pull off a complete racial flip-flop from the 2002 election, when he won with overwhelming European American votes (85 percent), to the 2006 election, when he would win one of the closest elections in the city's history (52 to 48 percent) with vast (approximately 80 percent) African American support.[106] But appearances can be deceiving. In their analysis of New Orleans electoral politics, Liu and Vanderleeuw found that the share of the "white" vote (21 percent) Nagin received in the 2006 general election fit the reelection pattern of previous African American mayors who received a substantial number of European American votes only in the absence of viable European American candidates. In brief, Nagin's win in 2006 was really not exceptional; it was instead consistent with the city's historical pattern of racial politics.[107]

Although African American voters may have won a symbolic victory in their ability to reelect an African American major in a racial and political environment that seemed hostile to their very existence in their own hometown of New Orleans, that does not mean they remained content having Ray Nagin as their mayor. As mayor Nagin approached his final year in office—his term ended in May 2010—his approval rating as of April 2009 dropped from 31 percent the previous year to just 24 percent, the lowest approval rating recorded for a mayor in New Orleans since the poll was begun more than two decades ago.[108] There was certainly reason for New Orleans residents to be dissatisfied with the pace of recovery of the city. A report by the Brookings Institution found that despite some progress, four years later New Orleans and its surrounding region still faced the challenges of "massive blight, affordable housing for low-income workers, and significant flood risk."[109]

By the time the next mayoral election came around, citizens of every color were looking for a change. Due to term limits, Mayor Nagin was not eligible to run for reelection. But even if he had been able to run again, there was little chance that he would have been reelected. Not only had New Orleanians had their fill of Ray Nagin, but there was a widely shared sentiment that what the city needed to manage its recovery was a skillful politician who could more successfully "navigate the state and federal bureaucracy," not a businessman. The Nagin administration ended with the landslide election of Mitch Landrieu in February 2010—with strong African American support—as the first European American mayor of New Orleans since his father held that office in the late 1970s.[110]

Just as the Mayor Giuliani case example made it clear that the urban racial state did not end with the passing of the 1960s, this Mayor Nagin case illustration forces us to move beyond the wishful thinking that the urban racial state somehow dissolves with the election of politicians of color.

Before I conclude this chapter, I will briefly discuss three other examples of highly racialized urban politics, policies, and practices that can be analyzed with the help of the urban racial state concept. With the changing racial demographics of the United States, much of the urban racial state's activity will increasingly involve complexities that go beyond "black" and "white" racial conflict. Two of the research proposals outlined below capture such racial complexities.

SUGGESTIONS FOR THREE URBAN RACIAL STATE RESEARCH PROJECTS

The 2001 Racial Unrest in Cincinnati

New York City was just one of many U.S. cities in the 1990s and early 2000s where African Americans felt that their young men were victims of unwarranted killings by racially bigoted police officers. On April 7, 2001, a European American police officer killed an unarmed African American teenager in Cincinnati's impoverished Over-the-Rhine neighborhood as he fled arrest for various minor misdemeanors, like his failure to fasten his seat belt. Timothy Thomas was the fifteenth African American male who was shot to death by a Cincinnati police officer over the six-year-period from 1995 to 2001. Most of those men were unarmed, and the problem appeared to be escalating. Indeed, Thomas was just the latest of five African Americans killed by the police since September of the previous year. Two days later racial unrest broke out when what began as a peaceful protest turned violent. That ensuing violence, which lasted several days, included a powerful symbol of political discontent, the breaking of more than two dozen windows at city hall.[111]

There seems to be ample case history events and documents for an analysis of the behavior of various components of Cincinnati's URS and other levels of the racial state before, during, and after the civil disorders. They include the appointment of a mayor's commission to study race relations in the city; a U.S. Department of Justice investigation of the Cincinnati police; a mediator appointed to resolve conflict over the issue of racial profiling; the "Collaborative Agreement" involving the Cincinnati city government, its police department, the U.S. Justice Department, and the American Civil Liberties Union; and a nearly seven-year NAACP economic boycott of the city.[112] The Cincinnati case history could be done as a study in its own right or as part of a nationwide analysis of urban racial states and police misconduct.

The Attacks on Asian Immigrant Students in Philadelphia

On December 3, 2009, at least thirty Chinese and other Asian immigrant students were attacked by large groups of mostly African American students at South Philadelphia High School in apparent retaliation for an attack on a disabled African American student by two Asian students the day before. In their testimonies about the incident, Asian immigrant students made clear their belief that the attacks were not simply reactive or sporadic. They reported that for years they had been "victimized," "often as school staffers stood by, encouraged the attacker, or hurled racial slurs."[113]

Although Philadelphia has an African American mayor and African Americans in high-level positions within the public school system (both the school superintendant and the principal of South Philadelphia High School were African American), those leaders did not seem to respond very quickly, decisively, or compassionately to the concerns raised about the civil rights violations of the Asian immigrants to the "city of brotherly love." The school superintendent initially rejected a request for a meeting with Asian students, parents, and activists, and the city's Commission of Human Relations did not announce its plans to get all relevant parties together until a day after the Asian American Legal Defense and Education Fund made known its intention to file a federal lawsuit against the school district.[114] The frustration of trying to get prompt and decisive action also manifested itself in a traffic-stopping protest about six weeks after the attacks occurred when two hundred and fifty people demanded an end to such violent assaults in the city's public schools.[115] This sad Philadelphia story reminds us once again that just because the local political power structure is controlled by people of color does not necessarily mean that it will be responsive to issues of civil rights and racial injustice, especially for members of racialized ethnic groups who are not well represented in the political system. This case should be examined closely to see what it reveals about whether the historical memory of a racialized ethnic group does or does not pressure leaders from that group to be more responsive to the discrimination complaints of other racialized ethnic groups. Such research could suggest steps to be taken to pressure an urban racial state to more quickly and decisively respond to the violation of such widely shared social justice ideals.

Sanctuary Cities and Backlash Cities in the United States: Conflict over Illegal Immigrants

For the foreseeable future, a major source of conflict over urban politics, policies, and practices will involve the basic question of who should be allowed to live in U.S. cities. When Asian immigrant students are physically attacked in schools, the not so implicit message is that they don't belong there.[116] There is, indeed, a strong sentiment among large segments of this nation's population that immigrants, especially immigrants of color, and most especially illegal immigrants to color, don't belong.[117] Fueled by what might best be referred to as immigration racism, political and policy debates over how to deal with illegal immigration from the U.S.'s southern border have divided not only many citizens of the United States but many of its cities and towns as well. There are a growing number of cities that find themselves in the opposing ideological and public-policy camps of "backlash" cities and "sanctuary" cities. Backlash cities tend to be small cities and towns like Albertville, Alabama; Hazelton, Pennsylvania; Green Bay, Wisconsin; and East Haven, Connecticut,[118] whereas sanctuary cities include many large cities like New York, Los Angeles, Houston, and San Francisco, as well as numerous smaller cities and towns like New Haven, Connecticut; Aurora, Colorado; and De Leon Springs, Florida.[119] Backlash cities have enacted policies and practices intended to force out illegal immigrants and to discourage others from moving in, such as English-only laws and laws that penalize landlords who rent to illegal immigrants and employers who hire them. In stark contrast, at a minimum, sanctuary cities forbid their police from inquiring into the immigrant status of residents unless they are reasonably suspected of engaging in criminal activity, and may enact other illegal-immigrant-friendly measures, like the provision of identification cards that facilitate their various business and other legal transactions.[120]

A study of the urban racial state's handling of illegal immigration might use both qualitative and quantitative methods to compare a sample of backlash cities to a group of sanctuary cities, controlling for factors like size, region of the country, racial and ethnic composition, governmental structure, the racialized identities of mayors and other key politicians, and their political affiliations. It could be especially revealing to compare adjoining or otherwise nearby cities with opposing policies and practices, like New Haven and East Haven, Connecticut, and to examine conflicts over state law and city government policies like the resistance to the controversial immigration law in Arizona by elected officials in Phoenix, that state's largest city. An examination of such conflict could reveal the importance of the fit or lack of fit between the politics, policies, and practices of the racial state at the federal, individual, and local urban state levels of its governmental core.

CONCLUSION

As you have seen from the New York and New Orleans case examples and the suggested new research projects, the potential of the urban racial state concept is in no way limited to explaining the workings of community action programs in the 1960s or to analyzing the city administrations headed by European American politicians. In the conclusion chapter I examine in greater detail the various lessons of those two more-recent New York and New Orleans case examples and how they relate to the findings of the book's New Haven and Syracuse case histories. I also summarize the findings of previous chapters, discuss the lessons learned about the urban racial state, and end by identifying URS conceptual work that remains to be done.

Conclusion

Summaries of Findings, Lessons Learned for Understanding Today's Urban Racial State, and What We Still Need to Know

The end of a book that is intended to introduce a new analytical concept is like a commencement exercise, where the focus is not really on the completion of the journey but on the new journeys to come. I hope that I have done enough in this book to give the fledgling urban racial state (URS) concept the wings it needs to fly into the arms of other scholars who will fix what they might find to be broken and expand upon what they think remains to be fleshed out and refined. To that end, in this final chapter of *The Urban Racial State*, I summarize the main findings of the previous chapters, discuss the lessons this book offers regarding the nature, organization, and workings of the urban racial state, and conclude with suggestions for further study.

SUMMARIES OF FINDINGS

The Urban Racial State's examination of the workings of the set of social structures and processes I have dubbed the urban racial state has revealed an interplay between the two that can be quite complex. Still the goal of the urban racial state is simple. While it ultimately maintains the racial status quo, the URS is the mechanism through which political leaders and their subordinates manage what are often competing racial demands within their geopolitical borders. Both this complexity and the ultimate function of the urban racial state are evident as I review the book's major case history and case example findings.

Overview of Case History Findings

Through its New Haven and Syracuse case histories *The Urban Racial State* documents the design of community action programs by the executive branch governmental core of those and other urban racial states in the late 1950s and early 1960s with the encouragement and financial sponsorship of the federal racial state and private foundations like the Ford Foundation. This was done to better manage the social problems and political volatility that accrued from the growing number of low-income African Americans who were concentrated in racial ghettos due to well-established policies and practices of housing segregation. We also saw that as the civil rights movement grew, spread northward, and increasingly focused on the concerns of impoverished ghetto residents, those community action programs were deployed by mayors to manage race relations by balancing to their benefit the growing aspirations, and sometimes protests, of African Americans against white racial resentment and periodic white backlash. The URS administration often, but not always with the support of its federal racial state counterpart, accomplished that difficult balancing act by expanding social-protest- and neighborhood-resident-participation-centered community action in response to rising African American aspirations and protest and by restricting such community action in reaction to white racial resentment and backlash. For example, in its quest to manage race relations consistent with its leader's own political needs and interests, the URS administration in cities such as New Haven used community action programs to dispense jobs and other resources to co-opt African American leaders. I also showed, however, that to the extent that community action programs could function independently of URS mayors they could actually be used to promote African American insurgency, which you saw happen for a short period of time in Syracuse. Finally, I found that the particular actions taken by the federal and urban racial states in regard to community action reflected and influenced the state of race relations both nationally and locally as the urban racial state shifted from its racially oblivious mode, where racial issues are routinely ignored, to its racially ameliorative status, to a racially repressive response, and then back again to its racially oblivious mode.

Next I compare this book's New Haven and Syracuse case histories and the more recent New York and New Orleans case examples.

Similarities and Differences in the Case Histories and Examples

As I noted earlier, the most obvious difference is that whereas the mayors of New Haven, Syracuse, and New York were viewed as being racially "white," the mayor of New Orleans was commonly perceived as being "black." Another apparent difference is that unlike what appeared to be true for the Nagin, Lee, and Walsh administrations in their URS capacities, the Giuliani URS administration made little or no attempt to balance the demands of different racialized groups in the city. Mayor Giuliani's URS administration also differed from the others in that it relied almost exclusively on its repressive state apparatus to control race relations, consistent with its perceived interests, whereas the Nagin administration depended more on the ideological state apparatus of its Bring New Orleans Back Commission in a way that was reminiscent of how in the 1960s mayors in cities like New Haven and Syracuse deployed community action programs.

When we take a closer look, we see that there are more similarities than differences in these four URS executive branch governmental cores. First, it is clear that the existence of a URS administration is not determined by the "race" of a mayor. The Lee, Walsh, Giuliani, and Nagin administrations all had fully functioning urban racial state components. This makes sense because, as you have seen, a URS does not simply disappear with the election of an African American or Latino/a American mayor and other legislative- and judicial-branch officials. Second, when we took a closer look at the Nagin URS administration during its two terms, we saw less of an attempt to balance the demands of the city's "black" and "white" racialized groups than initially appeared to be the case. Rather than seek racial balance, Nagin, like Giuliani, tended to play to the extremes. The major difference is that whereas Giuliani stuck with the dominant racialized group as his constituent base, the more racially nimble Nagin switched as needed. Third, those two more recent URS case examples were also similar in that, like the Walsh administration within its URS capacity, they were both conservative and business-centered. Fourth, as we saw for the 1960s Syracuse and New Haven case histories, the actions and reactions of the New York and New Orleans URS administrations were closely linked to those of other branches and levels of the racial state. Fifth, like the Lee URS administration but less like the more hands-off Walsh URS administration, both the Giuliani and Nagin URS administrations were very opportunistic. Similar to Lee and Giuliani, Nagin crafted and honed political positions, especially his racial decisions, to fit his changing political ambitions, challenges, and calculations. Finally, by examining these two more recent case examples of the workings of the urban racial state in New York City and in New Orleans, it is clear that despite claims that America is inextricably moving toward, or has already somehow "morphed" into a post-racial society, the urban racial state not only persists but in different times and various places since the post-civil rights movement era has actually been more intense than it was in this book's 1960s community action program case histories.

This Study's Contributions to the Urban Theory, Racism Theory, and Racial State Theory Literatures

In this book I introduced the concept of the urban racial state as a conceptual nexus that connects three bodies of social science literature that are essential to explaining the political workings of modern cities and their suburbs: urban theory, racism theory, and racial state theory.

Urban Theory

More than any other theoretical conceptualization, the urban racial state places racism at the center of urban theory. It not only acknowledges the existence of racism as being central to urban politics, and names and describes that phenomenon; it also provides analytical tools for explaining how it works, when, and why. By doing so the urban racial state concept takes a significant step toward the promise of the new urban paradigm to help restore the credibility of American urban sociology by bringing to its forefront racism and other manifestations of power and conflict that are not limited to a city's political boundaries. As you have also seen, as an analytical tool the urban racial state concept brings to the study of urban politics a way of examining not only the actions of political elites but of those of various elites and nonelites who mobilize the resources available to them to challenge the racial status quo. Another strength of the urban racial state concept is its ability to elucidate, at a more micro level of analysis, how urban systems operate by focusing on the key roles of their various bureaucratic managers. These include URS managers who may at times actually align themselves and the agencies they run with those who challenge their political bosses.

Racism Theory

All too often the sparse scholarship that has actually bothered to examine racism directly and explicitly has been either social-structurally blind—with its spotlight shone on the racially bigoted attitudes and behaviors of individuals, or at the other extreme, sightless to human agency in its focus only on the impersonal workings of institutionalized racism. The urban racial state concept provides a conceptual bridge that allows us to examine how racism works at both the macro and micro levels of analysis. For example, as we have seen, it places the racial actions of powerful political elites and their subordinates within the context of often competing demands made upon them by economic elites, white public opinion, and the articulation of the aspirations of the racially oppressed. Through such an examination, we can better understand both the structures and processes of systemic racism. And unlike most racism theory, which tends to focus exclusively on the personal or institutional perpetrators of racial oppression, the urban racial state concept stresses the importance of examining both the actions of those who support the racial status quo and those who organize to change it. That is, as you have seen in this book, its conceptualization of the URS views racial oppression as a structure and process in which the racially dominant group uses its power to maintain its privileged position while the racially oppressed mobilize whatever power they can muster to challenge that oppression in whatever ways they can.

Racial State Theory

As you have seen in this book, the concept of the racial state is useful in analyzing the link between changing race relations and state actions. It is only through such a macro-level analytical perspective that it is possible to place state actions within their broader socio-historical context. And while at the micro-level of analysis much of the literature on the racial state tends to be largely descriptive and thus provides few insights as to *how* the racial state actually operates, this analysis of the urban racial state shows how by deploying the managerial perspective of the state one can easily examine the roles and actions of individual urban racial state managers. Studies such as this one that focus on the state as a highly racialized entity also have the potential to force the large body of class-focused, but mostly racism-blind, state theory to incorporate the existence and workings of systemic racism, to acknowledge the relative autonomy of state actors, and to specify the actual mechanisms through which the state caries out its various functions. This study of the urban racial state has also brought much-needed attention to the functioning of the state at the local level of government, with particular focus, of course, on how it works in the urban context of cities and their suburbs. In addition, it has shown how at a particular point in time, based on the various circumstances and interests of their leaders, different branches and levels of the governmental core of racial states can operate either in harmony or in conflict.

LESSONS LEARNED FOR UNDERSTANDING TODAY'S URBAN RACIAL STATE

This study offers a number of lessons about the organization and function of the urban racial state. And as you saw in the previous chapter when I suggested ideas for additional research on the topic, the usefulness of the urban racial state concept is in no way limited to the community action programs in New Haven and Syracuse in the 1960s.

You have seen that the URS is relatively autonomous in its operation. That is—even though the urban racial state is unequally pressured by powerful interest groups like business elites, a larger "white" public, and racially oppressed groups—mayors, other politicians, and their various URS managers have significant freedom to shape its actions consistent with their ideologies and needs. You have also seen that consistent with the theory work of Carter A. Wilson, with this autonomy the urban racial state operates in a way that is both indeterminate (i.e., dependent on the outcome of political struggle) and paradoxical (e.g., at times it provides some ameliorative policy and program relief for the racially oppressed even though its ultimate function is the maintenance of the racial status quo).

This study has shown that although the main action of the urban racial state governmental core tends to be centered in its executive branch at the local level, it also operates in conjunction with two other governmental branches and levels of a society's larger racial state. You have also seen how the URS shifts from different modes of racial management (i.e., the racially oblivious, the racially ameliorative, and the racially repressive) to meet the changing demands of race relations and the shifting needs of politicians and their various URS managers. This analysis has also found that in making these shifts urban racial states can deploy, as appropriate, either the carrot of their ideological state apparatuses (e.g., schools and special programs) or the stick of their repressive status apparatuses (e.g., the police and local courts).

These case histories and examples have also revealed that racial dynamics are not the only social forces that shape the urban racial state. For example, class and gender relationships are also important. Moreover, you also saw—especially through the New Haven case history—that the forms and actions taken by the URS are heavily influenced by the particular era of urban politics in which it operates. And finally, through the New York City and New Orleans case examples, you have seen that the URS does not simply disappear over time, or with improvements in race relations, or with the election of African American or Latinoa politicians. For example, no matter what the color of the mayor, the ultimate function of all branches of the URS remains the maintenance of the racial status quo.

SUGGESTIONS FOR FURTHER STUDY

In keeping with the aspiration that social science knowledge should be cumulative, and its related expectation that the end of one study should mark the beginning of additional scholarly work, I include the following list of ideas for further study and refinement of the urban racial state concept:

1. The various relationships among the executive, judicial, and legislative branches of the urban racial state governmental core.
2. The urban racial state administration's transactions with different levels and branches of the federal racial state and the individual state governmental cores.
3. The relationship between the city and suburban components and branches of the urban racial state governmental core.
4. The relationship between the urban racial state administration and private foundations and other not-for-profit entities that influence the formulation and implementation of public policies.
5. The relationships between the governmental core branches of the urban racial state, economic elites, and various class relations challenges.
6. The relationships between the governmental core branches of the urban racial state, male dominance, sexuality-based oppression, and various gender or sexuality-based relations challenges.
7. The interrelationship of racial-, class-, gender-, and sexuality-based relations in influencing, and in turn being influenced by, the activities of the governmental core branches of the urban racial state.
8. What comparative research involving different levels of the racial state (e.g., the urban racial state and the federal racial state, the urban racial state and the individual state racial state, and the urban racial state and the local town racial state or rural racial state) can tell us about what, if anything, is distinctly *urban* about the urban racial state.
9. The origins and nature of the urban racial state, aside from its more obvious state actions.
10. How the urban racial state administrations of dominant "race" mayors compare to those of mayors from racially oppressed groups.
11. What an understanding of the urban racial state can contribute to a more comprehensive understanding of the origins, nature, organization, and operations of the state.
12. How the urban racial state works in other nations.

I hope that others who share my interest in urban politics will both add to this list and continue the important work that remains to be done in conceptualizing the urban racial state.

Notes

NOTES TO INTRODUCTION

1. By "racialized" I mean the stratification of societies and other social structures based on a widespread and dominant ideology that there exist biological differences among groups that rank them within a social hierarchy based on criteria like physical attractiveness, intelligence, and moral character. The salience of racial stratification varies from society to society and changes over time within a single society consistent with changing socio-historical conditions.

2. Although I realize that metropolitan counties, suburbs, and regional governments—including commissions and boards—can also function as the governmental cores of urban racial states, my focus in this study is on what happens within the political boundaries of city governments and, even more specifically, on the actions of their executive branches.

3. In this chapter new analytical terms to be used in this study are placed in italics as they are introduced. By the *urban racial state* I mean the political structure and processes of a city and its suburbs that manage race relations in ways that foster and sustain both its own immediate political interests and, ultimately, white racial supremacy. This definition and its various conceptual components are discussed in greater detail in the next chapter.

4. As you will see in chapter 6 when I discuss the Nagin URS administration in New Orleans, this primary goal of the urban racial state persists today even in cities with African American or Latino/a American mayors because white business and political interests that extend far beyond the borders of a particular urban area typically set the limits of what those governments may and may not do in the way of addressing racial inequality or initiating other social programs that could benefit large numbers of racially oppressed people.

In other words, these mayors of color serve largely as figureheads in urban racial states over which they rarely have the ultimate control. In this way they tend to provide the appearance of significant racial change as they legitimize the persistence of the racial and economic status quo. Adolph Reed Jr., "The Black Urban Regime: Structural Origins and Constraints," in *Power, Community and the City*, Volume 1, ed. Michael Peter Smith, 138–89 (New Brunswick, NJ: Transaction Books, 1988).

5. This concept is discussed more extensively as "race population control" in chapter 6 of Kenneth J. Neubeck and Noel A. Cazenave, *Welfare Racism: Playing the Race Card Against America's Poor* (New York: Routledge, 2001). Here I use the term *racially-targeted population control*, which I believe is more specific and therefore more easily understood.

6. Such changes are consistent with Hayward Horton's population and structural change thesis, which holds that demographic changes involving racially oppressed populations combine with the social structure they impact "to produce changes in the nature of racial inequality." Hayward Derrick Horton, "Critical Demography and Racism: The Case of African Americans," *African American Research Perspectives* 6, no. 2 (2000): 1–6.

7. Although in the 1960s there was an overall slight decline in the number of African Americans who migrated out of the South, and states in the north central region of the United States experienced a significant drop in the number of African Americans moving there, both the West and the northeast received even larger numbers of African Americans during that decade than they did in the 1950s. William Issel, *Social Change in the United States: 1945–1983* (New York: Schocken, 1987), 10.

8. Charles E. Silberman, "The City and the Negro," *Fortune*, March 1962, 89.

9. For a discussion of these and other "push" and "pull" factors associated with the African American migrations, see Doug McAdam, *Political Process and the Development of Black Insurgency, 1930–1970* (Chicago: University of Chicago Press, 1982), 77–78.

10. Marilyn Miller and Marian Faux, eds., *The New York Public Library American History Desk Reference* (New York: Macmillan, 1997), 107.

11. U.S. Census Office, *The Social and Economic Status of the Black Population in the United States: A Historical View, 1790–1978*, Current Population Reports, Special Studies Series P-23, no. 80 (Washington, DC: U.S. Government Printing Office, 1979), 7, 15.

12. Ibid., 7, 13, 15.

13. Silberman, "The City and the Negro," 88.

14. Carter A. Wilson, *Racism: From Slavery to Advanced Capitalism* (Thousand Oaks, CA: Sage, 1996), 58–79, 159–65. Also see the historical stages of racism identified in Loïc Wacquant, "From Slavery to Mass Incarceration: Rethinking the 'Race Question' in the U.S.," *New Left Review* 13 (January–February 2002): 42, 47.

15. Ghettoization has been defined as referring to "the underlying and interrelated social processes that produce and maintain *ghetto* areas." Anmol Chaddha and William Julius Wilson, "Reconsidering the 'Ghetto,'" *City & Community* 7, no. 4 (December 2008): 384.

16. Richard Sennett, *Flesh and Stone: The Body and the City in Western Civilization* (New York: Penguin, 2002), 237; see also Wacquant, "From Slavery to Mass Incarceration," 51.

17. Wacquant, "From Slavery to Mass Incarceration," 41. For a symposium on the historic and contemporary social science use of and debates about the term *ghetto*, see "Symposium on the Ghetto," *City & Community* 7, no. 4 (December 2008): 347–98. Like Wacquant, Gans, and others, I view ghettos and the process of ghettoization that produces and maintains them as being largely involuntary. Gans has defined ghetto as "a place to which the subjects or victims of the involuntary segregation process are sent" and as "the spatial representation of the social political process of involuntary segregation." Herbert J. Gans, "Involuntary Segregation and the Ghetto: Disconnecting Process and Place," *City & Community* 7, no. 4 (December 2008): 353, 355.

18. Silberman, "The City and the Negro," 89. Silberman noted that "between 1950 and 1960," when "the twelve largest U.S. cities lost over two million white residents[,] they gained nearly two million Negro residents."

19. Douglas S. Massey and Nancy A. Denton, *American Apartheid: Segregation and the Making of the Underclass* (Cambridge, MA: Harvard University Press, 1993), 45. Massey and Denton cite a survey that found "in 1962, 61% of white respondents agreed that 'white people have a right to keep blacks out of their neighborhoods if they want to, and blacks should respect that right'" (49).

20. Susan Welch, Lee Sigelman, Timothy Bledsoe, and Michael Combs, *Race & Place: Race Relations in An American City* (Cambridge: Cambridge University Press, 2001).

21. Issel, *Social Change in the United States*, 106.

22. Noel A. Cazenave, *Impossible Democracy: The Unlikely Success of the War on Poverty Community Action Programs* (Albany, NY: SUNY Press, 2001), 3; Joseph H. Helfgot, *Professional Reforming: Mobilization for Youth and the Failure of Social Science* (Lexington, MA: Lexington Books, 1981), 11–13; Frances Fox Piven and Richard A. Cloward, *Regulating the Poor: The Functions of Public Welfare* (New York: Vintage Books, 1993), 223.

23. Cazenave, *Impossible Democracy*, 141.

24. Piven and Cloward, *Regulating the Poor*, 212, 223. According to Piven and Cloward, not only did migration increase the number of African American voters but they "came to be located in states of the most strategic importance in presidential contests." In making this point, Piven and Cloward note that "in 1960, 90 per cent of all Northern blacks were concentrated in just 10 of the most populous Northern states—states with the largest number of electors" (251).

25. For a history of the civil rights movement in the North, see Thomas J. Sugrue, *Sweet Land of Liberty: The Forgotten Struggle for Civil Rights in the North* (New York: Random House, 2008).

26. For a discussion of how such transformations perpetuate racism in public assistance attitudes, policies, and practices, see Neubeck and Cazenave, *Welfare Racism*, 12, 37.

27. I will sometimes use the term the racial state in a very general sense to refer to its workings at any or all levels and branches of its governmental core.

28. See table 1.1 in chapter 1 to preview a more detailed representation and discussion of the nine racial state entities.

29. Harvard Sitkoff, *The Struggle for Black Equality: 1954–1992* (New York: Hill and Wang, 1993), 21–23, quotation at 24.

30. Ibid., 23. I am not implying that before the Brown decision there were no protest-focused civil rights activities or that such grassroots activism did not, in turn, influence the Brown decision and other court actions. As examples of studies that incorporate that subtlety and other complexities, see Charles Payne, *I've Got the Light of Freedom: The Organizing Tradition and the Mississippi Freedom Struggle* (Berkeley: University of California Press, 1995), and Johnny Williams, *African American Religion and the Civil Rights Movement in Arkansas* (Jackson: University Press of Mississippi, 2003).

31. Williams, *African American Religion*, 37.

32. Sitkoff, *Struggle for Black Equality*, 28–31.

33. Cazenave, *Impossible Democracy*, 21.

34. For example, the federal government was concerned when the juvenile delinquency rate doubled from 1948 to 1958. U.S. Department of Health, Education, and Welfare, *Report to the Congress on Juvenile Delinquency* (Washington, DC: U.S. Government Printing Office, 1960), 3–4.

35. Sitkoff, *Struggle for Black Equality*, 61–62, 64, 88–89, 91.

36. Cazenave, *Impossible Democracy*, 33, 49.

37. Issel, *Social Change in the United States*, 179–80.

38. Sitkoff, *Struggle for Black Equality*, 136.

39. Cazenave, *Impossible Democracy*, 16.

40. For an analysis of racial conflict involving War on Poverty community action programs in Los Angeles, see Robert Bauman, *Race and the War on Poverty* (Norman: University of Oklahoma Press, 2008).

41. Cazenave, *Impossible Democracy*, 156–58.

42. Ibid., 174, 179, 182.

43. Ibid., 185.

44. Martin Gilens, *Why Americans Hate Welfare* (Chicago: University of Chicago Press, 1999), 113–14.

45. Cazenave, *Impossible Democracy*, 142. See also Thomas Byrne Edsall and Mary D. Edsall, *Chain Reaction: The Impact of Race, Rights, and Taxes on American Politics* (New York: W. W. Norton, 1992), 59.

46. Senate Select Committee to Study Government Operations with Respect to Intelligence Activities and the Rights of Americans, 94th Cong., 2nd sess., S. Rep. 755 (Washington, DC: U.S. Government Printing Office, 1976).

47. Kenneth O'Reilly, "Federal Bureau of Investigation (FBI)" in *Civil Rights in the United States*, ed. Waldo E. Martin Jr. and Patricia Sullivan, 274–75 (New York: Macmillan, 2000).

48. Yohuru Williams, *Black Politics/White Power: Civil Rights, Black Power, and the Black Panthers in New Haven* (St. James, NY: Brandywine Press, 2000), 81.

49. Cazenave, *Impossible Democracy*, 167–68.

50. *Report of the National Advisory Commission on Civil Disorders* (New York: Bantam Books, 1968), 1.

51. The methodological appendix also contains a section that explains why I chose to organize the study's case history material around a blending of historical narrative and more conceptually focused sociological analysis. Cazenave, *Impossible Democracy*, 183–85.

52. The study's New Haven and Syracuse case *histories* are quite detailed and are based on extensive oral history and archival data collected specifically for this study, whereas the relatively brief case *examples* and suggestions for additional research are based largely on newspaper and magazine articles and, when available, books and journal articles.

NOTES TO CHAPTER 1

1. Whenever I use the term *racism*, I refer to systemic racism. Therefore, I do not limit its meaning to the racist beliefs or ideologies that form the ideological core of systems of racial oppression or to the racially bigoted attitudes and behaviors of individuals. When using the word *race*, I will normally place it in quotation marks to acknowledge not only that the race concept is problematic because it is conceptually ambiguous, but more importantly, that its use is problematic because it is both erroneous and socially injurious. See Noel A. Cazenave, "Conceptualizing 'Race,' and Beyond," *Association of Black Sociologists Newsletter* (February 2004): 4–6.

2. Joe R. Feagin, *The New Urban Paradigm: Critical Perspectives on the City* (Lanham, MD: Rowman and Littlefield, 1998), 2. In her history of Robert Park, a leader of the Chicago School of sociology who was especially influential in helping to shape the dominant American sociology paradigms for both urban sociology and race and ethnic relations, Barbara Ballis Lal notes that Park's emphasis on culture, ethnicity, and other subjective processes; the influence of his former boss and mentor, racial accommodationist Booker T. Washington; and Park's de-emphasis of power and conflict resulted in his discounting the impact of racial oppression in urban politics. Barbara Ballis Lal, *The Romance of Culture in An Urban Civilization: Robert E. Park on Race and Ethnic Relations in Cities* (London: Routledge, 1990), 21, 68.

3. Peter Saunders, *Social Theory and the Urban Question* (New York: Holmes and Meier, 1981), 1–2.

4. Feagin, *The New Urban Paradigm*, 8, 14, 17.

5. Ibid., 10.

6. Susan J. Smith, "Residential Segregation: A Geography of English Racism?" in, *Race and Racism: Essays in Social Geography*, ed. Peter Jackson, 25–49 (London: Allyn and Unwin, 1987), 44.

7. Jill Quadagno, *The Color of Welfare: How Racism Undermined the War on Poverty* (New York: Oxford University Press, 1994), v. Also see Steve Valocchi, "The Racial Basis of Capitalism and the State, and the Impact of the New Deal on African Americans," *Social Problems* 41 (August 1994): 347–62.

8. Ronald John Johnston, *Residential Segregation, the State and Constitutional Conflict in American Urban Areas* (London: Academic Press, 1984), 54; Kenneth T. Jackson, *Crabgrass Frontier: The Suburbanization of the United States* (New York: Oxford University Press, 1985), 198, 201, 203, 206, 208–9, 211, 293.

9. For a discussion of how racial segregation has helped shape U.S. cities spatially since World War II and has impacted both urban and national politics in such a way that has encouraged politicians and the public to accept social inequality as natural and inevitable, see William W. Goldsmith, "From the Metropolis to Globalization: The Dialectics of Race and Urban Form," in *Readings in Urban Theory*, ed. Susan Fainstein and Scott Campbell, 129–39 (Oxford: Blackwell, 1997), 130–31.

10. Nicholas Lemann, "The Myth of Community Development," *New York Times Magazine*, January 9, 1994, 31. As Smith puts it, "by linking supposedly race-related problems to the division of urban space, governments have created the illusion of tackling fundamental social and economic issues, while avoiding any vigorous commitment to the anti-racist cause." Susan J. Smith, "Residential Segregation and the Politics of Racialization," in *Racism, the City and the State*, ed. Malcolm Cross and Michael Keith, 128–43 (London: Routledge, 1993), 134. For a provocative analysis of this and other reasons for "placed-based" anti-poverty policies and of their limitations, see Margaret Weir, "Poverty, Social Rights, and the Politics of Place in the United States," in *European Social Policy: Between Fragmentation and Integration*, eds. Stephan Leibfried and Paul Pierson, 329–54 (Washington, DC: Brookings Institution, 1995).

11. For an influential article that shares many Marxist assumptions as it explains the limitations placed on mayors by wealthy business leaders upon whom city administrations headed by Africans Americans are dependent for campaign contributions and other forms of support, see Adolph Reed Jr., "The Black Urban Regime: Structural Origins and Constraints," in *Power, Community and the City*, Volume 1, ed. Michael Peter Smith, 138–89 (New Brunswick, NJ: Transaction Books, 1988). Also see Christopher Pickvane, "Marxist Theories of Urban Politics," in *Theories of Urban Politics*, ed. David Judge, Gerry Stoker, and Harold Wolman, 253–75 (London: Sage Publications, 1995), 257.

12. Bryan D. Jones, "Bureaucrats and Urban Politics: Who Controls? Who Benefits?" in Judge, Stoker, and Wolman, *Theories of Urban Politics*, 72–95, quote at 73.

13. Clarence Stone, Robert K. Whelan, and William J. Murin, *Urban Policy and Politics in a Bureaucratic Age* (Englewood Cliffs, NJ: Prentice Hall, 1986), 134–40, 378.

14. Jones, "Bureaucrats and Urban Politics," 91.

15. Joe R. Feagin, *Systemic Racism: A Theory of Oppression* (New York: Routledge, 2006), 7, 16.

16. Joe R. Feagin, *The White Racial Frame: Centuries of Racial Framing and Counter-Framing* (New York: Routledge, 2010), 9–10, 18–20.

17. Stokely Carmichael and Charles V. Hamilton, *Black Power: The Politics of Liberation* (New York: Vintage Books, 1967), 5.

18. Ibid., 6. Robert L. Allen, *Black Awakening in Capitalist America: An Analytic History* (New York: Anchor Books, 1969), 2, 8, 13–14, 17.

19. Robert Blauner, *Racial Oppression in America* (New York: Harper and Row, 1972), 12-13; Mark A. Chesler, "Contemporary Sociological Theories of Racism," in *Toward the Elimination of Racism*, ed. Phyllis A. Katz, 21-71 (New York: Pergamon, 1976), 56.

20. This emphasis on multiple dimensions fits Horan's analysis of "urban regimes" as "three way relationships shaped by the interconnected logics of state,

economy, and race." Cynthia Horan, "Racializing Regime Politics," *Journal of Urban Affairs* 24, no. 1 (Spring 2002): 22.

21. Joe R. Feagin and Clairece Booher Feagin, *Racial and Ethnic Relations* (Upper Saddle River, NJ: Prentice Hall, 1999), 48, 53.

22. Blauner, *Racial Oppression in America*, 32–33, 36.

23. Carter A. Wilson, *Racism: From Slavery to Advanced Capitalism* (Thousand Oaks, CA: Sage, 1996), 24–32.

24. Blauner, *Racial Oppression in America*, 37–38.

25. For a provocative discussion of the limits of what they characterize as political sociology's "exclusive focus on the nation-state," see Kevin T. Leicht and J. Craig Jenkins, "New and Unexplored Opportunities: Developing a Spatial Perspective for Political Sociology," in *The Sociology of Spatial Inequality*, ed. Linda M. Lobao, Gregory Hooks, and Ann R. Tickamyer, 63–84 (Albany, NY: SUNY Press, 2007), 68–71.

26. Johnston, *Residential Segregation*, 55.

27. Although the racism-centered theory of the state I am proposing is heavily influenced by the managerial perspective on the state, it is also informed by the class perspective in its underlying assumptions of how power relations work to shape state policy.

28. Gerhard Jacoby, *Racial State: The German Nationalities Policy in the Protectorate of Bohemia-Moravia* (New York: Institute of Jewish Affairs of the American Jewish Congress and World Jewish Congress, 1944). The notion of a racial state was implicit in even earlier scholarship on "race" and the nation state. For example, see Eric Voegelin, *Race and State*, trans. Ruth Heim (Baton Rouge: Louisiana State University Press, 2000); original German edition published in 1933.

29. Michael Omi and Howard Winant, *Racial Formation in the United States: From the 1960s to the 1990s* (New York: Routledge, 1994); David R. James, "The Transformation of the Southern Racial State: Class and Race Determinants of Local-State Structures," *American Sociological Review* 53, no. 2 (April 1988): 191–209.

30. Despite its contributions to our understanding of the racial state, Wilson's *Racism* fits this unfortunate pattern.

31. Jack Niemonen, "The Role of the State in the Sociology of Racial and Ethnic Relations: Some Theoretical Considerations," *Free Inquiry in Creative Sociology* 23, no. 1 (1995): 27, 28.

32. Among specific limitations of state theory that contribute to its inability to adequately explain the link between the state and racial domination, Hall argues, are the influence of neo-Marxism, which tends to treat other important issues involving the state as epiphenomenal to class domination, and the tendency to treat the state as an intervening variable to other factors like racial group conflict or dominance, with little autonomy in the pursuit of its own interests. Jarvis A. Hall, "Linking Two Theoretical Traditions: Toward Conceptualizing the American Racial State in a Globalized Milieu," *National Political Science Review* 9 (2003): 173–75, 181–82.

33. Wilson, *Racism*, 16, 20, 165.

34. Louis Althusser, "Ideology and Ideological State Apparatus (Notes Toward an Investigation)," in *Lenin and Philosophy and Other Essays* (New York: Monthly Review Press, 1971), 127–86. Gordon L. Clark and Michael Dear, *State Apparatus: Structures and Languages* of Legitimacy (Boston: Allen & Unwin, 1994), 142–143.

35. Clark and Michael Dear, *State Apparatus*, 45–46, 67, 140–43.

36. Although I acknowledge that modern systemic white racism has its roots in various forms of economic exploitation, I believe that both vulgar Marxist theorists who treat racism as ancillary to economic oppression and neo-Marxist scholars who allow for at least some "relative" autonomy of racial oppression are wrong. Both discount the significance of systemic racism as a social formation, and neither can explain why the racial state persists at all levels of its governmental core under socialist states.

37. Patricia Hill Collins, *Black Feminist Thought: Knowledge, Consciousness, and the Politics of Empowerment* (New York: Routledge, 2000), 66–67. Sexual identity is another factor that may work alone or in conjunction with these other three factors that shape the functions and actions of the urban racial state.

38. Johnston, *Residential Segregation*, 54–55.

39. The need for this racial balancing function of the racial state is conceptualized by Omi and Winant as being rooted in a "racial order" that exists in a state of "unstable equilibrium." It is the job of the racial state to act when that order is threatened by "racial disequilibrium." Omi and Winant, *Racial Formation in the United States*, 84–85.

40. Ibid., 86–87. Once these programs became sites of racial battles, they served an "insulation" function for the racial state by enabling it to limit "demands to terrains that are, if not entirely symbolic, at least not crucial to the operation of the racial order."

41. To the extent that activist African Americans were able to subvert or control community action programs, instead of supporting the existing "culture of domination" the programs could provide a "free" and "safe" space and other resources for the mobilization of the "oppositional consciousness" necessary for them to challenge the local white power structure. Aldon Morris and Naomi Braine, "Social Movements and Oppositional Consciousness," in *Oppositional Consciousness: The Subjective Roots of Social Protest*, ed. Jane Mansbridge and Aldon Morris, 20–37 (Chicago: University of Chicago Press, 2001), 25–26, 29–31; Jane Mansbridge, "The Making of Oppositional Consciousness," in Mansbridge and Morris, *Oppositional Consciousness*, 1–19, esp. 7–8.

42. Clark and Michael Dear, *State Apparatus*, 140–43.

43. Noel A. Cazenave, *Impossible Democracy: The Unlikely Success of the War on Poverty Community Action Programs* (Stony Brook, NY: SUNY Press, 2007), 141–42; Frances Fox Piven and Richard A. Cloward, *Regulating the Poor: The Functions of Public Welfare* (New York: Vintage Books, 1993), 234n24; James W. Button, *Black Violence: Political Impact of the 1960s Riots* (Princeton, NJ: Princeton University Press, 1978), 32–33; Daryl B. Harris, *The Logic of Black Urban Rebellions: Challenging the Dynamics of White Domination in Miami* (Westport, CT: Praeger, 1999), 53, 102.

44. Although I have laid out here a logical sequence of urban racial state modalities and responses congruent with the unfolding of events to be detailed in this study, they need not occur in this order and may overlap. This ability to account for such varying forms and actions is one of the reasons I prefer the term *urban racial state* over *urban racist state*, which can leave the false impression that racial structures and processes are not dynamic and variable. The more general concept

of the racial state allows for the fact that the state is neither monolithic nor static in its character or actions.

NOTES TO CHAPTER 2

1. Howard W. Hallman, Community Progress, Inc., "Supplement, Annual Program Review for the Ford Foundation," May 1, 1965, reel 2557, 62-328, sec. 1, p. 28, Ford Foundation Archives.

2. See, for example, Johnny E. Williams, "Race and Class: Why All the Confusion?" in *Race and Racism in Theory and Practice*, ed. Berel Lang, 215–27 (New York: Rowman & Littlefield, 2000), and Melvin Thomas, "Anything But Race: The Social Science Retreat from Racism," *African American Research Perspectives* 6, no. 1 (2000): 79–96.

3. Joe R. Feagin, *The White Racial Frame: Centuries of Racial Framing and Counter-Framing* (New York: Routledge, 2010), 9–10.

4. For more on the centrality of the denial of systemic racism, see Noel A. Cazenave and Darlene Alvarez Maddern, "Defending the White Race: White Male Faculty Opposition to a White Racism Course," *Race and Society* 2, no. 1 (1999): 25–50.

5. This tendency to reduce American's systemic white racism problem to its "Negro problem" has been duly noted by African American intellectuals for some time. For example, in *The Souls of Black Folk*, originally published in 1903, W. E. B. Du Bois lamented the tendency of "white sociologists" to "gleefully count" "black" "bastards" and "prostitutes." W. E. B. Du Bois, *The Souls of Black Folk* (Greenwich, CT: Fawcett, 1961), vii, 20.

6. Jackson notes, for example, that it was politics that "assured that the poverty planners would define the nature and causes of poverty in cultural and behavioral rather than structural economic and political terms." Consequently, structural problems like "systemic racism in employment and union practices . . . did not shape the characteristics or justifications of programs." Thomas F. Jackson, "The State, the Movement, and the Urban Poor: The War on Poverty and Political Mobilization in the 1960s," in *The "Underclass" Debate: Views from History*, ed. Michael B. Katz, 403–39 (Princeton, NJ: Princeton University Press, 1995), 416.

7. Gordon L. Clark and Michael Dear, *State Apparatus: Structures and Languages of Legitimacy* (Boston: Allen & Unwin, 1994), 45–46. This avoidance of the systematic racism that creates and maintains racial ghettos is facilitated by the tendency of social scientists and public policy makers in the United States to conveniently conflate racial-discrimination-driven disparities with those rooted primarily in social class. See Williams, "Race and Class."

8. This expansion/contraction deployment of community action by the URS in its regulation of race relations is supported by the findings of James Button and of Daryl Harris. Button documents how the federal government, through agencies like the Office of Economic Opportunities and the Department of Justice, increased either government resources or punishment in response to the urban rebellions of the mid- and late 1960s. He finds, for example, that "the *black riots had a greater direct, positive impact than any other independent variable upon total OEO expenditure increases in the latter 1960s*, as well as upon most individual poverty

program increases." Button also notes that the early unrest (1963–1966) was met with greater federal government generosity than that which occurred later (1967–1968), which was more likely to receive a harsher response in line with the white racial backlash. See James W. Button, *Black Violence: Political Impact of the 1960s Riots* (Princeton, NJ: Princeton University Press, 1978), 11, 32–33, 37, 158. For information on other federal agencies that offered "ameliorative programs" to African American communities in response to the urban rebellions of that time included the Department of Housing and Urban Development and the Department of Health, Education and Welfare, see Daryl B. Harris, *The Logic of Black Urban Rebellions: Challenging the Dynamics of White Domination in Miami* (Westport, CT: Praeger, 1999), 53. In addition, Model Cities program funds were also increased at the federal level, and local governments increased public assistance. See James W. Button, "The Outcomes of Contemporary Black Protest and Violence," in *Violence in America*, vol. 2, *Protest, Rebellion, Reform*, ed. Ted Robert Gurr, 286–386 (Newbury Park, CA: Sage, 1989), esp. 295–96.

9. Allan R. Talbot, *The Mayor's Game: Richard Lee of New Haven and the Politics of Change* (New York: Harper & Row, 1967), 167–69.

10. Yohuru Williams, *Black Politics/White Power: Civil Rights, Black Power, and the Black Panthers in New Haven* (St. James, NY: Brandywine Press, 2000), 50, 55–57.

11. Terry Preston, "Mitchell Sviridoff, 81, Dies: Renewal Chief," *New York Times*, October 23, 2000; Mitchell Sviridoff, interview with author, March 24, 1992, 2.

12. Sviridoff, "Memo on Problems of Leadership in the Negro Community," 1959, copy provided to author by Mitchell Sviridoff.

13. Ibid., 1.

14. Ibid., 1, 2.

15. Ibid., 2, 3. Again, because the use of race/color terms such as "race," "black," and "white" is conceptually ambiguous, factually erroneous, and socially injurious, I usually use pan-ethnic terms like African American or European American. For consistency's sake, in cases where such racial terminology is used in statistical reports that are cited, they will be also be used in this book but placed within quotation marks. No quotation marks will be used for commonly used terms that fit specific social and historical contexts like white backlash, black power, or white power structure.

16. Sviridoff, "Memo on Problems of Leadership," 2, 3.

17. Ibid., 4–6. Sviridoff notes that while it is important to strengthen alliances with moderate African American leaders, cutting off communication with radical leaders would encourage "irresponsibility."

18. As Russell Murphy notes, "there was no room for complacency since . . . population projections indicated that within twenty years the blacks would constitute almost a majority of the population." Russell D. Murphy, *Political Entrepreneurs and Urban Poverty: Strategies of Policy Innovation in New Haven's Model Anti-Poverty Project* (Lexington, MA: Heath Lexington Books, 1971), 19.

19. Ibid., 17.

20. When Murphy compared those six problem-burdened neighborhoods to the city as a whole, he found that 15 percent of New Haven's population was African American compared to 26 percent of those "inner city" neighborhoods he

identified and that a quarter of the city's families had incomes of less than $4,000 compared to nearly a third in those six neighborhoods. Ibid., 16.

21. Ibid., 19–20.

22. James R. Lowe, *Cities in a Race with Time: Progress and Poverty in America's Renewing Cities* (New Haven, CT: Random House, 1967). Also see Robert A. Warner, *New Haven Negroes: A Social History* (New York: Arno Press, 1969). Warner concludes that despite their long history in New Haven, their assimilation, and their remarkable advances, the African American experience was one that was more similar to that of a racial caste than of equal opportunity (iii, ix).

23. Talbot, *Mayor's Game*, 165.

24. Murphy, *Political Entrepreneurs*, 24; Howard Hallman, interview with author, August 18, 1992, 7.

25. Murphy, *Political Entrepreneurs*, 26.

26. Hallman, interview with author, 5.

27. Ford Foundation Grant to City of New Haven, April 12, 1962, reel 2560, 62-328, Mid-5, p. 12, Ford Foundation Archives; Reference Chronology: 1961–1964, Poverty and Urban Policy (supplemental materials), John F. Kennedy Library.

28. Murphy, *Political Entrepreneurs*, 16–17. If the U.S. census "non-white" designation was used to derive the number of African Americans in New Haven, that number may have been somewhat inflated since in 1960 the "non-white" category included "1,169 city residents who were born in Puerto Rico or had parents who were born in Puerto Rico." Talbot, *Mayor's Game*, 165.

29. "Opening Opportunities: New Haven's Comprehensive Program for Community Progress," April 4, 1962, reel 2560, 62-328, Mid-5, Community Progress, Inc., 1962–1968, Ford Foundation Archives.

30. People interviewed who were involved in the planning or administration of those projects (e.g., Mobilization for Youth's Richard Cloward) sometimes referred to their respective proposals as the "telephone book." Richard Cloward, interview with author, May 28, 1992, 10.

31. "Opening Opportunities," 7, 39; "Application for a Ford Foundation Grant to Carry Out New Haven's Comprehensive Program for Community Progress," April 4, 1962, reel 2560, 62-328, Mid-5, Community Progress, Inc., 1962–1968, Ford Foundation Archives.

32. Sviridoff, interview with author, 4–5.

33. "Opening Opportunities," 31. The proposal notes that the rate of juvenile delinquency, based on the number of children ages seven to fifteen who were referred to the juvenile court in 1961, was more than twice as high in the project's seven target neighborhoods (35.3 per thousand) than in the city as a whole (16.5 per thousand).

34. "Application for a Ford Foundation Grant," 12.

35. Ibid.; "Opening Opportunities," 29.

36. "Opening Opportunities," 29.

37. "Application for a Ford Foundation Grant," 10.

38. Ibid.; "Opening Opportunities," table of contents.

39. For example, the CPI proposal claimed that community schools would become "truly a community institution." "Application for a Ford Foundation Grant "; "Opening Opportunities," 6.

40. Alinsky criticized the council of social agencies approach to community organization as one that was superimposed on area residents by social work professionals. He depicted his own community organization strategy as being based on "indigenous leadership." Noel A. Cazenave, "Chicago Influences on the War on Poverty," *Journal of Policy History* 5, no. 1 (1993): 52–68.

41. Much later Hallman indicated that his opposition to CAPs like CPI promoting social protest against local power structures lessened as "it began to be more acceptable in the late sixties." His revised and more nuanced position was "it's possible, but you've got to do it with discretion, and you're better to work through an intermediary, rather than a public agency doing it directly." Hallman, interview with author, 34–35.

42. This, of course, refers to the reform government ideal. In practice, the Lee administration and other reform city governments at that time were still knee-deep in some aspects of machine politics, like patronage jobs for their supporters.

43. For a continuum of different public policy responses to racism that range from "racism driven" to "racism blind" to "racism cognizant" to "racism sensitive" and, finally, to "racism targeted," see Kenneth J. Neubeck and Noel A. Cazenave, *Welfare Racism: Playing the Race Card Against America's Poor* (New York: Routledge, 2001), 221–22.

44. Clarence N. Stone, Robert K. Whelan, and William J. Murin, *Urban Policy and Politics in a Bureaucratic Age* (Englewood Cliffs, NJ: Prentice Hall, 1986), 110, 136–37. For a more detailed analysis of this link that was heavily influenced by their work, see Noel A. Cazenave, *Impossible Democracy: The Unlikely Success of the War on Poverty Community Action Programs* (Albany, NY: SUNY Press, 2001), 57.

45. "New Battle for Connecticut Negroes: Birmingham Stirs Demands for Civil Rights and Comprehensive Attacks on Slum Living," *Connecticut Life*, June 6, 1963, 10–11.

46. Edgar S. Cahn and Jean C. Cahn, "The War on Poverty: A Civilian Perspective," *Yale Law Journal* 73, no. 8 (July 1964): 1317–52. In the next chapter I will discuss this article, the controversy it caused, and a response written by another CPI attorney in defense of the agency and the democratic theory it employed.

47. As Dowdy put it, "I was there on an everyday basis. Because I was on their staff. Part of the deal was, I got paid through them. Part of my salary came from them, and I had a desk there." Richard S. Dowdy Jr., interview with author, July 10, 1992, 2, 23.

48. Peter Marris and Martin Rein, *Dilemmas of Social Reform: Poverty and Community Action in the United States* (Chicago: University of Chicago Press, 1982), 172.

49. Ibid., vi, 172.

50. Robert A. Dahl, *Who Governs? Democracy in an American City* (New Haven: Yale University Press, 1961).

51. Marris and Rein, *Dilemmas of Social Reform*, vi, 172.

52. Sviridoff, interview with author, 37.

53. Lowe, *Cities in a Race with Time*, surmised that the "human relations" advisor part of Dowdy's job title was, indeed, a "euphemism for Negro relations" (512); "City's Human Relations Adviser Resigning to Attend Law School," *New Haven Journal-Courier*, August 28, 1963, clipping provided by Richard S. Dowdy.

54. Dowdy, interview with author, 7.

55. Ibid. As Dowdy put it, "These are young white fellows and a white professor, who'd have no access to the heart of the black community" (11); "Role in Cloud Trial is Described by Dowdy," *New Haven Register*, March 18, 1963, clipping provided by Richard S. Dowdy. My purpose in not naming the rape victim here is to avoid any further intrusion on her privacy.

56. That witness testified he saw Cloud with a European American woman in his shop, although he could not say it was the alleged victim. "Cloud Convicted of Kidnapping, Assault; Could Get 105 Years," *New Haven Journal-Courier*, March 7, 1963; "A Sound Sentence—And a Serious Question," *New Haven Register*, March 13, 1963, clipping provided by Richard S. Dowdy.

57. "A Sound Sentence." In a later article in that same newspaper, Dowdy indicated that although Mayor Lee was aware of his actions, the mayor neither authorized them nor instructed him to do so. "Role in Cloud Trial is Described by Dowdy," *New Haven Register*, March 18, 1963, clipping provided by Richard S. Dowdy.

58. See Clark and Dear, *State Apparatus*, 45–46.

59. "Balanced 'Human Relations' in the Mayor's Office," *New Haven Register*, March 22, 1963, clipping provided by Richard S. Dowdy.

60. "NAACP Levels Blast at Cloud Case Defense," *New Haven Register*, March 26, 1963.

61. Zoe Cornwall, *Human Rights in Syracuse: Two Memorable Decades; A Selected History from 1963 to 1983* (Syracuse, NY: Human Rights Commission of Syracuse and Onondaga County, 1987), 1, 5.

62. Alan K. Campbell et al., *The Negro in Syracuse: His Education, Employment, Income and Housing* (Syracuse, NY: University College, Syracuse University, 1964), 5; *Syracuse Action for Youth: An Action Program for Disadvantaged Youth* (Syracuse, NY: Mayor's Commission for Youth, Inc., 1964), II-4.

63. *Syracuse Action for Youth*, II-5.

64. Campbell et al., *Negro in Syracuse*, 20, 31, 38.

65. Nick Kotz and Mary Lynn Kotz, *A Passion for Equality: George Wiley and the Movement* (New York: W. W. Norton, 1977), 105.

66. Syracuse University Youth Development Center, "The First Five Years: 1958–1963," 7, Daniel Knapp Papers, box 19, Crusade for Opportunity Grants: 63002, 64016, Correspondence and Reports, John F. Kennedy Library.

67. Ibid.

68. Kotz and Kotz, *Passion for Equality*, 104.

69. Campbell et al., *Negro in Syracuse*, 21–24.

70. For an analysis of the role of local business interests and their allies in such downtown urban renewal efforts, see Robert M. Fogelson, *Downtown: Its Rise and Fall, 1880–1950* (New Haven, CT: Yale University Press, 2001), 319–20, 344.

71. Cornwall, *Human Rights in Syracuse*, 6.

72. "Syracuse: How Far From Birmingham?" 1963, n.p., George Wiley Papers, box 6, folder 3, Wisconsin Historical Society.

73. *Syracuse Action for Youth*, II-20.

74. Ibid., II-15.

75. Ibid., II-33.

76. Douglas Massey and Nancy Denton, *American Apartheid: Segregation and the Making of the Underclass* (Cambridge, MA: Harvard University Press, 1993).

77. For example, reading scores were lower than the city average, three fourths of the students in the SAY proposal's Action Areas A and B schools received at least one failing grade, nearly half the students in Area A schools were suspended at least once, and the 1960 dropout rate for Area A was four times greater than for the rest of the city. *Syracuse Action for Youth*, III-23, 27–29.

78. Ibid., III-31.

79. Ibid., III-34.

80. Ibid, IV-17, 19.

81. Ibid., IV-22.

82. August Meier and Elliot Rudwick, *CORE: A Study in the Civil Rights Movement, 1942–1968* (Urbana: University of Illinois Press, 1975), 243, 305–6.

83. Kotz and Kotz, *Passion for Equality*, 113.

84. Cornwall, *Human Rights in Syracuse*, 13.

85. For more on the importance of such indigenous resources for African American insurgency, see Doug McAdam, *Political Process and the Development of Black Insurgency, 1930–1970* (Chicago: University of Chicago Press, 1999).

86. Kotz and Kotz, *Passion for Equality*, 115.

87. "Syracuse: How Far From Birmingham?" n.p.

88. Cornwall, *Human Rights in Syracuse*, 10.

89. Betty Baer, interview with author, November 25, 1992, pp. 2, 6, 7, 12, 15. The CORE protests also helped develop some of the grassroots leadership that would later be employed in community action programs in the city. They included Inez Heard (known as "Mrs. CORE") and Anna Mae Williams, who would be hired by CATC. Kotz and Kotz, *Passion for Equality*, 108, 114.

90. "First Five Years," 59.

91. Ibid.

92. S. M. Miller, "Poverty, Race and Politics," 6, 7, 8, 19, 21, Syracuse University Youth Development Center, January 1963, George Willey Papers, box 6, folder 7, Wisconsin Historical Society. For a detailed analysis and critique of Ohlin's paper and the idea of elite outsiders fostering indigenous leadership, see Cazenave, *Impossible Democracy*, 40–43.

93. Miller, "Poverty, Race and Politics," 19, 23–26.

94. I use the words *relative radicalization* to make it clear that I am not implying that these reform-oriented social scientists were really radicals who sought to fundamentally restructure U.S. society. They were only "radical" relative to their pre–civil rights movement positions and to the political orientations of most European Americans at that time.

95. John Bartlett and Justin Kaplan, eds., *Bartlett's Familiar Quotations* (Boston: Little, Brown and Company, 1992), 58, column 15.

96. Daniel Knapp and Kenneth Polk, *Scouting the War on Poverty: Social Reform Politics in the Kennedy Administration* (Lexington, MA: Heath Lexington Books, 1971), 46.

97. For example, President's Committee on Juvenile Delinquency and Youth Crime officials noted that the name of the Syracuse project was to be changed from the Mayor's Commission for Youth "so that it is not confused with the Gov-

ernmental structure in the City." Memorandum from Bernard Russell, director, to Mr. Hackett, Mr. Ellinger, Dr. Kravitz, Dr. Frankel, Mr. Boone, and Mr. Lang, "Weekly Report—Syracuse," December 16, 1963, Department of Health, Education and Welfare, Office of Juvenile Delinquency and Youth Development, PCJD-OJD Background Materials, Projects, Comprehensive Demonstrations, Syracuse, Daniel Knapp Papers, box 19, John F. Kennedy Library.

NOTES TO CHAPTER 3

1. Betty Baer, interview with author, November 25, 1992, 3, 14–15. I was first exposed to the conceptualization of first, second, and third forces in my oral history interview with Betty Baer. The third force has been defined as "one or more nations, political parties, or other organizations occupying an intermediate position between two other opposed forces." *Random House Webster's College Dictionary* (New York: Random House, 1992), 1387, s.v. "third force."

2. Here I paraphrase Robert Burns. John Bartlett and Justin Kaplan, eds., *Bartlett's Familiar Quotations* (New York: Little, Brown and Company, 1992), 361, #6.

3. Noel A. Cazenave, "War on Poverty," in *Civil Rights in the United States*, ed. Waldo E. Martin and Patricia Sullivan, 776–77 (New York: Macmillan, 2000).

4. Those projects are the focus of my previous book, *Impossible Democracy: The Unlikely Success of the War on Poverty Community Action Programs* (Albany, NY: SUNY Press, 2007). See especially chapters 4 and 6.

5. Charles E. Silberman's *Crisis in Black and White* (New York: Vintage Books, 1964) was funded through a grant from the Public Affairs Program. Paul Ylvisaker directed for the Ford Foundation. Research by Charles Silberman on the City and the Negro, reel R0160, grant PA 62-416, sec. 1, 2, Program Action Form, Charles Silberman, July 26, 1962, Ford Foundation Archives. For more on the Ford Foundation funding of Silberman's book and how Silberman challenged what he considered to be the paternalism of the foundation's approach to community action, see Cazenave, *Impossible Democracy*, 35–37, 45, 198n23.

6. Silberman, *Crisis in Black and White*, 352. In his own book, Alan Talbot, who replaced Howard Hallman as the number-two person in the administration of CPI, recalled that "CPI countered his and similar criticisms with the argument that 'more meaningful' participation of the poor had been achieved through the establishment of strong neighborhood organizations and the hiring of large numbers of indigenous workers." Allan R. Talbot, *The Mayor's Game: Richard Lee of New Haven and the Politics of Change* (New York: Harper & Row, 1967), 218; Kenneth Matthews, "H. Hallman Quitting As CPI Deputy, Talbot to Get Executive Post," *New Haven Journal-Courier*, January 25, 1965.

7. Silberman, *Crisis in Black and White*, 38–39.

8. Ibid., 354–55. For more on Ylvisaker's views on community reform in general, and on acculturation theory and democratic theory in particular, see Cazenave, *Impossible Democracy*, 35–37.

9. Adam Yarmolinsky, Sargent Shriver's assistant during the planning of the War on Poverty, recalled that the Cahn and Cahn article was one "of the basic documents" that influenced that process. Adam Yarmolinsky, interview with

Michael L. Gillette, AC 82-21, 82-22, interview II, October 21, 1980, Lyndon Baines Johnson Library.

10. Here I refer to the official "publication date" cited on the article because I don't know when its journal issue was actually published. For example, it could have been released shortly before or shortly after President Johnson signed the Economic Opportunity Act of 1964 on August 20. Edgar S. Cahn and Jean C. Cahn, "The War on Poverty: A Civilian Perspective," *Yale Law Journal* 73, no. 8 (July 1964): 1317–52.

11. Clarence N. Stone, Robert K. Whelan, and William J. Murin, *Urban Policy and Politics in a Bureaucratic Age* (Englewood Cliffs, NJ: Prentice-Hall, 1986), 135–37.

12. For a more detailed discussion of the various conceptual points along this racism and public-policy continuum, see Kenneth J. Neubeck and Noel A. Cazenave, *Welfare Racism: Playing the Race Card Against America's Poor* (New York: Routledge, 2001), 221–22.

13. Cahn and Cahn, "War on Poverty," 1318.

14. Cazenave, *Impossible Democracy*, xi, 181.

15. Cahn and Cahn, "War on Poverty," 1320.

16. Ibid., 1322.

17. Ibid., 1326. Clarence N. Stone, "Race, Power, and Political Change," in *Power in the City: Clarence Stone and the Politics of Inequality*, ed. Marion Orr and Valerie C. Johnson, 161–84 (Lawrence: University Press of Kansas, 2008), esp. 162–64.

18. Cahn and Cahn, "War on Poverty," 1326, 1328.

19. Letter from Richard Oliver Brooks to Mr. James O. Freedman, December 7, 1964, 1, reel 2557, 62-328, Community Progress, Inc., 1962–1968, Ford Foundation Archives. On December 16, 1964 a copy was sent to Christopher Edley of the Ford Foundation. In my oral history interview with Mitchell Sviridoff decades later, he recalled that Brooks wrote that letter "entirely on his own" and not as an official response from CPI. Sviridoff also indicated that he thought Brooks "went to the other extreme" and that he would not have written that response to the Cahns' article. Mitchell Sviridoff, interview with author, March 24, 1992, 38. I believe Marris and Rein were correct in referring to Brooks' letter as "a semi-official reply to the Cahns' paper." Peter Marris and Martin Rein, *Dilemmas of Social Reform: Poverty and Community Action in the United States* (Chicago: University of Chicago Press, 1982), 175.

20. Letter from Brooks to Freedman, 2.

21. Ibid., 3–4.

22. Ibid., 4.

23. Ibid., 8–10.

24. Stone, "Race, Power, and Political Change," 162–64.

25. Yohuru Williams, *Black Politics/White Power: Civil Rights, Black Power, and the Black Panthers in New Haven* (St. James, NY: Brandywine Press, 2000), 50, 54, 62–63; Mandi Isaacs Jackson, *Model City Blues: Urban Space and Organized Resistance in New Haven* (Philadelphia: Temple University Press, 2008), 124.

26. Fred Harris, interview with author, July 9, 1992, 24–25; Williams, *Black Politics/White Power*, 71. Jackson indicates that Fred Harris and his wife, Rose,

were also concerned about "racism in the curriculum and in the classroom." Jackson, *Model City Blues*, 124.

27. Fred Harris, interview with author, 6–8.

28. Ibid., 8–10.

29. Richard Lee, interview with author, June 8, 1992, 24.

30. Williams, *Black Politics/White Power*, 69–70. Williams also noted that unlike the local NAACP and CORE chapters there was no national office HPA needed to answer to. So HPA could set its own agenda without fear that national officials might interfere because of pressure from Mayor Lee.

31. Walsh served as Mayor of Syracuse from 1962 through 1969. City of Syracuse, "Mayors of Syracuse, New York,"www.syracuse.ny.us/Mayors_of_Syracuse.aspx?ekmensel=9050e624_52_66_718_5.

32. James A. Tillman Jr. and Mary Norman Tillman, *Why America Needs Racism and Poverty: An Examination of the Group Exclusivity Compulsion in America as the Natural Enemy of Rational Social Change in Race and Poverty Relations* (n.p.: Four Winds, 1969), 206.

33. President's Committee on Juvenile Delinquency and Youth Crime, "Counter-Attack on Delinquency: The Program of the Federal Government to Stimulate Communities to Develop Rational Answers to a Growing Crisis," August 8, 1963, 69–70, Published Background Material 1961–1964, Daniel Knapp Papers, box 1, John F. Kennedy Library; Mayor's Commission for Youth, Inc., *Syracuse Action for Youth: An Action Program for Disadvantaged Youth* (Syracuse, NY: Mayor's Commission for Youth, Inc., 1964), I-7.

34. Letter from Mayor William F. Walsh to Mr. Irving G. Berman, April 10, 1964 in Mayor's Commission, *Syracuse Action for Youth*, iv.

35. Mayor's Commission for Youth, Inc., "Developing Youth Opportunities: A Planning Proposal, City Hall, Syracuse, New York," 10, Crusade for Opportunity Grants, 63002, application 5/11/62, Daniel Knapp Papers, box 19, John F. Kennedy Library.

36. President's Committee, "Counter-Attack on Delinquency," 70.

37. This included a $141,284 check and an additional $11,268 to be provided later. "Syracuse Given $141,284 for Delinquency Study," *Syracuse Post-Standard*, October 6, 1962, clipping from President's Committee on Juvenile Delinquency and Youth Crime, "A Newspaper History of the Federal Anti-Delinquency Program," Daniel Knapp Papers, box 1, Published Background Material 1961–1964, John F. Kennedy Library.

38. Mayor's Commission, *Syracuse Action for Youth*, title page.

39. Ibid., I-24, I-26.

40. Ben Zimmerman, interview with author, December 8, 1992, 3.

41. Mayor's Commission, *Syracuse Action for Youth*, viii, VII-2, 3–5, 9.

42. Ibid., VII-72.

43. Ibid., VII-86.

44. Ibid., viii, xii, I-12; Zoe Cornwall, *Human Rights in Syracuse: Two Memorable Decades, a Selected History from 1963 to 1983* (Syracuse, NY: Human Rights Commission of Syracuse and Onondaga County, 1987), 10–11.

45. "Planning Grant History Syracuse," n.d., 2–3, 5, Working Files, Daniel Knapp Papers, box 52, John F. Kennedy Library.

46. Mayor's Commission, *Syracuse Action for Youth*, VII-7.

47. Ibid., VII-9, 10. For more on Ohlin and Cottrell's positions with PCJD and their intellectual influence on its conceptualization of community action as well as the similarities and differences between that PCJD approach and Saul Alinsky's strategy and tactics, see Cazenave, *Impossible Democracy*, 38–45.

48. Mayor's Commission, *Syracuse Action for Youth*, VII-11.

49. Ibid., VII-12–14.

50. For more on this conundrum, which I refer to as impossible democracy, see Cazenave, *Impossible Democracy*, x, 133–34.

51. Baer, interview with author, 3–4.

52. Ibid., 4–5.

53. Daniel Knapp and Kenneth Polk, *Scouting the War on Poverty: Social Reform Politics in the Kennedy Administration* (Lexington, MA: Heath Lexington Books, 1971), 49, 171. This was their way of solving what I refer to as the "impossible democracy" dilemma of community action programs using federal government funds to sponsor social protest against city hall and other components of local power structures. Cazenave, *Impossible Democracy*, xi, 15.

54. "Summary of Minutes of Demonstration Projects Review Panel Meeting, May 13–16, 1964, Department of Health, Education, and Welfare, Welfare Administration, Office of Juvenile Delinquency and Youth Development," 11–13, 16, PCJD-OJD Background Materials, Minutes and Reports of Technical and Demonstration Review Panels 4/64–12/64, Daniel Knapp Papers, box 7, John F. Kennedy Library.

55. Robert S. Pickett, "The Genesis of the Community Action Training Center of Syracuse University: A Study of a City's Response to Community Development, 1962–1964," January 1967, 4–5, CATC, box 1, Community Action Training Center 1962–1964, George Arents Library, Syracuse University. Pickett concludes that "in the haste to get out the proposal, which due to its tremendous size, had come to be called the 'telephone book,' the mayor had signed it without reading it in detail" and notes that Mayor Walsh would later claim to have not read its community development section.

56. Knapp and Polk, *Scouting the War on Poverty*, 50.

57. Tillman and Tillman, *Why America*, 207.

58. Memorandum from Bernard Russell to Mr. Hackett, Mr. Ellinger, Dr. Kravitz, Dr. Frankel, Mr. Boone, and Mr. Lang, "Weekly Report—Syracuse," Department of Health, Education, and Welfare, Office of Juvenile Delinquency and Youth Development, PCJD-OJD Background Materials, Projects, Comprehensive Demonstrations, Syracuse, Daniel Knapp Papers, box 19, John F. Kennedy Library.

59. Jonathan Andrew Freedman, *A Sociological Approach to Rapid Change Conditions* (Ph.D. diss., Brandeis University, 1973; Ann Arbor, MI: University Microfilms, 1973), 248n3.

60. Knapp and Polk, *Scouting the War on Poverty*, 172.

61. Pickett, "Genesis of the Community Action Training Center," 4–5.

62. Zimmerman, interview with author, 16. As Zimmerman recalled, "Warren was only interested in the community development piece.... He really just wanted there to be a community development piece. He wanted an Alinsky program. So to that extent he was critical of what we were doing" (16).

63. Cazenave, *Impossible Democracy*, 2, 14–15.
64. "A Proposal for a Community Development, Demonstration, Training and Research Project. Submitted to the Office of Economic Opportunity Community Action Program by Syracuse University," December 7, 1964, 1–2, CATC, box 6, George Arents Library. The proposal consists of thirty-six pages plus a three-page personnel appendix.
65. Ibid., 12–14, 16.
66. Knapp and Polk, *Scouting the War on Poverty*, 173–74.
67. Pickett, "Genesis of the Community Action Training Center," 13, 31–33.
68. Memorandum from Clifford L. Winters Jr. to Vice President Clark Ahlberg, "Memorandum on Events, Social [sic] Action Training Center," January 25, 1965, 3, CATC, box 6—Correspondence, Washington 1966, George Arents Library, Syracuse University; Pickett, "Genesis of the Community Action Training Center," 1, 6; Erwin Knoll and Julis Witcover, "Fighting Poverty—and City Hall," *The Reporter*, June 3, 1965, 19. Knapp and Polk, *Scouting the War on Poverty*, 176.
69. Knapp and Polk, *Scouting the War on Poverty*, 174.
70. For a discussion of the treatment of African Americans and their concerns by Syracuse's major newspapers, see chapter 6 of Cornwall, *Human Rights in Syracuse*, 62–70. For example, it is noted in that commission history that because "the media in Syracuse was owned and run by whites and presented the white perspective," African Americans had to lure "the press into covering events that might otherwise have been ignored" (62).
71. Cartoon editorial, "No Way to Fight a War!!!," *Syracuse Herald-Journal*, February 7, 1965, clipping from CATC, box 1, George Arents Library, Syracuse University.
72. "War on Poverty Enlists More High Price Generals Then Low Paid Non Coms," *Syracuse Herald-Journal*, February 2, 1965, clipping from CATC, box 1, George Arents Library, Syracuse University.
73. Pickett, "Genesis of the Community Action Training Center," 9.
74. "S.U.'s Own Anti-Poverty War . . . Who Approved for Community?" *Syracuse Herald American*, February 21, 1965, clipping from CATC, box 1, George Arents Library, Syracuse University.
75. Pickett, "Genesis of the Community Action Training Center," 26.
76. Baer, interview with author, 23–24.
77. Bill Hutchinson, "Haggstrom 'Intolerant' CATC Leader Criticized," *Syracuse Post-Standard*, December 3, 1965, clipping from CATC, box 6, Newspaper Clippings, George Arents Library, Syracuse University.
78. Eleanor Rosebrugh, "9 Groups Vote Fight for CATC," *Syracuse Post-Standard*, December 3, 1965, clipping from CATC, box 6, Newspaper Clippings, George Arents Library, Syracuse University.
79. "SCDA Knock Crusade," *Syracuse Herald-Journal*, December 8, 1965, clipping from CATC, box 6, News Clippings, George Arents Library, Syracuse University.
80. Eve Edstrom, "An Outside Viewpoint . . . CATC Impact Flops. Crusade to Try," *Syracuse Herald American/Post-Standard*, November 28, 1965, 58.
81. "Crusaders: Not City Hall Tool," *Syracuse Post-Standard*, December 3, 1965, 5.
82. Winters also asserted that Shriver was seeking such a compromise "way out" to fund the project. Letter from Clifford L. Winters Jr. to Warren

Haggstrom, December 19, 1966, Community Action Training Center, CATC, box 6—Haggstrom, Warren Memos to and from (Second Grant), December 1966 and December 1967 Letters, George Arents Library, Syracuse University. When asked whether he believed CFO would have funded a SCDA proposal, Ben Zimmerman responded, "Yes, without a doubt." Ben Zimmerman, March 1966, 2, CATC, box 3—Interviews Conducted by Inez Heard, March and April 1966, George Arents Library, Syracuse University.

83. Alfred Friendly, "Who Talks for Poor . . . Ventriloquists?" *Syracuse Journal-Herald*, January 11, 1966, clipping from CATC, box 1—CATC News Clippings, George Arents Library, Syracuse University.

84. Office of Economic Opportunity Administrative History, vol. 1, "The Syracuse Situation," 86–87, 91, Lyndon Baines Johnson Library; "Powell to Blast Shriver on CATC," *Syracuse Herald-Journal*, December 9, 1965, 27; Robert E. Baker, "OEO Switches Policy on Syracuse Project," *Washington Post*, December 2, 1965, clipping from CATC, box 6—Newspaper Clippings, George Arents Library, Syracuse University.

85. "Powell to Blast Shriver," 27.

86. An article in a local Syracuse newspaper concluded that "perhaps it was not so much pressure from a Republican mayor in Syracuse that led to a reversal of top policy in the OEO as it was fear in the White House of possible CATC upheavals in Democratically-controlled cities." "End of Bad Program? Democrats Fear CATC," *Syracuse Post-Standard*, December 2, 1965, clipping from CATC, box 6—Newspaper Clippings, George Arents Library, Syracuse University.

87. Richard F. Long, "Syracusans Detail Fund Shift Protest," *Syracuse Post-Standard*, December 8, 1965, clipping from CATC, box 6—News Clippings, George Arents Library, Syracuse University.

88. OEO Administrative History, 87, 91.

89. Robert S. Pickett, interview with author, June 23, 1992, 11–13.

90. Ibid., 13–14.

91. Clifford Winters, interview with author, October 20, 1992, 25–26.

92. Mary Norman Tillman, interview with author, October 22, 1992, 4–5.

93. Ibid., 7–8.

94. Ibid., 5–6.

NOTES TO CHAPTER 4

1. Zoe Cornwall, *Human Rights in Syracuse: Two Memorable Decades, A Selected History from 1963 to 1983* (Syracuse: Human Rights Commission of Syracuse and Onondaga County, 1989), 46.

2. Joe R. Feagin, *The New Urban Paradigm: Critical Perspectives on the City* (Lanham, MD: Rowman and Littlefield, 1998), 2.

3. Manuel Castells, *The City and the Grassroots: A Cross-Cultural Theory of Urban Social Movements* (Berkley: University of California Press, 1983), xviii, 49.

4. Carter A. Wilson, *Racism: From Slavery to Advanced Capitalism* (Thousand Oaks, CA: Sage, 1996), 16, 20, 165.

5. Aldon Morris and Naomi Braine, "Social Movements and Oppositional Consciousness," in *Oppositional Consciousness: The Subjective Roots of Social Protest*, ed. Jane Mansbridge and Aldon Morris, 20–37 (Chicago: University of Chicago Press, 2001), esp. 23, 25–26, 29; Jane Mansbridge, "The Making of Oppositional Consciousness," in Mansbridge and Morris, *Oppositional Consciousness*, 1–19.

6. Activism within CFO was limited largely to the participation- and control-focused challenges involving CFO administrators, board members, staff, and action-area residents within the project's governance boards, rather than protests directed at external components of the local white power structure.

7. Similar to the point I made in the previous note regarding CFO's rather narrow brand of activism, these "protests" consisted mostly of various extraordinary and dramatic procedural maneuvers by action-area residents to win control of the project's board, as well as whatever public skirmishes accrued from them.

8. Noel A. Cazenave, *Impossible Democracy: The Unlikely Success of the War on Poverty Community Action Programs* (Albany, NY: SUNY Press, 2007), 141.

9. Erwin Knoll, "Shriver Mayors Make Up: Role of Poor Limited in War," *Syracuse Herald-Journal*, January 17, 1966, 4; Cazenave, *Impossible Democracy*, 153.

10. Robert Fisher, *Let the People Decide: Neighborhood Organizing in America* (Boston: Twayne, 1984), 117; Cazenave, *Impossible Democracy*, 167, 242–43n154.

11. August Meier and Elliot Rudwick, *CORE: A Study in the Civil Rights Movement, 1942–1968* (Urbana: University of Illinois Press, 1975), 358, 364.

12. Keesing's Research Report, *Race Relations in the USA, 1954–68* (New York: Charles Scribner's Sons, 1970), 227.

13. Richard G. Case, "CATC Gets Last U.S. Handout: S.U. Program for Organizing Poor Will Be Phased Out," *Syracuse Herald-Journal*, March 30, 1966, clipping from CATC, box 1—News Clippings, George Arents Library, Syracuse University.

14. Crusade for Opportunity news release, July 7, 1966, CATC, box 7, Crusade for Opportunity Board Meeting, 1965–1966, George Arents Library, Syracuse University.

15. Lawrence Davis, "Syracuse: What Happens When the Poor Take Over," *Reporter*, March 21, 1968, 19.

16. James Tillman could probably best be described as what Dora Pantell and Edwin Greenidge refer to as a "moderate black militant." Not only were these moderate black militants of the mid- and late 1960s who were committed to working to improve conditions within black ghettos opposed to both the separatism and violence of the "black extremists," but unlike both black extremists and "the traditional moderate Negro," their "moderate militant movement" saw the solution to "the 'Negro problem'" as militantly working "within the existing structure of American society." This included using the resources provided by the War on Poverty community action programs to engage "the black ghetto resident in working out his own destiny" generally and more specifically in regard to those programs "to develop indigenous leadership, operation, and control." Dora Pantell and Edwin Greenidge, *If Not Now, When? The Many Meanings of Black Power* (New York: Dell Publishing Company, 1969), 5–6, 9.

17. Eleanor Rosebrugh, "Report Ignores Problems: Crusade Praises Achievements," *Syracuse Post-Standard*, January 23, 1967, clipping from CATC, box 1, George Arents Library, Syracuse University.

18. James A. Tillman and Mary Norman Tillman, *Why America Needs Racism and Poverty: An Examination of the Exclusivity Compulsion in America as the Natural Enemy of Rational Social Change in Race and Poverty Relations* (n.p.: Four Winds, 1969), 167, 170 (emphasis original). Although the fact that some of the existing publications in which Tillman's own words survive are sketchy, when existent at all, can be explained to some extent by his desire to work behind the scenes while the poor spoke for themselves—the Tillmans' book, for example, was not published until two years after James Tillman left CFO—it is important to note that Tillman's account also went unreported in a local history of human rights in Syracuse that was published decades later in 1989. See chapter 4 of Cornwall, *Human Rights in Syracuse*; Morris and Braine, "Social Movements," 25–26; Mansbridge, "Making of Oppositional Consciousness," 1.

19. Tillman and Tillman, *Why America Needs Racism*, 184–85.

20. Ibid., vii, viii, 3.

21. Ibid., 6.

22. Ibid., 9-10. The Tillmans' reform vision fit what Omi and Winant refer to as "political projects" that drive "racial movements." Such projects are formulated by "intellectuals" who "seek to transform (or rearticulate) the dominant racial ideology," often through the way that social problems are conceptualized. Michael Omi and Howard Winant, *Racial Formation in the United States: From the 1960s to the 1990s* (New York: Routledge, 1994), 86.

23. Tillman and Tillman, *Why America Needs Racism*, 10–11.

24. Davis, "Syracuse," 20.

25. Tillman and Tillman, *Why America Needs Racism*, 212.

26. Cornwall, *Human Rights in Syracuse*, 42.

27. Ibid.

28. Tillman and Tillman, *Why America Needs Racism*, 208–10, 212, 214–15 (emphasis original). As evidence of the success of Tillman's efforts to increase the involvement of action-area residents in CFO, the Tillmans noted that whereas only 12 percent of those eligible voted in CFO's neighborhood board elections in 1965, that number increased to 22 percent in October of 1966, a rate they indicated the Office of Economic Opportunity touted as the highest for any city in the nation.

29. Ibid., 173.

30. Ibid., 174–75 (emphasis original).

31. Mary Norman Tillman, interview with author, October 22, 1992, 14–15.

32. Ibid., 15–16.

33. Eleanor Rosebrugh, "Poor Seek Control: CFO Board Choices Challenged," January 23, 1967, *Syracuse Post-Standard*, clipping from CATC, box 1, George Arents Library, Syracuse University.

34. Ibid.

35. Tillman and Tillman, *Why America Needs Racism*, 239, 241.

36. "Poor Must Be Heard. But CFO Takeover Is Unwise," *Syracuse Post-Standard*, January 24, 1967; "Power Clash in Crusade," January 25, 1967, Syracuse Herald-Journal, from catg box 1, George Arents Library, Syracuse University.

37. Eleanor Rosebrugh, "Norman Hill Elected Chairman of Crusade: Anti-Poverty Group Meet Has SRO Crowd," *Syracuse Post-Standard*, January 26, 1967, 8; Sandra Hughes, "Neighborhood People Win Battle for Crusade Control," *Syracuse*

Herald-Journal, January 26, 1967, clipping from CATC, box 1, George Arents Library, Syracuse University; Davis, "Syracuse," 20.

38. Hughes, "Neighborhood People Win."
39. Tillman and Tillman, *Why America Needs Racism*, 241.
40. Ibid.
41. Noel A. Cazenave and Darlene Alvarez Maddern, "Defending the White Race: White Male Faculty Opposition to a 'White Racism' Course," *Race and Society* 2, no. 1 (1999): 26–27, 40–41.
42. Clifford Winters, interview with author, October 20, 1992, 14.
43. Norman Hill, interview with author, June 22, 1992, 13.
44. Ibid., 17.
45. Davis, "Syracuse," 20; Cornwall, *Human Rights in Syracuse*, 47.
46. Hill, interview with author, 2, 5–6. At the time Hill was elected chairman of the Crusade for Opportunity board, he was a recently discharged twenty-seven-year-old Vietnam War veteran who had become involved with a CFO neighborhood center and as a member of a neighborhood board.
47. Davis, "Syracuse," 20. Eleanor Rosebrugh, "21 Quit Crusade after Chairman's Action: Hill Tells Member to 'Shut Up,'" *Syracuse Post-Standard*, June 15, 1967, 1.
48. Davis, "Syracuse," 20.
49. Rosebrugh, "21 Quit Crusade," 1; Davis, "Syracuse," 20–21.
50. Ernest L. Boston, interview with author, July 23, 1992, 5, 24–25.
51. Cazenave, *Impossible Democracy*, 150–51.
52. William Walsh, interview with author, June 24, 1992, 22.
53. Davis, "Syracuse," 21.
54. Cazenave, *Impossible Democracy*, 153, 166–67.
55. Cornwall, *Human Rights in Syracuse*, 47–48.
56. Davis, "Syracuse," 21; Tillman and Tillman, *Why America Needs Racism*, 233.
57. Davis, "Syracuse," 20.

NOTES TO CHAPTER 5

1. Letter to Mayor Richard Lee, August 20, 1967, Richard Charles Lee Papers (MS 318), box 87, folder 1570, Manuscripts and Archives, Yale University Library. I deleted the name and address of the person who sent the letter.
2. Clarence N. Stone, Robert K. Whelan, and William J. Murin, *Urban Policy and Politics in a Bureaucratic Age* (Englewood Cliffs, NJ: Prentice Hall, 1986), 75.
3. Ibid., 137.
4. Letter from Clifford J. Campbell to Paul N. Ylvisaker, June 15, 1966, 5–6, reel 2557, 62-328, Mid-4, Ford Foundation Archives.
5. Earl Williams, interview with author, June 6, 1992, 9.
6. Edwin Edmonds, interview with author, June 8, 1992, 13.
7. Richard Belford, interview with author, June 9, 1992, 2, 19.
8. Russell D. Murphy, *Political Entrepreneurs and Urban Poverty: The Strategies of Policy Innovation in New Haven's Model Anti-Poverty Project* (Lexington, MA: Heath Lexington Books, 1971), 16, table 2-3, 22, table 2-5.

9. Richard Balzer, *Street Time: Text Based Conversations with Fred Harris* (New York: Grossman, 1972), 12; Yohuru Williams, *Black Politics/White Power: Civil Rights, Black Power, and the Black Panthers in New Haven* (St. James, NY: Brandywine Press, 2000), 70–71.

10. Williams, *Black Politics/White Power*, 68–69.

11. Ibid., 70; Fred Powledge, *Model City: A Test of American Liberalism; One Town's Efforts to Rebuild Itself* (New York: Simon Schuster, 1970), 155–56.

12. Williams, *Black Politics/White Power*, 70.

13. Balzer, *Street Time*, 13.

14. Williams, *Black Politics/White Power*, 74.

15. In the 1960 census, African Americans made up 13 percent of the Hill's population. Murphy, *Political Entrepreneurs*, 16, table 2-3. However, that statistic underestimates the extent of racial ghettoization in the Hill because, as Powledge notes, within the Hill, there was significant racial segregation within census tracts. Powledge, *Model City*, 115.

16. Raymond E. Wolfinger, *The Politics of Progress* (Englewood Cliffs, NJ: Prentice-Hall, 1974), 201.

17. Balzer, *Street Time*, 24.

18. Powledge, *Model City*, 162–63.

19. Harris also recalled that it was CPI neighborhood workers who suggested they submit a proposal. Fred Harris, interview with author, July 9, 1992, 27; Balzer, *Street Time*, 24.

20. I mean "radical" only in relative political terms. I am not suggesting that these grassroots activists were political revolutionaries.

21. Balzer, *Street Time*, 24, 26–27.

22. Ibid., 25.

23. U.S. Congress, "Investigation into the Operations of Community Progress, Inc.," 90th Cong., 2nd sess., *Congressional Record*, vol. 114, pt. 1, January 15–29, 1968 (Washington, DC: U.S. Government Printing Office, 1968), 167.

24. Harris, interview with author, 27.

25. Balzer, *Street Time*, 26.

26. Keesing's Research Report, *Race Relations in the USA, 1954–1968* (New York: Charles Scribner's Sons, 1970), 219, 227. The owner of the restaurant who did the shooting was identified as being "white" in the chronological narrative of those events prepared by the city's Commission on Equal Opportunities. Commission on Equal Opportunities, "Narrative Concerning the Disturbances in New Haven Beginning August 19, 1967," 1. A copy of this report was given to me by Richard Belford, the CEO executive director at that time.

27. For example, one author noted that whereas Mayor Lee and others referred to it as a "disturbance," "white radicals" deemed it a "riot," and "black militants" called it a "rebellion." Powledge, *Model City*, 113.

28. *Report of the National Advisory Commission on Civil Disorders* (New York: Bantam Books, 1968), 286.

29. Ibid., 286, 308.

30. A common racist stereotype in the United States is that of African Americans as apes or other animals who inhabit places that are so plagued with violence and other uncivilized behavior that they are more like jungles than neighbor-

hoods. Apelike images have frequently been evoked by European American critics of President Obama.

31. "Investigation into the Operations of Community Progress," 164; James Mutrie Jr., "Giaimo Calls CPI Failure; Raps Salaries, Expenses, Warns City is Nearing 'Jungle Law,'" *New Haven Register*, January 2, 1968, 1, 37.

32. Powledge, *Model City*, 164, 166.

33. Commission, "Narrative Concerning the Disturbances," 1.

34. Belford, interview with author, 11.

35. Commission, "Narrative Concerning the Disturbances," 5, 7–8.

36. Ibid., 11–12.

37. Ibid., 14, 17–18.

38. Ibid., 19–21.

39. Ibid., 24–26.

40. Ibid., 26, 30–32.

41. Williams, *Black Politics/White Power*, 87. Belford recalled the transfer of his deputy director, who would later become New Haven's first African American mayor, to another city agency as an example of how Mayor Lee had begun to withdraw his support from the agency. Belford, interview with author, 12–13. In his study of New Haven, Powledge quotes Belford as saying that Lee told him "that it was my job as executive director to quote keep down people like Harris." And regarding what might be referred to as the URS administration function of CEO Belford stated that it "was intended for us to be window-dressing, a showcase to look as if we're providing equal opportunities, but really as a pacifying agency so we can absorb the shock of any kind of protest without embarrassing the city." Powledge, *Model City*, 182.

42. Williams notes that, "throughout 1968, New Haven's city fathers sought to minimize the damage of the city's riot. It was referred to as a nonracial disturbance perpetrated by a few miscreants not representative of New Haven's mostly peaceful minority population." For example, the city's police department noted the involvement of European Americans in the civil disturbance to discount the view that its participants were overwhelmingly African American. Williams, *Black Politics/White Power*, 84, 87.

43. Richard Lee, interview with author. June 8, 1992, 28.

44. "Human Story: 1967. Annual Report of Community Progress, Inc," reel 2559, 62-328, Mid-5, p. i, Ford Foundation Archives.

45. Ibid., ii.

46. Ibid.

47. Robert Kilpatrick and Robert A. Jordon, "Real Causes Deep-Rooted, Most Agree," *New Haven Register*, August 21, 1967, 1 2.

48. Fred Harris, interview with author, 28.

49. Statement by Hill Parents Association, August 24, 1967, Richard Charles Lee Papers (MS 318), box 87, folder 1570, Manuscripts and Archives, Yale University Library.

50. Ibid.

51. Balzer, *Street Time*, 35.

52. Letter to Mayor Lee, August 1967[?], Richard Charles Lee Papers (MS 318), box 87, folder 1570, Manuscripts and Archives, Yale University Library.

53. Ibid.

54. Gail Sheehy, *Panthermania: The Clash of Black against Black in One American City* (New York: Harper and Row, 1971), 86–87.

55. Stephen Hand, "'Black Men' Attack CPI," *New Haven Journal-Courier*, October 3, 1967, 1.

56. Balzer, *Street Time*, 38.

57. Ibid., 39; Powledge, *Model City*, 172; Williams, *Black Politics/White Power*, 88.

58. Louis Althusser, "Idealogy and Ideological State Apparatus (Notes Toward an Investigation)," in Lenin and Philosophy and Other Essays (New York: Monthly Review Press, 1971), 127–86. *Commission on Civil Disorders*, 308.

59. Williams concludes that Mayor Lee ignored community complaints about the police and completely turned matters over to them. Williams, *Black Politics/White Power*, 88–89. Green and Cheney reported that there was speculation in the city at that time that Mayor Lee was hands-off when it came to the behavior of the police due to a political debt he owed New Haven's police chief. Peter M. Green and Ruth A. Cheney, "Urban Planning and Urban Revolt: A Case Study," *Progressive Architecture* 49 (January 1968): 143.

60. "Report of the Committee to Enumerate Harassment and Repression as Presented to the Rally Sponsored by the Coalition of Concerned Citizens, November 5, 1967," 1. Copy of document given to author by Richard Belford.

61. Ibid., 1–2. In specific reference to CPI, the report charged that programs being designed with maximum feasible participation of project-area residents were a rarity. Instead, CPI "jealously" guarded "its own control" of the programs it administered in "an atmosphere of paternalism" and "mutual hostility between CPI and grassroots people" (4).

62. Ibid., 2–6; Powledge, *Model City*, 172–73.

63. Harris, interview with author, 20–21.

64. During our interview Harris noted in explaining why he didn't remember some things, "I was on drugs at that time. I was a heroin addict." Ibid., 20. In another interview Harris indicated that "before I started with HPA, when I was out on the West Coast, I had been on stuff. But I hadn't tried to hide it, I admitted it before I began working with HPA." Balzer, *Street Wise*, 41. Green and Cheney stated that Harris's supporters and others were suspicious of the police arrest of Harris at that time because the Lee administration claimed to have known that Harris had been addicted to heroin for two years. Green and Cheney, "Urban Planning," 154.

65. Ibid., 140.

66. Paul von Zielbauer, "Richard C. Lee, 86, Mayor Who Revitalized New Haven," *New York Times*, February 4, 2003.

67. Fred Powledge, "The Flight From City Hall: Four Mayors Who Aren't Running Again," *Harper's*, November 1969, 76, 79. Hugh Price, the then-current leader of New Haven's Black Coalition, rooted what he saw as Mayor Lee's "downfall," especially as a national leader, in the fact that despite the excellent job he had previously done as mayor his "political style was such that he wasn't able to make the shift into the mid-Sixties." Powledge, *Model Cities*, 207–8.

68. For example, in his oral history interview with me, after having initially concluded that the HPA leadership "didn't do anything which was positive," Mayor Lee qualified that statement by saying, "maybe they had the establishment stop and rethink the past, and the way they were going." Lee, interview with author, 28.

69. "Human Story: 1967," iii.

70. Letter from Clifford J. Campbell, August 7, 1967, 1–2, reel 2557, 62-328, sec. 1, Ford Foundation Archives. Because I was not able to find an actual copy of the report during my archives research, I have relied on newspaper accounts of its contents.

71. "Ford and CPI Sit on Report," *New Haven Register*, March 24, 1968, clipping from reel 2557-2560, 62-328, sec. 1, Ford Foundation Archives.

72. Donald Dallas, "Ford Report on CPI Asks Stronger Effort, Resident Involvement," *New Haven Register*, March 24, 1968, 1, 3.

73. Ibid., 3.

74. Ibid.

75. Ibid.

76. Ibid.

77. Memorandum from Clifford J. Campbell to S. M. Miller, January 4, 1968, 1, reel 2257, 62-328, sec. 1, Ford Foundation Archives. Miller was a member of the review team Campbell chaired that visited the CPI project in June.

78. Ibid., 2. Sviridoff was reported to have suggested that with his skills to work with the social changes that were then occurring things would have turned out better for CPI had he remained its head. Powledge, *Model Cities*, 331–32. I don't think what you have seen about Sviridoff's leadership style, program philosophy, and relationships with outspoken African Americans supports that claim.

79. Lawrence Spitz, interview with author, October 20, 1992, 35.

80. For an informative analysis of the social movement consequences of such divided loyalties, see Lori G. Waite, "Divided Consciousness: The Impact of Black Elite Consciousness on the 1966 Chicago Freedom Movement," in *Oppositional Consciousness: The Subjective Roots of Social Protest*, ed. Jane Mansbridge and Aldon Morris, 170–203 (Chicago: University of Chicago Press, 2001), esp. 171, 174–75.

81. Wolfinger, *Politics of Progress*, 73.

82. Robert A. Jordon, "Ex-Employee Asks Reorganization, CPI Tagged 'Inevitable Failure,'" *New Haven Register*, January 22, 1968, 36.

83. Frank Donegan, "CPI Castigated on Staff Politics by Ex-Employee," *New Haven Journal-Courier*, January 22, 1968, clipping from reel 2259, 62-328, Mid-5, Ford Foundation Archives.

84. Ibid.

85. Edmonds, interview with author, 13, 18–19.

86. Paul Bass and Douglas W. Rae, *Murder in the Model City: The Black Panthers, Yale and the Redemption of a Killer* (New York: Basic Books, 2006), 52.

87. Ibid.

88. Balzar, *Street Wise*, 45.

89. Powledge, *Model City*, 206–7.

90. Letter from Lawrence Spitz to Mitchell Sviridoff, reel 2557, 62-328, sec. 1, Ford Foundation Archives; Keesing's, *Race Relations in the USA*, 262.

91. Spitz, interview with author, 22.

92. Powledge, *Model City*, 204–5.

93. "Black Coalition Explains Plans for CPI Phase Out," March 2, 1968, clipping from MSS B 61, Community Progress, Inc., New Haven Records, 1962–1976, Newspaper Clippings, New Haven Colony Historical Society.

94. Dallas, "Ford Report on CPI," 3.

95. Donald Dallas, "Want Full Control, Negro Groups Draft Plan to Take Over Jobs Funds," *New Haven Register*, March 27, 1968, 1–2. As part of that consortium arrangement, CPI would also have a vote, as would another Hill-area organization, and in the case of a tie, the Black Coalition would cast the deciding vote.

96. Powledge, *Model City*, 264–65.

97. Williams, *Black Politics/White Power*, 75.

98. Robert Kilpatrick, "CPI Directors Seeking to Determine Exact Role for Neighborhood Workers," *New Haven Register*, September 21, 1967, clipping from MSS B 61, Community Progress, Inc., New Haven Records, 1962–1976, Newspaper Clippings, New Haven Colony Historical Society.

99. "Neighborhood Units, Resigning Spitz, CPI Board Urge Breaking Up Agency," *New Haven Register*, May 2, 1968, 1–2.

100. Donald Dallas, "Downey Tells Professional Men: Neighborhood Control Concept Needs Public Support," *New Haven Journal-Courier*, December 16, 1968, 1.

101. James Mann, "CPI Changes: 3 Effects," *New Haven Journal-Courier*, December 17, 1968, 1, 4; James Mann, "Mostly in Talk Stage, CPI Decentralization Bogged," *New Haven Journal-Courier*, December 16, 1968, 1, 21.

102. James Mann, "Spitz Raps CPI 'Spin-Off' Timetable," *New Haven Journal-Courier*, December 18, 1968, 1, 5.

103. Jonathan Bunge, "The Movement to Decentralize Social Services in New Haven in the Late 1960s" (paper delivered at New Haven Seminar, New Haven Colony Historical Society, December 14, 1983), 6–7, 10, 12–13.

104. "Jefferys Picked as President of CPI Directors," *New Haven Register*, June 11, 1968, clipping from CPI Clippings, New Haven Free Public Library.

105. William J. Jecusco, "Brown Seeking Top CPI Post," *New Haven Journal-Courier*, May 9, 1968, 4; Mark Melady, "Brown Chosen as New CPI Director," *New Haven Journal-Courier*, June 21, 1968, 1, 19.

106. Jack Millea, "CPI is Dead," *New Haven Register*, October 6, 1976, 72. Two years later the City of New Haven Board of Aldermen finally got its way in setting up its own antipoverty program when it established a new private, not-for-profit, antipoverty agency, which still exists today, called the Community Action Agency of New Haven. See www.caanh.net.

NOTES TO CHAPTER 6

1. Christopher Cooper, "Old-Line Families Escape Worst of the Flood and Plot the Future; Mr. O'Dwyer, at His Mansion, Enjoys Highball with Ice; Meeting with the Mayor" *Wall Street Journal*, September 8, 2005.

2. Michael Goldfield, *The Color of Politics: Race and the Mainsprings of American Politics* (New York: New Press, 1997), 311–12.

3. I am not suggesting that during this period the Democrats were not adept at finding ways to exploit white racist sentiments to their political advantage. For cogent examples of Democrats' exploitation of white racism, see Goldfield's discussion of how Jimmy Carter appealed to white racist sentiments in both his gubernatorial and presidential campaigns, and Neubeck and Cazenave's reference to President Clinton's skillful playing of the race card with his 1992 campaign promise to "end welfare as we know it." Goldfield, *Color of Politics*, 8, 313–14; Kenneth J. Neubeck and Noel A. Cazenave, *Welfare Racism: Playing the Race Card against America's Poor* (New York: Routledge, 2001), 4.

4. Goldfield, *Color of Politics*, 314.

5. Ibid., 8, 316. Manning Marable, *Race, Reform, and Rebellion: The Second Reconstruction and Beyond in Black America, 1945–2006* (Jackson: University Press of Mississippi, 2007), 236, 246.

6. Marable, *Race, Reform, and Rebellion*, 221.

7. W. E. B. DuBois, *The Souls of Black Folk: Essays and Sketches* (Greenwich, CT: Fawcett, 1961), vii.

8. Jack Newfield, *The Full Rudy: The Man, the Myth, the Mania* (New York: Thunder Mouth/Nation, 2002), 69. Newfield quotes a 1996 newspaper article that reported that while the number of European American males that worked in city agencies under the mayor's control increased, slightly since Giuliani assumed office the number of African Americans employed there decreased by 4,632.

9. Ibid., 67.

10. Wayne Barrett, *Rudy! An Investigative Biography of Rudolph Giuliani* (New York: Basic Books, 2000), 328–29.

11. Carrie Melago, "Big City Payout, Few Convictions in Other NYPD Cases before Bell," *New York Daily News*, April 27, 2008.

12. Andrew Kirtzman, *Rudy Giuliani: Emperor of the City* (New York: William Morrow, 2000), 204–5.

13. Ibid., 205–6.

14. Ibid.

15. Ibid., 206–7.

16. Ibid.

17. Ibid.

18. Henry Goldman, "The Trial to Open for 5 N.Y. Officers in Attack on Immigrant. They are Accused of Beating and Sodomizing a Haitian at a Police Station. The Case Spurred a Backlash against the Police and the Mayor," *Philadelphia Inquirer*, May 4, 1999.

19. Melago, "Big City Payout."

20. Michael Cooper, "Officer Acquitted in Squeegee Man's Shooting," *New York Times*, July 9, 1999.

21. Patrice O'Shaughnessy, "Squeezee Man Goes Home," *New York Daily News*, June 28, 1998.

22. Cooper, "Officer Acquitted."

23. Howard Chua-Eoan, "Black and Blue," *Time*, March 6, 2000, 24, 26.

24. Byrna J. Fireside, *The Trial of the Police Officers in the Shooting Death of Amadou Diallo: A Headline Court Case* (Berkeley Heights, NJ: Enslow, 2004), 7.

25. Ibid., 8–9, 13.

26. Ibid., 7.
27. Ibid., 12, 16.
28. Kirtzman, *Rudy Giuliani*, 247; Barrett, *Rudy!* 291.
29. Kirtzman, *Rudy Giuliani*, 249.
30. Melago, "Big City Payout."
31. Barrett, *Rudy!* 332.
32. Eric Lipton, "Giuliani Cites Criminal Past of Slain Man," *New York Times*, March 20, 2000.
33. Mark Riley, "You'll Kill Us All, Blacks Taunt NY Police," *Sydney Morning Herald* (Australia), March 21, 2000; Kirtzman, *Rudy Giuliani*, 273.
34. Kirtzman, *Rudy Giuliani*, 273–74. Kirtzman states that Giuliani's aides and other supporters urged him to show more compassion in his handling of the Dorismond shooting, but Giuliani felt reaffirmed in his position to stand firm in support of the police by the Diallo shooting verdict. Another Giuliani biographer reported that the NYPD "ransacked" Amadou Diallo's apartment after he was killed to find any information that might be used to discredit him. Barrett, *Rudy!* 330.
35. Lipton, "Giuliani Cites Criminal Past."
36. Newfield, *Full Rudy*, 115. The only actual convictions in Dorismond's public record were for two disorderly conduct charges he faced as an adult. Lipton, "Giuliani Cites Criminal Past."
37. Lipton, "Giuliani Cites Criminal Past." Not only had Dorismond been an altar boy; he had attended the same Catholic high school as had Giuliani. Newfield, *Full Rudy*, 115.
38. Newfield, *Full Rudy*, 115.
39. Brent Staples, "Editorial Observer: The Mayor Can Defuse the Dorismond Case," *New York Times*, March 25, 2000.
40. Joe Mahoney, "Gov Apology in Cop Shoot: Says Sorry to Dorismond Mom," *New York Daily News*, June 7, 2000.
41. There were other expressions of concern at the New York state racial state level. For example, by the end of that month, a joint public hearing of three state assembly committees examined whether Mayor Giuliani violated state law by having his police commissioner release Dorismond juvenile arrest record. New York State Assembly, Assembly Standing Committee on Codes, Assembly Standing Committee on Judiciary, Assembly Standing Committee on Children and Families, *Joint Public Hearing to Consider Potential Violations of New York State Law Committed in Connection with the Apparent Review and Release of Information from Sealed Records Following the Death of Patrick Dorismond* (Mineola, NY: En-De Reporting Services, 2000).
42. Kirtzman, *Rudy Giuliani*, 276; Editorial Desk, "Lessons from the Dorismond Funeral," *New York Times*, March 28, 2000.
43. Kirtzman, *Rudy Giuliani*, 276.
44. William Glaberson, "City Settles Suit in Guard's Death by Police Bullet," *New York Times*, March 13, 2003.
45. Tim Wise, *Between Barack and a Hard Place: Racism and White Denial in the Age of Obama* (San Francisco, CA: City Lights Books, 2009), 26. Wise's book also provides a good critique of the claim that the Obama win signified the end of racism in the United States.

46. Urban regime theory is a body of urban politics political science literature advanced by the work of Clarence Stone that has focused on the dominance of business interests in urban coalitions. See Marion Orr and Valerie C. Johnson, "Power and Local Democracy, Clarence N. Stone and American Political Science," in *Power in the City: Clarence Stone and the Politics of Inequality*, ed. Marion Orr and Valerie C. Johnson, 1–30 (Lawrence: University of Kansas Press, 2008); Clarence N. Stone. "Urban Regimes and the Capacity to Govern: A Political Economy Approach," in Orr and Johnson, *Power in the City*, 76–107. Adolph Reed Jr. applies urban regime theory specifically to the conundrum I discuss that many African American mayors face in trying to balance the needs and aspirations of economically struggling African Americans against the often diametrically opposed economic and political agendas of the largely European American business elites. See Adolph Reed Jr., "The Black Urban Regime: Structural Origins and Constraints," in *Power, Community and the City*, Volume 1, ed. Michel Peter Smith, 138–89 (New Brunswick, NJ: Transaction Books, 1988). As I will discuss later in comparing how the political and economic elite of Atlanta and New Orleans made very different strategic decisions about business, politics, and race relations, there is literature that suggests that because of its extreme political, economic, and racial conservatism New Orleans did not develop an effective urban regime coalition. Without going into those and other urban regime theory issues, debates, and nuances, I simply take away from that work the importance of the conundrum African American (and Latino American) mayors face in trying to simultaneously meet the needs and demands of these two, often competing, constituencies. For an empirically based critique of the limitations of urban regime theory in explaining racialized politics, see Neil Kraus, "The Significance of Race in Urban Politics: The Limitations of Regime Theory," *Race and Society* 7 (2004): 95–111.

47. Nagin was born in New Orleans's Charity Hospital and won a baseball scholarship to Tuskegee University where he earned a degree in accounting. He later received an MBA from Tulane University and, before becoming mayor, worked his way up to become Cox Communication's vice president responsible for cable operations for southeast Louisiana. He was also a part owner of a minor league hockey team in New Orleans. "Profile: Ray Nagin," *BBC News*, May 21, 2006, http://news.bbc.co.uk/2/hi/americas/4623922.stm; Douglas Brinkley, *The Great Deluge: Hurricane Katrina, New Orleans, and the Mississippi Gulf Coast* (New York: William Morrow, 2006), 26.

48. Brinkley, *Great Deluge*, 21.

49. Ceci Connolly and Manuel Roig-Franzia, "A Shrinking New Orleans: Mayor Says Infrastructure Can't Support Previous Population," *Washington Post*, October 26, 2005.

50. D. Osei Robertson, "Property and Security, Political Chameleons, and Dysfunctional Regime: A New Orleans Story," in *Seeking Higher Ground: The Hurricane Katrina Crisis, Race, and Public Policy Reader*, ed. Manning Marable and Kristen Clarke, 39–63 (New York: Palgrave Macmillan, 2008), 44.

51. Brinkley, *Great Deluge*, 21–22. As Brinkley puts it, "Even as Nagin represented oil and gas millionaires, shipping magnates, blue bloods, and nouveau-riche developers, he was a buffer zone between New Orleans' blacks and whites." See also Jesse McKinnon, "The Black Population: 2000," Census 2000

Brief, August 2001, 7, tab. 3, www.census.gov/prod/2001pubs/c2kbr01-5.pdf; "The Living Wage Movement: A New Beginning," *Black Commentator*, May 8, 2002, www.blackcommentator.com/wage_1.html; Tim Padgett, "Can New Orleans Do Better?" *Time*, October 16, 2005.

52. Robertson, "Property and Security," 44.

53. Beverly H. Wright and Robert D. Bullard, "Black New Orleans: Before and After Hurricane Katrina," in *The Black Metropolis in the Twenty-First Century: Race, Power, and the Politics of Place*, ed. Robert D. Bullard, 173–97 (Lanham, MD: Rowman and Littlefield, 2007), 187.

54. Padgett, "Can New Orleans Do Better?"

55. Chester Hartman and Gregory D. Squires, "Pre-Katrina, Post-Katrina," in *There is No Such Thing as a Natural Disaster: Race, Class, and Hurricane Katrina*, ed. Chester Hartman and Gregory D. Squires, 1–11 (New York: Routledge, 2006), 3.

56. "Washing Away," *New Orleans Times-Picayune*, June 2002, five part special report, www.nola.com/hurricane/content.ssf?/washingaway/index.html.

57. Baodung Liu and James M. Vanderleeuw, *Race Rules: Electoral Politics in New Orleans, 1965–2006* (Plymouth, UK: Lexington Books, 2007), 5; Editors of *Time* Magazine, *Hurricane Katrina: The Storm that Changed America* (New York: Time, Inc., 2005), 90; Michael Eric Dyson, *Come Hell or High Water: Hurricane Katrina and the Color of Disaster* (New York: Perseus, 2006), 58–59. Dyson also quotes an Amtrak spokesman who indicated that the Nagin administration declined their offer to carry several hundred people to the safer ground of Macomb, Mississippi, as Amtrak moved some of its equipment out of harm's way (57–58); Brinkley, *Great Deluge*, 22–23.

58. Editors, *Hurricane Katrina*, 7–8.

59. Ibid., 90.

60. Dyson, *Come Hell or High Water*, 170–71.

61. For a detailing of those and other rumors and the actual facts, see Editors, *Hurricane Katrina*, 55.

62. Louisiana is organized into political jurisdictions of parishes rather than counties.

63. Aside from the fact that most of my family and kin lost their homes when the levees broke after Katrina hit, one of my most emotionally painful post-Katrina moments came as I read a *Hartford Courant* column written by a fellow University of Connecticut professor and former neighbor. To make his case as to why New Orleans should not be rebuilt, he stereotyped those residents who endured the storm and its immediate aftermath as "looters and shooters."

64. Center for Media and Democracy, "George W. Bush: Hurricane Katrina," www.sourcewatch.org/index.php?title=George_W._Bush:_Hurricane_Katrina; Kenneth T. Walsh, "Hurricane Katrina Left a Mark on George W. Bush's Presidency," *U.S. News and World Report*, December 11, 2008. The President's mother, former first lady Barbara Bush, added to his woes when she was quoted as saying that because many of the evacuees she met in a Houston shelter "were underprivileged anyway," "this is working out very well for them." "Barbara Bush Calls Evacuees Better Off," *New York Times*, September 7, 2005.

65. Susan Page and Maria Puente, "Views of whites, blacks differ starkly on disaster," *USA Today*, September 13, 2005.

66. Lisa de Moraes, "Kanye West's Torrent of Criticism, Live on NBC," *Washington Post*, 3 September 2005, C1.

67. Dan Fromkin, "A Polling Free Fall among Blacks," *Washington Post*, October 13, 2005.

68. "Troops Told 'Shoot to Kill' in New Orleans," *ABC News Online*, September 2, 2005, www.abc.net.au/news/newsitems/200509/s1451906.htm.

69. Brinkley, *Great Deluge*, 470. Brinkley also indicates that Governor Blanco deployed National Guard troops to block other bridges and exit points from the city.

70. Rochelle Smith, "Rochelle Smith," in *Overcoming Katrina: African American Voices from the Crescent City and Beyond*, ed. D'Ann R. Penner and Keith C. Ferdinand, 121–29 (New York: Palgrave, Macmillan, 2009), 128.

71. Bring New Orleans Back Fund, James J. Reiss Jr., http://masgateway.com/portal.aspx?portal=31+tabid=25; Cooper, "Old-Line Families." One journalist stated that Mayor Nagin's Bring New Orleans Back Commission, the business-elite-dominated entity he charged to develop a plan to rebuild the city, had its roots in that meeting. Mike Davis, "Who Is Killing New Orleans?" *Nation*, March 23, 2006, www.thenation.com/article/who-killing-new-orleans.

72. "Ethnic Cleansing," http://balkansnet.org/ethnicl.html.

73. Dan Baum, "*Letter* from New Orleans: The Last Year, Behind the Failure to Rebuild," *New Yorker*, August 21, 2006; Bring New Orleans Back Fund, "Donald T. 'Boysie' Bollinger," http://masgateway.com/portal.aspx?portal=31+tabid=13.

74. Stephen Sackur, "One Year On: Katrina's Legacy," *BBC News*, August 24, 2006; Baum, "*Letter* from New Orleans;" Gary Rivlin, "A Mogul Who Would Rebuild New Orleans," *New York Times*, September 29, 2005.

75. Rivlin, "Mogul Who Would Rebuild New Orleans."

76. Joel Havemann, "A Shattered Gulf Coast; New Orleans' Racial Future Hotly Argued; The U.S. Housing Chief Expresses Doubt About Rebuilding, and Draws Anger and Concern," *Los Angeles Times*, October 1, 2005.

77. Dyson, *Come Hell or High Water*, 91.

78. Ibid., 154.

79. Richard Allen Greene, "Post-Flood City Wrestles with Race Issue," *BBC News*, August 25, 2006.

80. James Dao, "In New Orleans, Smaller May Mean Whiter," *New York Times*, January 22, 2006.

81. Dyson, *Come Hell or High Water*, 116.

82. "Bring New Orleans Back Fund: Commission Members," www.bringneworleansback.org/Commission_Members.

83. Ibid.; "Co-Chair Maurice L. Lagarde III, Bring New Orleans Back," www.bringneworleansback.org/Mel_Lagarde/index.html.

84. Baum, "*Letter* from New Orleans."

85. Rivlin, "Mogul Who Would Rebuild New Orleans."

86. Louisiana Committee for a Republican Majority, "Wendy Vitter Backs 'Operation Clean House': LA Committee for a Republican Majority Launches Website," December 4, 2006, www.lcrmnow.com/news.asp.

87. Rivlin, "Mogul Who Would Rebuild New Orleans."

88. Urban Land Institute, "A Strategy for Rebuilding New Orleans, Project Description," www.project-neworleans.org/urbandesign/uli1.html.

89. The Urban Land Institute was founded in 1936 as the research component of the National Association of Real Estate Boards. It became an independent organization in 1940 and today has more than forty thousand members worldwide engaged in both "private enterprise and public service." Urban Land Institute, "Learn about ULI," www.uli.org/LearnAboutULI.aspx.

90. "Bring New Orleans Back Fund: Joe Canizaro," http://masgateway.com/portal.aspx?portal=31&tabid=17.

91. Urban Land Institute, "Strategy for Rebuilding."

92. Dyson, *Come Hell or High Water*, 31.

93. President Bush was also wrong because his statement ignored the obvious fact that, as I noted earlier, the city's poor—who as you have seen, are much more likely to be African American—had fewer resources to leave the city before Katrina hit.

94. Of course, as Mayor Nagin would soon come to appreciate as he prepared his reelection campaign, there were politically important exceptions of more affluent and/or whiter neighborhoods in the city's lowlands.

95. Davis, "Who Is Killing New Orleans?"

96. Urban Land Institute, "Strategy for Rebuilding."

97. Ibid; Kenneth M. Reardon, "The Shifting Landscape of New Orleans: While Planners and Developers Redraw the City Map, Displaced Residents Struggle to Have a Role," *Shelterforce: Journal of Affordable Housing and Community Building*, Spring 2006, www.shelterforce.org/article/793/the_shifting_landscape_of_new_orleans.

98. Manuel Roig-Franzia, "Hostility Greets Katrina Recovery Plan: Residents Assail Eminent Domain and Other Facets of New Orleans Proposal," *Washington Post*, January 12, 2006.

99. Glen Ford and Peter Gamble, "Fighting the Theft of New Orleans: The Rhythm of Resistance," *Black Commentator* 167, January 19, 2006, http://blackcommentator.com/167/167_cover_fighting_no_theft.html.

100. Gwen Filosa, "Nagin Says He'll Oppose Building Moratorium; Any Homeowner Can Rebuild, Mayor Vows to Residents during Lakeview Appearance," *New Orleans Times Picayune*, January 22, 2006.

101. Davis, "Who Is Killing New Orleans?"

102. John Pope, "Evoking King, Nagin Calls N.O. 'Chocolate' City, Speech Addresses Fear of Losing Black Culture," *New Orleans Times-Picayune*, January 17, 2006.

103. "Nagin Apologizes for 'Chocolate' City Comments," *CNN.com*, January 17, 2006, http://articles.cnn.com/2006-01-17/us/nagin.city_1_majority-african-american-city-mayor-ray-nagin-dark-chocolate?_s=PM:US. In explaining his comments, Nagin stated that they were intended to make it clear that African Americans "understand they are welcomed in this city" by addressing an "unspoken thing about who's coming back, who should come back, [and] what type of city we are going to have in the future."

104. Pope, "Evoking King." During his 2006 mayoral campaign, Nagin stressed what was racially at stake in the election when campaigning in New Orleans and

to displaced evacuees in Houston and Atlanta. For example, in New Orleans his campaign had billboards that referred to Nagin as "our mayor," and in a speech he gave in Houston Nagin specifically noted that none of the other candidates looked like him. Robertson, "Property and Security," 49.

105. The political context of Nagin's "Chocolate City" speech was obvious to observers of the New Orleans political scene. See Dao, "Smaller May Mean Whiter." In explaining his "Chocolate City" remarks, Nagin stated that they were simply a response to his being "emotionally drained" by accusations from other African Americans in reaction to his "taking an inclusive approach to government" that he was a "Ray Reagan," and a "white man in black skin" who "does not care about black people," combined with the hopelessness and sense that they were not welcome back in New Orleans he got when he spoke to evacuees in different cities. Filosa, "Nagin Says He'll Oppose." Although there is no debate among political scientists that racial politics was the driving force behind Nagin's "Chocolate City" speech, there is disagreement as to which political science theory best applies. For Jay Arena, Nagin's actions were a clear example of the dilemma African American mayors face in negotiating the often conflicting demands of urban regime politics. See Jay Arena, "The Contradictions of Black Comprador Rule: Understanding Nagin's 'Chocolate City,' Remark," January 22, 2006, www.zcommunications.org/the-contradictions-of-black-comprador-rule-by-jay-arena.pdf. In their analysis of electoral politics in New Orleans, however, Liu and Vanderleeuw question whether the characteristics of urban regime politics specified by Clarence Stone in his study of Atlanta applied to New Orleans, whose white leadership was unwilling to pursue a course of racial moderation as a means of growing the city's economy. They conclude that what mattered in explaining Nagin's "Chocolate City" speech and other aspects of New Orleans politics was old-fashioned racial politics, not urban regime politics. Liu and Vanderleeuw, *Race Rules*, 17–18, 23, 73.

106. Robertson, "Property and Security," 45, 50.

107. Liu and Vanderleeuw, *Race Rules*, 24.

108. That drop was 36 percent among African Americans—from approximately half that the previous year—and only 5 percent among "whites." John Schwartz, "Term Limits Say New Orleans Mayor Can't Return: Residents Say They Don't Mind," *New York Times*, May 4, 2009.

109. Amy Liu and Allison Plyer, "The New Orleans Index, Summary of Findings, New Orleans Four Years after Katrina," August 2009. Brookings Institution Metropolitan Policy Program & Greater New Orleans Community Data Center, www.brookings.edu/reports/2007/08neworleansindex.aspx?emc=lm&m=217818&l=35&v=1030447.

110. Campbell Robertson, "Another Contest for New Orleans This Weekend," *New York Times*, February 5, 2010. Landrieu, whose previous office was Lieutenant Governor, won 66 percent of the total vote compared to only 14 percent for his main opponent, Troy Henry, an African American businessman. Richard Fausset, "New Orleans Picks Mayor: It's Landrieu," *Los Angeles Times*, February 7, 2010.

111. "Cincinnati Civil Disorders (2001)," Ohio Historical Society, www.ohiohistorycentral.org/entry.php?rec=1647; "Protesters Loot, Set Fires in Cincinnati," *CNN.com*, April 11, 2001, http://archives.cnn.com/2001/US/04/10/cincinnati.protest.04/.

112. "Cincinnati: 2001 Year of Unrest," *Cincinnati Enquirer*, December 30, 2001, www.enquirer.com/unrest2001/.

113. Kristen A. Graham, "Asian Students Describe Violence at South Philadelphia High," *Philadelphia Inquirer*, December 10, 2009.

114. Kristen A. Graham and Jeff Gammage, "Federal Complaint Expected on School Violence," *Philadelphia Inquirer*, December 12, 2009.

115. Jeff Gammage, "Marchers Demand End to Philadelphia School Violence," *The Philadelphia Inquirer*, January 19, 2010, B1.

116. A useful concept for understanding such behavior is the "racially motivated 'blocking of space.'" Joe R. Feagin and Melvin P. Sikes, *Living with Racism: The Black Middle-Class Experience* (Boston: Beacon Press, 1994), 21.

117. Such immigration racism may serve the function of "immigration-focused race population control." Neubeck and Cazenave, *Welfare Racism*, 147-48.

118. Tony Favro, "American Cities Debate English-Only Legislation," *City Mayors*, June 25, 2009, www.citymayors.com/society/us-english-only.html; Chris Harcum, "A Difficult Year for Latinos in East Haven," *New York Times*, December 27, 2009.

119. Steve Salvi, "The Original List of Sanctuary Cities, USA," *Ohio Jobs & Justice PAC*, www.ojjpac.org/sanctuary.asp.

120. Tony Favro, "U.S. Cities Offer Very Different Ways of Dealing with Illegal Immigration," *City Mayors*, May 31, 2007, www.citymayors.com/society/us-illegals.html.

Index

acculturation theory, 59
Action Area, 49–51, 71
Addington, Harold E., 76
Aesop, 54
affirmative action, 136, 138
African Americans: aspirations of, *28*; class-based alliances for, 53; co-optation of leadership of, 66, 104–6, 108; as inferior, 34; insurgency of, 13, 54–55, 57–58, 60, 66; leadership by, 35–36, 108, 125, 129–31, 133; location of, 3–4; mayors, 148, 150, 160, 162, 203n46; migration of, 3–5, 27, 37, 47, 175n24; social protest by, 8, 29, 86, 118, 129
Albertville, AL, 163
Alinsky, Saul, 41, 58, 76, 80–82, 184n40; Alinsky-style CAPs, 47, 54, 68–69, 71, 74–75, 82, 190n62; confrontational strategies of, 54, 61, 72
Althusser, Louis, 24, 35
American Civil Liberties Union, 162
Amtrak, 204n57
Anemone, Lou, 139
"Angry Young Black Men's" rally, 118
antipoverty programs, 34, 47, 68, 79–80, 101

anti-Semitism, 4
Arena, Jay, 207n105
Arkansas National Guard, 7
Asian American Legal Defense and Education Fund, 162
Asian students, immigration of, 162–63
Audubon Place neighborhood, 154, 158
Aurora, CO, 163
aversive racism, 4

backlash. *See* racial backlash
Baer, Betty, 186n89, 187n1; CFO and, 77; SAY and, 52, 57, 69, 71–72
Baez, Anthony, 139–40
Baker, Richard, 155
Belford, Richard, 107, 113–15, 119, 197n41
Belton, Curtis, 117
Bender, Harvey, 158
bias: coalitional, 62, 64; of middle-class, 128; in research, 15
Birmingham, AL, 7, 43
Birmingham jail letter, of King, 59
Black Coalition, 127–28, 131–32, 198n67, 200n95
"black extremists," 193n16

209

black ghettos, 17, 21
black nationalists, 10, 36, 89
Black Panther Party, 10
Black Power (Carmichael and Hamilton), 20
Black Power movement, 9, 66, 81–83, 85, 89, 92
"black uplift," 91
Blanco, Kathleen, 150, 153–54, 205n69
Blauner, Robert, 21
BNOB. *See* Bring New Orleans Back Commission
Bollinger, Donald ("Boysie"), 154–57
Boss, Kenneth, 143
Boston, Ernest L., 101
Braine, Naomi, 86, 89
branches of government, 27
Brewer, Kingston, 128
Bring New Orleans Back Commission (BNOB), 154–59, 167, 205n71
Brookings Institution, 160
Brooks, Richard Oliver, 62–64, 188n19
Brown, Michael, 152
Brown, Milton, 132
Brown decision, 6
Bunge, Jonathan, 131
Bush, Barbara, 204n64
Bush, George H. W., 137
Bush, George W., 137, 152–55, 157, 204n64, 206n93
busing, 136
Button, James, 181–82n8

Cahn, Edgar, 60–64, 187n9; "The War on Poverty: A Civilian Perspective," 60–61
Cahn, Jean, 43–44, 60–64, 187n9; "The War on Poverty: A Civilian Perspective," 60–61
Campbell, Alan K., 48
Campbell, Clifford J., 105–6, 122, 124–25, 199n70
Canada, 46
Canizaro, Joseph, 155–57, 159
Canizaro Commission. *See* Bring New Orleans Back Commission
CAPs. *See* community action programs

Carmichael, Stokely, *Black Power*, 20
Carter, Jimmy, 201n3
Castells, Manuel, 16–17, 86
CATC. *See* Community Action Training Center
Cazenave, Noel A., *Impossible Democracy*, 11–12, 87
census, U.S., 48, 150, 183n28, 196n15
Central High School, 7
CEO. *See* Commission on Equal Opportunities
CFO. *See* Crusade for Opportunity
Cheney, Ruth A., 198n59, 198n64
Chicago School of sociology, 16–17, 177n2
"Chocolate City" speech, of Nagin, 159, 206n103, 207n105
Cincinnati, 161–62
civil disorder, in New Haven, 111–12
Civilian Complaint Review Board, 140
civil rights movement, 18; acceleration of, 7–8; CAPs and, 53–54; CPI and, 41, 63; decline of, 88, 148; expansion of, 35; federal racial state and, 6–7; "maximum feasible participation of the poor" policy and, 8; militancy in, 34, 58, 90, 92, 105, 129; racial backlash to, 8–11; social protest in, 6–8; URS and, 5–6; War on Poverty and, 57–83
Clark, George L., 24
class-based segregation, 62
class-centered state theories, 26
classical sociology, 17
class paternalism, 42
class relationships, 17, 26
Clinton, Bill, 201n3
Clinton, Hillary, 146–47
Cloud, Harold, 41–43, 45, 185n55, 185n56
Cloud rape case, 42–43, 44, 45
Cloward, Richard, 50, 183n30
coalitional bias, 62, 64
COINTELPRO. *See* Counter Intelligence Program
colonialism, internal, 20–21
color line, 137

Commission on Equal Opportunities (CEO), 107, 113–15
Committee on Employment Opportunity, 40
community action programs (CAPs), 28, 29; Alinsky-style, 47, 54, 68–69, 71, 74–75, 82, 190n62; civil rights movement and, 53–54; as ISAs, 24–25; participation activities of, 5, 29–30; public policy and, 33; as racial forces, 58; as racially targeted population control, 27–28, 33–35, 38–39; racism blindness of, 34–35; rationale for, 51–52; in Syracuse, 46–54; URS use of, 28; War on Poverty and, 8–9, 11, 24, 39, 54–55, 60, 68, 80, 83, 85, 87, 100–101
Community Action Training Center (CATC), 47, 74–82, 87, 92, 97, 101; "maximum feasible participation of the poor" policy and, 74, 78, 82; OEO and, 74, 79; War on Poverty and, 76, 79
Community Progress, Inc. (CPI), 13, 36–37, 104–33; action plans, 40–41; civil rights movement and, 41, 63; criticism of, 58–64; goals of, 39; Lee and, 104–6, 115–16, 129–32; "maximum feasible participation of the poor" policy and, 109, 121, 130, 198n61; militancy of, 61; neighborhood focus of, 61–63; OEO and, 109, 122, 125; paternalism of, 58–59; planning of, 38–39; racial status quo for, 55; racism blindness of, 42; War on Poverty and, 43, 112
Compass, Eddie, 151–52
Comprehensive Management Plan, of New Orleans, 151
conflict-avoidance ideology, 105
Congress of Racial Equality (CORE), 7–8, 186n89, 189n30; in New Haven, 64, 66, 106, 108; in Syracuse, 51–52, 75, 88, 98; Walsh and, 51
Connecticut Life, 43
consensus-centered view, 59–60

consensus-centered view, of government, 59–60
conservatives, of African American leadership, 36
Constitution, Fourteenth Amendment to, 6
co-optation: of African Americans' leadership, 66, 104–6, 108; racial, 110–11; self-determination *vs.*, 109–11
Coordinated Community Services, 40
CORE. *See* Congress of Racial Equality
Cottrell, Leonard, 70–71, 190n47
Council of Churches, 114
Council of Social Agencies, 128
Counsel, Willie, 116, 120
Counter Intelligence Program (COINTELPRO), 10
courts, legal, 6
CPI. *See* Community Progress, Inc.
Crisis in Black and White (Silberman), 58–59
Crusade for Opportunity (CFO), 13, 47, 52–53, 72–83, 85–102, 194n28; Baer and, 77; OEO and, 92, 99–101, 194n28; Walsh and, 73, 75, 77, 79–80, 87–88, 95–96, 98; War on Poverty and, 73–74, 86, 98; Zimmerman and, 77, 80, 89, 190n62, 192n82
culture of domination, 180n41
culture of poverty, 16, 71
cycle of URS responses to changing race relations, 31

Dahl, Robert, *Who Governs?*, 44
Daley, Richard J., 80
Dear, Michael, 24
De Leon Springs, FL, 163
democracy, 59
demographics, racial, 3, 46–47
Detroit, 112, 116
Deutscher, Irwin, 47–48, 52–53
Diallo, Amadou, 1, 142–46, 202n34
Dilemmas of Social Reform (Marris and Rein), 43, 44
Dinkins, David, 138, 141
Dixwell Avenue, New Haven, 45

Dixwell neighborhood, New Haven, 38
Dorismond, Patrick, 145–47, 202n34
Dowdy, Richard, 43–46, 184n47, 185n55
Downey, Joseph, 131
dual process, of state intervention, 24, 28–29
Du Bois, W. E. B., 137, 181n5

East Haven, CT, 163–64
Economic Opportunity Act, 8–10, 58–61, 87, 100–101, 188n10
Edmonds, Edwin, 106–7, 127, 130, 132
Eisenhower, Dwight, 7
employment: decline in, 4; discrimination, 47; labor, 3, 46; migration due to, 3; in Syracuse, 50
Equal Employment Practices Commission, 138
ethnoracial prison, 4
European Americans: mayors, 147–48, 160–61; migration of, 3, 4
"exclusivity compulsion," 89
executive branch, of government, 27, 29; of city government, 1, 2, 34; of federal government, 100, 155

Faubus, Orval, 7
FBI. *See* Federal Bureau of Investigation
Feagin, Joe: *The New Urban Paradigm*, 16–17, 86; systemic racism approach of, 19–20; on white racial frame, 19, 34
Federal Bureau of Investigation (FBI), 10
Federal Emergency Management Agency (FEMA), 151, 154
federal racial state, 30, 132; civil rights movement and, 6–7; race relations and, 86–91; URS and, 25, 27, 30, 35, 62, 100–102, 171
FEMA. *See* Federal Emergency Management Agency
15th Ward, of Syracuse, 48, 51
Flake, Floyd, 144
Ford Foundation, 38–41, 166; Gray Areas programs, 7, 58–60; in New Haven, 105, 122–28, 131; paternalism of, 58, 187n5; in Syracuse, 47, 62

Freedman, James O., 188n19

gender-based relations challenges, 26, 171
ghettoization, 17–18, 42, 174n15, 175n17; in New Haven, 124, 196n15; segregation from, 4; in Syracuse, 46–50
ghettos, 3–5; black, 17, 21; control of, 5; goals for, 43; Jewish, 4; social problems in, 34
Giaimo, Robert, 112–13
Gilens, Martin, 9
Giuliani, Rudolph, 1; *Leadership*, 149; racially targeted police misconduct under, 137–47; RSA of, 138–47, 167; URS administration of, 138–39, 149, 167
Goldstein, Abraham, 45
government: branches of, 27; city government, executive branch of, 1, 2, 34; consensus-centered view of, 59–60; executive branch of, 27, 29; federal government, executive branch of, 100, 155; local participation in, 18; managerial perspective on, 21–22; race relations responses of, 30–31; racial goals of, 26–27; racial state entities of, 27; white racial supremacy in, 25–27, 173n3
Gramsci, Antonio, 23–24, 119
grassroots leadership, 24, 110, 126, 186n89
Gray Areas programs, 7, 58–60
Great Migration, 3; "push" and "pull" factors in, 3, 174n9
Great Mississippi Flood of 1927, 156
Green, Edith, 87
Green, Je Royd, 129
Green, Peter M., 198n59, 198n64
Green Amendment, 10, 87, 101
Green Bay, WI, 163
Greenidge, Edwin, 193n16
group *vs.* individual social mobility, 89

Haggstrom, Warren C., 52–53, 68–69, 74–82, 90–91

Hall, Jarvis A., 23, 179n32
Hallman, Howard, 33, 38, 44, 62–63, 105, 184n41
Hamilton, Charles, *Black Power*, 20
Harding, Ray, 140
Harlem Globetrotters, 44
Harlem Youth Opportunities Unlimited–Associated Community Teams, 11–12, 58
Harris, Daryl B., 181–82n8
Harris, Fred, 64–65, 108–11, 114–20, 128, 188n26, 198n64
Harris, Rose, 114, 116, 188n26
Hastert, Dennis, 155
Hazelton, PA, 163
Heard, Inez, 186n89
hegemonic ideologies, 20, 24–25, 119
Hill, Norman, 97–100, 195n46
Hill Parents Association (HPA), 64–66, 106–11, 114–26, 130, 133
Hitler, Adolf, 22
Holden, Reuben, 116, 123
Holder, Melvin, 153
home, ownership of, 48–49
Horan, Cynthia, 178–79n20
Horton, Hayward, 174n6
Horton, Willie, 137
housing code enforcement, 121
Housing Opportunity, 40
Houston, TX, 163
HPA. *See* Hill Parents Association
human ecology approach, 16–17
human relations adviser's office, 45
Human Rights Commission of Syracuse, 51
Humphrey, Hubert, 80
Hurricane Betsy, 156
Hurricane Katrina, 13, 134, 147–61

ideological state apparatuses (ISAs), 24–25, 35, 45, 133, 170
illegal immigration, 1, 136, 163
immigration: Asian students and, 162–63; illegal, 1, 136, 163; racism against, 163–64, 208n117
immoderates/direct actionists, of African American leadership, 36

Impossible Democracy (Cazenave), 11–12, 87
indeterminate and paradoxical nature of state actions, 23, 30, 86, 170
indigenous leadership, 53, 68, 71, 108, 184n40
individual *vs.* group social mobility, 89
institutional stakes, in segregation, 21
insurgency: of African Americans, 13, 54–55, 57–58, 60, 66; of CAP, 92; racial, 10, 19, 26, 89, 118; in Watts, 10
internal colonialism theory, 20–21
ISAs. *See* ideological state apparatuses

Jackson, Alphonso, 155
Jackson, Thomas F., 181n6
Jefferys, Harry D., 132
Jewish ghettos, 4
Jim Crow system, of segregation, 4, 6, 9, 27
Johnson, Lyndon, 8–9, 26, 58, 60, 68, 112
Johnson, Ronald, 114
judicial branch of government, 27
"jungle law" metaphor, 112–13, 197n30

Kennedy, John F., 26, 38
Kennedy, Robert, 66
Kerner Commission report, 11, 20, 112–13
King, Martin Luther, Jr., 10–11, 81–82, 128, 159; Birmingham jail letter of, 59
Knapp, Daniel, 70, 72
Kravitz, Sanford, 77

labor, demand for, 3
Lagarde, Mel, 156
land, use of, 16
Landrieu, Mitch, 161, 207n110
Latino Americans, 13, 20, 138–39, 140, 155–56; mayors, 148–49, 167, 173n4, 203n46
leadership: African American, 35–36, 108, 125, 129–31, 133; conservative style of, 36; co-optation of African Americans', 66, 104–6, 108; grassroots, 24, 110, 126, 186n89; immoderate/direct actionist style of, 36;

indigenous, 53, 68, 71, 108, 184n40; moderate style of, 36
Leadership (Giuliani), 149
Lee, Richard, 35–37, 117–33, 167; CPI and, 104–6, 115–16, 129–32; URS administration of, 37, 58, 64, 107, 109, 115, 126, 167
legislative branch of government, 27
liberalism, racism blindness of, 91
Liberal Party, 140
Little Rock, Arkansas, 6–7
Liu, Baodung, 160, 207n105
Livoti, Frank, 139
Logue, Frank, 132
Los Angeles, CA: riots in, 9–10, 176n40; as "sanctuary" city, 163
Louima, Abner, 140–42, 144–45

machine politics era, 104
male dominance, 171
managerial perspective, on government, 21–22
Manpower employment program, 129
Mansbridge, Jane, 86, 89
Marable, Manning, 137
March on Washington for Jobs and Freedom, 7, 43
Marris, Peter, 43, 44
Marx, Karl, 89
Marxism, 16–18, 23, 178n11, 180n36; neo-Marxism, 179n32, 180n36
"maximum feasible participation of the poor" policy: CATC and, 74, 78, 82; civil rights movement and, 8; CPI and, 109, 121, 130, 198n61; racial backlash and, 83; in Syracuse, 85–102; War on Poverty policy of, 35, 61, 83, 102
mayoral administrations, 33; of New Haven, 12, 37; racially targeted population control by, 3; tasks of, 1–2
mayors: African American, 148, 150, 160, 162, 203n46; European American, 147–48, 160–61; Latino American, 148–49, 167, 173n4, 203n46. *See also specific mayors*

Mayor's Commission for Youth, 52, 67, 71, 73, 76
McGuire, Edward, 78
"Memo on Problems of Leadership in the Negro Community" (Sviridoff), 35–37
methodology, of qualitative historical sociology, 12
Metropolitan Transportation Authority, 144
Meyer, Michael, 141–42
MFY. *See* Mobilization for Youth
middle class: bias of, 128; as reactionary force, 93
migration: of African Americans, 3–5, 27, 37, 47, 175n24; due to employment, 3; of European Americans, 3, 4; Great Migration, 3, 174n9
militancy: in civil rights movement, 34, 58, 90, 92, 105, 129; of CPI, 61; "moderate black militants," 193n16; Tillman, J., and, 89
Miller, S. M., 52–53
minority-contracting programs, 138
mobility, social, 21, 53; individual *vs.* group, 89
Mobilization for Youth (MFY), 11–12, 39–40, 58, 68, 183n30
model city, New Haven as, 111–12, 116–18, 121
"moderate black militants," 193n16
moderates, of African American leadership, 36
Morris, Aldon, 86, 89
Morton, Paul, 150
Murin, William, 18; *Urban Policy and Politics in a Bureaucratic Age*, 60, 104–5
Murphy, Russell D., 182–83n20, 182n18
Muslim Americans, 53, 136

NAACP. *See* National Association for the Advancement of Colored People
Nagin, C. Ray, 13; background of, 149–50, 203n47; "Chocolate City" speech of, 159, 206n103, 207n105;

Hurricane Katrina and, 147–61; RSA of, 149, 153; URS administration of, 147, 152, 167, 173n4
National Association for the Advancement of Colored People (NAACP), 35, 189n30; in Cincinnati, 162; in New Haven, 45–46, 64–66, 106, 108, 114; in Syracuse, 98
National Association of Real Estate Boards, 206n89
nationalists, black, 10, 36, 89
National League of Cities, 80
National Urban League, 127
Nazi Germany, 22
necessitarians, new urban, 91, 122
Negro-Muslim movement, 53
"Negro problem," 3, 19–20, 34, 47, 181n5, 193n16
neighborhood autonomy, 70–71, 109
Neighborhood Center Boards, 93, 95, 99
Neighborhood Development Center, 71
neighborhood focus, of CPI, 61–63
Neighborhood Hill Action Group, 130, 132
neighborhoods, 61–62
neo-Marxism, 179n32, 180n36
Neubeck, Kenneth J., 201n3
Newark, 116
"New Battle for Connecticut Negroes: Birmingham Stirs Demands for Civil Rights, and Comprehensive Attacks on Slum Living," 43
New Deal, 17
New Haven, CT, 35; civil disorder in, 111–12; CORE in, 64, 66, 106, 108; Dixwell Avenue in, 45; Dixwell neighborhood of, 39; Ford Foundation and, 105, 122–28, 131; ghettoization in, 124, 196n15; mayoral administration of, 12, 37; as model city, 111–12, 116–18, 121; NAACP in, 45–46, 64–66, 106, 108, 114; RSA of, 118–21; as "sanctuary" city, 163–64; social revolution in, 38; social service agencies of, 37–38; urban renewal in, 37, 39, 107–8, 116, 128

New Haven Police Department (NHPD), 120
New Haven Redevelopment Agency, 38
New Haven Register, 45
New Orleans, LA, 12–13, 134, 147–61, 164, 166–67; Comprehensive Management Plan of, 151; 9th Ward of, 155–56, 158
new urban necessitarians, 91, 122
new urban paradigm, 17, 19, 86, 168
The New Urban Paradigm (Feagin), 16–17, 86
New York, NY, 134; police killings in, 1, 13, 20, 138–47; as "sanctuary" city, 163
New York Police Department (NYPD), 138–45, 202n34
NHPD. *See* New Haven Police Department
Niemonen, Jack, 22
9th Ward, of New Orleans, 155–56, 158
Nixon, Richard, 132, 136
"non-white" designation, 49, 183n28
NYPD. *See* New York Police Department

Obama, Barack, 136–37, 148, 197n30, 202n45
OEO. *See* Office of Economic Opportunity
Office of Economic Opportunity (OEO), 30, 52, 61, 87; CATC and, 74, 79; CFO and, 92, 99–101, 194n28; CPI and, 109, 122, 125
Ohlin, Lloyd, 50, 53, 71, 186n92, 190n47
Omi, Michael, 194n22
"Opening Opportunities," 39, 40
Operation Breakthrough, 110, 117, 129
Opportunities Industrialization Center, 129
opportunity theory, 50
"oppositional consciousness," 180n41

pacification, 91
pan-ethnic terms, 182n15
Pantell, Dora, 193n16

Park, Robert, 177n2
Parker, Caroline, 158
Parker, Henry, 127–28
Parker, Janette, 126–28
Parks, Rosa, 6
participatory politics, 8, 18, 35, 55, 91
Pataki, George, 146
paternalism: class, 42; of CPI, 58–59; of Ford Foundation, 58, 187n5; racial, 66, 91, 121, 124, 127
patronage, 138
PCJD. *See* President's Committee on Juvenile Delinquency and Youth Crime
Pennington, Richard, 150
People's War Council Against Poverty, 80
Philadelphia, MS, 136
Philadelphia, PA, 104, 162–63
Phoenix, AZ, 164
Pickett, Robert, 81, 190n55
place-based programs, 21
Police Benevolence Association, 139
police brutality, 137, 140
police killings, in New York City, 1, 13, 20, 138–47
police suppression, 35
political sociology, 21, 179n25
political structure, 25
politics, participation in, 50
Polk, Kenneth, 72
poor, participation of, 61
Poor People's Campaign, 10–11
population control. *See* racially-targeted population control
postrace society, 148, 167
post-reform urban politics, 18, 42, 54, 60, 121–29
poverty: antipoverty programs, 34, 47, 68, 79–80, 101; culture of, 16; racialization of, 9; from segregation, 50. *See also* War on Poverty
powerlessness, 50, 69, 73–74
Powledge, Fred, 129–30, 196n15, 198n67
presidential campaigns, 136, 175n24, 201n3

President's Committee on Juvenile Delinquency and Youth Crime (PCJD), 7, 38–39, 54, 60, 73
Prince Street School, 65
Proctor, Emory C., 99
"A Program for Community Improvement in New Haven," 38
programming race relations, 34–35
"promised land," 4
protest. *See* social protest
public policy, 4; of "backlash" cities *vs.* "sanctuary" cities, 163–64; CAPs and, 33; continuum from "racism driven" to "racism targeted," 184n43, 188n12; shifts in racism cognizance, 60–61, 105
"push" and "pull" factors, in Great Migration, 3, 174n9

qualitative historical sociology, methodology of, 12

race concept, 177n1
race relations, 25; federal racial state and, 86–91; government responses to, 30–31; programming, 34–35; regulation of, 1, 3, 6, 24–25, 27, 124, 181n8; URS response to, 31
racial backlash, 28–31, 29, 34–35, 74; "backlash" cities *vs.* "sanctuary" cities, 163–64; to civil rights movement, 8–11; "maximum feasible participation of the poor" policy and, 83; in Syracuse, 46; terminology of, 44; URS and, 29
racial co-optation, 110–11
racial framing, 19, 34
racial insurgency, 10, 19, 26, 89, 118
racialization, of poverty, 9
"racially motivated 'blocking of space'", 208n116
racially-targeted police misconduct, under Giuliani administration, 137–47
racially-targeted population control, 17; CAPs as, 27–28, 33–35, 38–39; by mayoral administrations, 3; by URS, 3, 12–13

racial paternalism, 66, 91, 121, 124, 127
racial state theory, 21–25, 168–69
racial status quo, 1, 2
racism: as aberrant, 22; aversive, 4; immigration and, 163–64, 208n117; as white illness, 91
Racism: From Slavery to Advanced Capitalism (Wilson), 4, 23
racism blindness, 16, 34, 184n43; of CAPs, 34–35; of CPI, 42; of liberalism, 91; as risk avoidance, 62; urban theory and, 16–18
racism theory: internal colonialism theory, 20–21; systemic approach to, 19–20, 34, 42, 177n1
radicalization, relative, 54, 186n94
reactionary force, middle class as, 93
Reagan, Ronald, 136
real estate interests, 21
Reed, Harold, 45
reform politics period, 18, 104
Reid, Antoine, 141–42
Rein, Martin, 43, 45
Reiss, James, 135, 154, 156, 158
relative radicalization, 54, 186n94, 196n20
repressive state apparatuses (RSAs), 24, 35, 45, 66; of Giuliani, 138–47, 167; of Nagin, 149, 153; of New Haven, 118–21
Republican Party, 136, 146, 149, 155, 157
research: additional needed, 161–64, 169–71; bias in, 15
residential segregation, 4, 17, 21, 59
"reverse discrimination," 136
Rezak, Nicolas, 99
risk avoidance, racism blindness as, 62
Roosevelt, Franklin D., 17
Ross, Fred, 71–76, 81
RSAs. *See* repressive state apparatuses
rural racial state, 171

Safir, Howard, 140, 146
"sanctuary" cities *vs.* "backlash" cities, 163–64
San Francisco, CA, 163

SAY. *See* Syracuse Action for Youth
SCDA. *See* Syracuse Community Development Association
school segregation, 4, 6, 50, 136
segregation: class-based, 62; from ghettoization, 4; institutional stakes in, 21; Jim Crow system of, 4, 6, 9, 27; poverty from, 50; residential, 4, 17, 21, 59; in schools, 4, 6, 50, 136; in Syracuse, 46–50, 62
self-determination *vs.* co-optation, 109–11
Sennett, Richard, 4
"separate but equal," 6, 11
separatism, 89, 193n16
SES. *See* socio-economic status
sexuality-based oppression, 171
Shriver, Sargent, 80, 87, 187n9, 192n82
Silberman, Charles, 58–59, 175n18, 187n5
slavery, 4, 46, 98
Smith, Susan, 17, 178n10
SNCC. *See* Student Non-Violent Coordinating Committee
social mobility, 21, 53; individual *vs.* group, 89
social protest, 6; by African Americans, 8, 29, 86, 118, 129; in civil rights movement, 6–8; as socio-therapeutic, 53; in Syracuse, 51–52
social revolution, 38, 63, 122
social science theory, 39
social stratification, 173n1
social-structure blindness, 168
socio-economic status (SES), 50
sociology, 2–3; Chicago School of, 16, 177n2; classical, 17; political, 21, 179n25; qualitative historical sociology, methodology of, 12; urban, 16–18, 168
socio-therapeutic value, of social protest, 53
"A Sound Sentence—And a Serious Question," 45
South Philadelphia High School, 162
Spitz, Lawrence, 116, 118, 123–25, 128–31

"squeegee man" shooting, 141–42
state: definition of, 21; indeterminate and paradoxical nature of actions of, 23, 30, 86, 170. *See also* federal racial state; urban racial state
Stone, Clarence, 18, 203n46; *Urban Policy and Politics in a Bureaucratic Age*, 60, 104–5
"stop and frisk" actions, 143
stratification, social, 173n1
Street Crime Unit, 142–44
Student Non-Violent Coordinating Committee (SNCC), 81, 106
suburbs, 4
Supreme Court, U.S., 6
Sviridoff, Mitchell, 39, 43–44, 59, 125, 127–30; "Memo on Problems of Leadership in the Negro Community," 35–37
Syracuse, NY: CAPs in, 46–54; CORE in, 51–52, 75, 88, 98; employment in, 50; 15th Ward of, 48, 51; Ford Foundation and, 47, 62; ghettoization in, 46–50; "maximum feasible participation of the poor" policy in, 85–102; NAACP in, 98; racial backlash in, 46; racial demographics in, 46–47; segregation in, 46–50, 62; social protest in, 51–52; urban renewal in, 48–49, 51–54
Syracuse Action for Youth (SAY), 39, 52–55; Action Area of, 49–51; Baer and, 52, 57, 69, 71–72; SAY proposal, 66–75, 186n77; Zimmerman and, 53
Syracuse Community Development Association (SCDA), 72, 78–80, 83, 87–88, 192n82
Syracuse University Youth Development Center. *See* Youth Development Center
systemic racism approach, 19–20, 34, 42, 177n1

Task Force on Police-Community Relations, 141
Thomas, Timothy, 161

Tillman, James, 80–82, 88–101, 105, 122, 193n16; *Why America Needs Racism and Poverty*, 89
Tillman, Mary Norman, 81–82, 90–94, 194n18; *Why America Needs Racism and Poverty*, 89
tokenism, 91
Trojan horse, 54
Trump, Donald, 155

ULI. *See* Urban Land Institute
Underground Railroad, 46
United Way, 52
Urban Land Institute (ULI), 157–59, 206n89
Urban League, 36, 40, 44, 127, 129
Urban Policy and Politics in a Bureaucratic Age (Stone, Whelan, and Murin), 60, 104–5
urban racial state (URS), 25–31, 28, 29; CAPs, use of, 28; civil rights movement and, 5–6; definition, 1, 25–26; federal racial state and, 25, 27, 30, 35, 62, 100–102, 171; Giuliani administration of, 138–39, 149, 167; goals of, 12–13; Lee administration as, 37, 58, 64, 107, 109, 115, 126, 167; Nagin administration of, 147, 152, 167, 173n4; race relations, cycle of responses to, 31; racial backlash and, 29; racially ameliorative, 2, 12–13, 37, 55, 57, 60, 83, 138; racially oblivious, 2, 12, 60, 166; racially repressive, 2, 13; racially targeted population control by, 3, 12–13; reason for, 5; responsiveness of, 30; urban theory and, 25–26, 168–69; Walsh administration of, 46, 66–67, 92–93, 100–101, 104, 167
urban reform, theories of, 59
urban regime theory, 19, 178–79n20, 203n46, 207n105
urban renewal, 8; in New Haven, 37, 39, 107–8, 116, 128; in Syracuse, 48–49, 51–54
urban sociology, 16–18, 168
urban theory: government, 18–19;

racism blindness, 16–18; URS and, 25–26, 168–69
URS. *See* urban racial state

Vanderleeuw, James M., 160, 207n105
Vasquez, Anthony, 145–46
Venice, Italy, 4
Volpe, Justice, 140–41
voter disenfranchisement, 137
voter registration drives, 9, 73–77

Wallace, George, 136
Walsh, William, 9, 51; CFO and, 73, 75, 77, 79–80, 87–88, 95–96, 98; CORE and, 51; URS administration of, 46, 66–67, 92–93, 100–101, 104, 167
Warner, Robert A., 183n22
War on Poverty: CAPs and, 1, 8–9, 24, 39, 54–55, 60, 68, 80, 83, 85, 87, 100–101; CATC and, 76, 79; CFO and, 73–74, 86, 98; civil rights movement and, 57–83; CPI and, 43, 112; critique of, 60; Economic Opportunity Act and, 8; ideological rationale for, 50; "maximum feasible participation of the poor" policy of, 35, 61, 83, 102; opportunity theory and, 50; origin of, 58
"The War on Poverty: A Civilian Perspective" (Cahn, E., and Cahn, J.), 60–61, 62, 63
Washington, Rudy, 144
Watts insurgency, 10
Whelan, Robert, 18; *Urban Policy and Politics in a Bureaucratic Age*, 60, 104–5
white backlash. *See* racial backlash

"white flight," 3, 4, 37
white racial frame, 19, 34
white racial supremacy, in government, 25–27, 173n3
white racism, 12, 34, 39, 40, 42, 46–47, 54, 112, 113
Who Governs? (Dahl), 44
Why America Needs Racism and Poverty (Tillman, J., and Tillman, M.), 89
Wiley, George, 51–52
Williams, Anna Mae, 186n89
Williams, Earl, 106
Williams, Yohuru, 197n42, 198n59
Wilson, Carter A., 30, 86, 170; *Racism: From Slavery to Advanced Capitalism*, 4, 23
Winant, Howard, 194n22
Winfrey, Oprah, 151
Winters, Clifford L., 79, 81, 97, 99, 192n82
Wolfinger, Raymond, 109, 126
Woolever, Frank, 85, 97

X, Malcolm, 9, 98

Yale Law Journal, 43, 60
Yale University, 65, 127–28
Yale University Law School, 45
Yarmolinsky, Adam, 187n9
Ylvisaker, Paul, 59, 105, 187n5
Youth Development Center, 47–48, 52, 74; philosophies of, 52–53; Zimmerman and, 67, 71

Zimmerman, Ben: CFO and, 77, 80, 89, 190n62, 192n82; SAY and, 53; Youth Development Center and, 67, 71

About the Author

Noel A. Cazenave is associate professor of sociology at the University of Connecticut. He is also on the faculty of the Urban and Community Studies program of UConn's Greater Hartford Campus. His recent and current work is in the areas of racism studies, U.S. poverty policy, political sociology, and urban studies. His coauthored book, *Welfare Racism: Playing the Race Card against America's Poor,* has won numerous awards. Professor Cazenave more recently published *Impossible Democracy: The Unlikely Success of the War on Poverty Community Action Programs.* He is currently working on a book which is tentatively entitled *Conceptualizing Racism*; a project he hopes will advance the emerging field of racism studies and its goal to study racism directly and explicitly.